D1436249

501 MUST-VISIT
DESTINATIONS

501 MUST-VISIT DESTINATIONS

Bounty Books

An Hachette UK Company
www.hachette.co.uk

First published in Great Britain in 2006 by Bounty Books,
a division of Octopus Publishing Group Ltd
Carmelite House
50 Victoria Embankment
London EC4Y 0DZ
www.octopusbooks.co.uk

First published in paperback in 2013
This revised edition published in 2016

Copyright © Octopus Publishing Group Limited 2006, 2013, 2016

All rights reserved. No part of this publication may be reproduced, stored in a retrieval system,
or transmitted, in any form or by any means, electronic, mechanical, photocopying, recording
or otherwise without the prior written permission of the publisher.

ISBN 978-0-7537-2982-3

A CIP catalogue record is available from the British Library

Printed and bound in China

10 9 8 7 6 5 4 3

Publisher: Samantha Warrington
Managing Editor: Karen Rigden
Editor: Phoebe Morgan
Senior Production Manager: Peter Hunt
Packaged by Emma Hill

PLEASE NOTE: Political situations arise very quickly and a city or country that was quite safe a short time ago
can suddenly become a 'no go' area. Check with the Foreign Office (www.gov.uk/foreign-travel-advice)
or your local embassy to ensure safe travel is sanctioned in this area before booking tickets and travelling.

CONTENTS

INTRODUCTION

Fifty or sixty years ago, travelling abroad for most people was an unrealizable dream. Only the wealthy with a lot of time on their hands could afford to travel to a foreign country for a holiday and even for them the idea of going to South America, Africa or Asia would have been pretty much unthinkable. The development of air transport over the past few decades has changed all that. Today your often-dreamed-of trip to Cambodia or Uganda or Bolivia or even Antarctica can so easily become reality. More and more people from many different countries and of all age groups are catching the travel bug all the time.

The most remote places on earth are today accessible to the intrepid traveller. Whether it be the remarkable Yemeni island of Socotra in the Indian Ocean or Lake Baikal in Siberia, or Aitutaki in the South Pacific, none of the destinations in this book should be much more than two days' total travelling time from a major airport – provided you have the determination, energy and money to go there, of course. Truly the world now is your oyster.

Some of the must-visit destinations featured are great wonders of nature, but the majority are creations of human beings – towns and cities, cathedrals, castles, museums, gardens and markets – all testament to the industry, ingenuity and perseverance of mankind. Some of them, like the Great Wall of China, the Taj Mahal or the Acropolis, are famous throughout the world but many are little known. Were you to visit the spectacular lagoon at Dakhla or the beautiful temple of Wat Tham Paplong for example there is still every chance that you would be the only tourist there.

It is likely that some – or maybe even all – of your own favourite destinations are not included in this book. So it needs to be stressed that the 501 destinations chosen are just a selection from the many thousands of beautiful and interesting places in this wonderful world of ours. Undoubtedly travel and tourism can have a damaging effect as visitors to some of the world's most famous cities and monuments can readily testify. Some particularly popular places, the city of Venice or Egypt's Valley of the Kings for example, can at certain times of year be – and feel – almost overwhelmed by the sheer number of visitors and your pleasure at finally reaching your eagerly awaited must-visit destination can be marred by the presence of just too many human beings. Sometimes you can dramatically improve the experience if you simply avoid making your trip during the busiest time of the year. Venice or Florence are still beautiful in the winter months. The Valley of the Kings is equally amazing in August.

Of course, travelling to your must-visit destination can often be as interesting and as much fun as arriving there. The people you meet, the hotels you stay at, the meals you eat, the trips you take on the local trains, buses or taxis – once you return home your memories of your visit will be of the journey and the whole experience and not just of the destination itself.

If you are the proverbial armchair traveller who, for whatever reason, travels in your mind rather than in reality, this book should help you indulge your fantasies. However if you have ever remotely considered visiting the destinations of your dreams, stop resisting. Take the plunge and go. Your mind and your life will be enriched by the experience.

AFRICA

GONDAR

Ethiopia

WHEN TO GO?
September, October and November are the best times to visit.

In the 16th and 17th centuries, the fortress city of Gondar – the Royal Enclosure – served as the residence of the Ethiopian emperor, Fasilides, who moved his capital here in 1636AD. By the late 1640s he had built a great castle here, the now restored Fasilades Palace. With its huge towers and looming battlement walls, it seems as if a piece of medieval Europe has been transported to Ethiopia.

Recognised as a UNESCO World Heritage site in 1979, the palace, surrounded by an impressive 900-m (2,953-ft) wall, stands in a compound filled with juniper and wild olive trees, amid Enqual Gemb, or Egg Castle, named after its domed roof, the royal archive, many impressive churches and monastaries and a stable. These exemplify architecture that is marked by both Hindu and Arab influences, subsequently transformed by the Baroque style that the Jesuit missionaries brought to Gondar, and have earned the city the nickname 'The Ethiopian Camelot'.

Beyond the city to the northwest, by the Qaha River, are the Fasilades Baths. A two-storeyed, rustic battlement sits on the steps leading to a rectangular pool, while the bathing pavilion stands on pier arches and contains several rooms that may be reached via a stone bridge.

DID YOU KNOW?
All of the churches were built within a century – according to legend, with the help of angels.

WHAT IS THERE TO SEE?
Eleven monolithic churches built in the 13th century.
WHEN SHOULD I VISIT?
September, October and November are best.
WHERE IS IT?
In the former province of Wollo.

LALIBELA

Ethiopia

Lalibela is Ethiopia's equivalent of Petra in Jordan. Surrounded on all sides by rugged and forbidding mountains to the north of the modern province of Wollo, Lalibela gives the impression that you've landed in a kingdom centuries past. The 11 medieval, monolithic churches of this 13th-century 'New Jerusalem' are Ethiopia's top attraction, and they inspire awe, regardless of whether you are interested in religion or religious architecture. The churches are cut straight from bedrock so their roofs are at ground level. A complex labyrinth of tunnels and narrow passageways with offset crypts, grottoes and galleries connects them all. It's a damp and silent subterranean world – apart from the echoing sounds of the chanting faithful.

AKSUM
Ethiopia

WHAT IS IT?
Ethiopia's holiest city.
WHY IS IT IMPORTANT?
Christianity was declared the national religion here in the fourth century.
WHAT IS THERE TO SEE?
One of the possible resting places of the Ark of the Covenant.

Aksum is considered the holiest city in Ethiopia. Christianity was declared the national religion here in the fourth century by the ruler, Ezana, who constructed much of the monumental architecture and converted much of the Axumite kingdom's population to Christianity around 330AD after his own conversion.

The modern city of Aksum is located in the northeastern portion of what is now Ethiopia, on the horn of Africa. It lies high on a plateau 2,195m (7,200ft) above sea level. According to the Ethiopian Orthodox Church, Aksum is where the original Ark of the Covenant, containing the Ten Commandments, is located. Just past the church's museum lies Aksum's impressive ancient stelae field. These are enormous carved pillars made from single granite blocks, the highest of which still standing is a looming 24m (79ft) tall.

SIMIEN NATIONAL PARK

Ethiopia

Massive erosion over the years on the Ethiopian plateau has created one of the most spectacular landscapes in the world. The Simien National Park, a UNESCO World Heritage Site, consists of a rocky massif – cut through by streams and gorges – that slopes dramatically down to grasslands and wide valleys. Not only are the views from the mountains breathtaking, but the park is also home to some extremely rare animals, such as gelada baboons, Simien foxes and Ethiopian wolves (the park was created primarily to protect the 1,000 walia ibex, a type of wild goat found nowhere else in the world). Trekking in the Simiens is excellent and the park is easily accessible from Debareq, 101km (63 miles) from Gondar, where guides are available to help you get the most from, and stay safe in, one of the world's must stunning natural wonders.

BE PREPARED FOR ALL CONDITIONS
Snow and ice commonly appear on the highest points of the Simien Mountains and temperatures at night often fall below 0°C (32°F).

WHAT IS IT? A World Heritage Site with dramatic scenery.
WHY IS IT IMPORTANT? Spectacular scenery, flora and fauna. Home of Ras Dejen, the highest point in Ethiopia.
WHERE IS IT? The Simien Mountains are in northwest Ethiopia, east of the highway from Gondar to Aksum.

AMBOSELI RESERVE

Kenya

Amboseli is renowned for its population of an estimated 650 elephants, as well as its large herds of wildebeest, zebra, impala, the endangered black rhino and elusive cheetah. The backdrop of the snow-capped peak of Mount Kilimanjaro, just 40km (25 miles) away and rising majestically above the clouds, dominates the reserve. Designated an international biosphere reserve and national park in 1974, Amboseli covers a mere 392 sq km (244 sq miles), but despite its small size and the fragility of its ecosystem, it manages to support a wide range of mammals. More than 50 of the larger species of mammals and over 400 species of birds can be found throughout the area. Keep an eye out for the arid lakebed that produces mirages in the sweltering heat and be sure to enjoy the views from Observation Hill.

WHEN SHOULD I GO?
Game viewing is best in high summer.
WORTH A TASTE:
Matoke (mashed plantains) and *nyama choma* (goat barbecue) washed down with a Tusker beer.

LITERARY INSPIRATION
With its rugged landscape and the romantic, mystical atmosphere of the great mountain looming above, it is no wonder that Amboseli inspired the big-game-hunting tales of Ernest Hemingway and Robert Ruark.

LAMU
Kenya

HOW TO GET THERE:
The best way to get to Lamu is to fly. The road to Lamu is rough and while there are buses, the journey is tedious and sometimes dangerous.
CULTURAL ETIQUETTE:
Lamu is strictly Islamic so be sensitive as to how you dress.

Lamu Island's long, white sandy beaches framed by rolling dunes are as unspoiled today as they were when the land was settled in the 14th century as a Swahili trading post. Lamu town is Kenya's oldest, and in its day it served as a thriving port for the export of timber, ivory and amber. Tourism arrived in the 1960s when the sleepy island turned into a hippy heaven, rivalled only by Kathmandu.

The island has, however, managed to retain its distinctive character and charm. Donkeys – the main mode of transport – wander through labyrinthine streets the width of an average pavement. Children's laughter echoes in the courtyards as they play in the dappled sunlight, while men chat in groups in the street and women wearing their black *buibui* veils scamper around behind the heavy, carved wooden doors for which the island is famous – offering another snapshot of paradise.

LAKE TURKANA

Kenya

Appearing mirage-like in the middle of a vast, lunar landscape of extinct volcanoes and lava beds is the world's largest desert lake. A World Heritage Site, Lake Turkana, the most northerly of Kenya's Rift Valley Lakes, is also known as the 'Jade Sea' for the array of blue and green hues produced by the algae it contains.

The Jurrassic-like setting of the lake, made all the more spectacular by its drastic contrast to the barren surroundings, is steeped in prehistory. The lake was first discovered by westerners in 1888 when an Austrian explorer found human skulls and bones here, and 80 years later was made famous by Richard Leakey's discovery of fossil remains dating back three million years at his excavation at Koobi Fora.

WHAT IS THERE TO SEE? 22,000 Nile crocodiles in addition to hippos, venomous snakes, Grevy's and plains zebras, reticulated giraffes, camels and more than 40 different species of fish. There are also plentiful numbers of migrating waterfowl, including flocks of flamingoes.

HISTORICAL SIGNIFICANCE

Lake Turkana is widely believed to be where man first walked upright.

MASAI MARA

Kenya

WORTH THE SPLURGE: Take a sunrise balloon ride for an incredible view over the vast plains.

A call comes over your guide's walkie talkie, a crackling message that lions have been sighted and the jeep speeds off in hot pursuit. It is just another hazy afternoon in the Masai Mara Game Reserve. As you approach the pride of lions basking lazily in the belting sun, you understand why this park, with its abundance of wildlife, rolling plains and grasslands, was chosen as the location for the film *Out of Africa*.

The park is in the southwestern corner of Kenya, close to the Tanzanian border and roughly 275km (171 miles) from Nairobi. Opened in 1974, the Masai Mara National Reserve comprises 1,510 sq km (938 sq miles) of plains and woodlands and is Africa's richest, and most-visited, wildlife reserve. 'The Mara' is home to an incredibly rich and varied wildlife, and is renowned as the only reserve where you can view the 'Big Five' in a single morning's game drive. From July to October you can also witness the amazing annual migration of more than 1.3 million wildebeest, zebras and gazelles from the Serengeti, quickly followed by lions, leopards, cheetahs and hyenas, together with the opportunistic vultures hovering above.

Hot-air ballooning is a favourite way to witness the majestic scenery and wildlife, particularly at sunrise. The experience of hovering above a seemingly endless parade of animals is unforgettable.

DID YOU KNOW?
It was Scottish explorer John Walter Gregory who first dubbed this geologic phenomenon the Rift Valley.

THE RIFT VALLEY

Kenya

WHERE IS IT?
West of Mount Kenya in the Kenyan highlands.
WHAT IS THERE TO SEE?
Volcanoes, hot springs and millions of birds.

Right: Local Masai warriors perfoming a traditional dance

Some 20 million years ago, the Earth's crust weakened and tore itself apart, causing a jagged rift thousands of kilometres long across the African continent. The land on either side then erupted, creating great volcanic mountains, while the valley floor gradually sank into a low, flat plain. This geologic phenomenon, named the Great Rift Valley, divides Kenya down the length of the country, essentially separating east from west. Today's Rift Valley is characterized by uninhabitable desert and fertile farmland, flat arid plains and steep escarpments. The Rift Valley is currently home to 30 active and semi-active volcanoes, a countless number of hot springs and a series of lakes rich in sodium carbonate, where millions of birds flock in order to feast on the abundant food supply. Quite a sight!

LAKE NAKURU

Kenya

Few words can accurately describe the incredible vision of a seemingly endless pink blanket of feathers laying at your feet. This is the astonishing beauty that greets you at Lake Nakuru National Park. Designated a bird sanctuary in 1960 and established as a national park in June 1968, it was created for the protection of its huge flocks of greater and lesser flamingoes. Tens of thousands of these flamingoes descend upon the shores of this shallow, alkaline lake.

The park is also an important site for both white and black rhinos. Around the lake zebras and Bohor's reedbuck can be seen, while clawless otters and hippos can be found in the lake itself or on its shores, and klipspringers and rock hyraxes live on the steep cliffs. This is an incredible place to view nature in the wild.

WHEN SHOULD I VISIT?

Waterfowl numbers generally swell from October–April. Antelopes and hippos have young in March, lions in April/May.

AWE-INSPIRING

Lake Nakuru is home to tens of thousands of pink flamingoes – sometimes numbering over a million. The best place to view the stunning array of birds is from Baboon Cliff.

TSAVO NATIONAL PARK

Kenya

DID YOU KNOW?

This is the largest game park in Kenya, and one of the largest in the world.

JUST HOW BIG IS IT?

The park is just over 21,000 sq km (8,108 sq miles) – larger than Jamaica!

WHY SO POPULAR?

It boasts more than 60 major species of mammals and 1,000 plant species.

After a very long, rough and bumpy bus ride, it is the endless expanse of dry grassland and the rich, dark red clay earth that makes the first impression on a traveller entering the Tsavo National Park. The park is divided into two areas – Tsavo East and Tsavo West – by the Nairobi–Mombasa highway. It is the largest game park in Kenya, and one of the largest in the world, and is the most popular destination in Africa for safaris. Known for its high concentration of elephants and lions, Tsavo National Park offers a stunning assortment of animals able to survive in the unforgiving arid, volcanic landscape – including the famed 'Big Five'. From one hotel, formerly a sisal plantation, you can watch the elephants through floor-to-ceiling glass windows as you dine by candlelight. It is like living in a wildlife programme as you witness these, and other animals, drink from an isolated pond within arms' length. The views of the various animals caught in the dim, torch-lit night as you watch them from your luxurious grass-covered hut, which is perched on stilts, are incredible

Tsavo East is less visited and only the southern area of the park, below the Galana River, is open to visitors. Sightings of elephants are virtually guaranteed here except in the wetter months of May, June and November, when the larger animals disperse.

MOUNT KENYA

Kenya

Opened to visitors in 1949 and designated a UNESCO World Heritage Site in 1997, Mount Kenya National Park offers one of the most impressive landscapes in all of East Africa.

There are 12 remnant glaciers on the mountain, all of which are receding rapidly, and four secondary peaks that sit at the head of the U-shaped glacial valley that is littered with wild flowers. With its rugged glacier-clad summits and forested middle slopes, Mount Kenya is simply spectacular.

The park has incredible lakes, tarns, glaciers, peaks and natural mineral springs. At the lower levels are dry upland forests that give way with height to montane forest with cedar and podo, then thick bamboo forest, upper forests of smaller trees and high-altitude moss and finally high-altitude heath and shrubs followed by open moorland, where animals like elephants, buffaloes, zebras and eland have been sighted as high as 4,000m (13,123 ft). Other animals of the forests include bushbuck, black and white Colobus monkeys and Sykes monkeys, while lower down the slopes the wide variety of wildlife includes black rhinos, leopards, hyenas, genet cats, olive baboons, waterbucks, black-fronted duikers, bush pigs and giant forest hogs.

WHEN SHOULD I GO?
Large animals are in the high elevations during dry seasons Jan–Mar and July–Oct. High elevation birds go to lower elevations during the rains of Mar–June and Oct–Dec.

DID YOU KNOW?
The mountain's highest point, named 'Wagagai', is located entirely within the country of Uganda.

BEST VIEW:
Mount Elgon itself is best seen from the Endebess Bluff, where you can get a panoramic view of the many gorges, lakes, mesas, rivers and hot springs that lie in the shadow of the mountain peaks.

Right: Mount Kenya

MOUNT ELGON

Kenya

Giving new meaning to the term 'salt lick', the Elephant Caves at Mount Elgon National Park provide these gentle giants with the vital mineral, and offer a once-in-a-lifetime opportunity for wildlife-watchers to witness a rare, natural phenomenon. Many herbivores experience what is known as 'salt hunger' because their diet doesn't supply them with adequate nutrients and minerals, including sodium, so they are forced to seek out an alternative source. In Mount Elgon National Park, the elephants have found their own source of salt and most people come to view the single, large herd of more than 100 individuals. Every night, they venture in convoy into the vast caves within the volcanic underground of this ancient caldera to lick the natural salt-rich deposits caused by Elgon's high rainfall leeching the soil from the rock.

ZUMA MARKET

Madagascar

DID YOU KNOW?
Zuma is widely claimed to be the second-largest market in the world.

Looking down on Analakely, you'll see an ocean of hundreds of huge, white umbrellas, under which vendors sell their wares. Anything you can think of can be found here. Bustling with people and filled with exotic scents, Zuma Market is an assault on the senses. There is a flower section bursting with vivid colours and amazing fragrance, a section for handicrafts including an abundance of leather, woodcarvings, straw hats as worn by the locals, batik and other fabrics, and even semi-precious stones and beads — all strewn across mats on the ground, on tables or on any other available surface. There are areas filled with fruits and vegetables, clothes, paintings, plants, tyres and housewares. A cacophony of sounds and even more stimulation for your eyes, Zuma is part Indian Bazaar, part country fair and part circus.

Also worth visiting are the Queen's Palace and Royal Village, or Rova, which was formerly the Merina Dynasty residence and the Tsimbazaza Zoological and Botanical Garden. In the spectacular natural surroundings of this otherwise noisy and somewhat polluted city, exist fantastic wildlife-viewing opportunities. Perinet, 140km (90 miles) from the capital, is a nature reserve where you can see a multitude of the famed indri, or tail-less lemurs, made popular by the cartoon, *Madagascar*.

LIVINGSTONIA

Malawi

WHAT IS THERE TO SEE?
The mission settlement and the Stone House, formerly the home of the Laws family, now a guest house and museum.
WHERE IS IT?
Above Lake Malawi at 900m (3,000ft)

Livingstonia, a mission settlement established in 1894 by Robert Laws, a disciple of David Livingstone, is situated high above Lake Malawi, with stunning views across to Tanzania. David Livingstone, the Scottish explorer, visited Lake Nyasa in 1859 and was shocked by the slave trade that he witnessed. He drew public attention to the situation when he returned to Europe, and by 1873 two Presbyterian missionary society bases had been established in the region. Stone House, where Robert Laws once lived, can now be rented overnight. Also worth a visit is the church, built in 1894 in Scottish style, with lovely windows depicting the arrival of Livingstone at Lake Malawi. Also of interest is the large bell, erected in honour of Laws and his family, as well as the stone cairn, in memory of where Dr Laws and his companions pitched their camp during their first night on the plateau.

LAKE MALAWI

Malawi

WHY IS IT IMPORTANT?
A scenic lake, noted for its importance in the study of evolution.
HOW BIG IS IT?
It's 560km (348 miles) long, 80km (50 miles) wide and 700m (2,297 ft) deep.

A designated World Heritage Site, Lake Malawi is second only in importance to the history of evolutionary study to that of the finches of the Galápagos Islands. Lake Malawi hosts the richest variety of tropical fish of any freshwater lake in the world. Nearly 500 species of cichlids are unique to its waters, encompassing 30 per cent of the entire group. Of particular interest is the brightly coloured 'mbuna' rock fish. There is a total of 28 other species endemic to the lake.

Dr David Livingstone claimed the honour of 'discovering' Lake Malawi, although he was most certainly not the first European to see its splendour. Livingstone described it as a 'lake of stars' because of its glittering surface. This area of spectacular scenery, forming the western part of the Rift Valley, encompasses several offshore islands, the Nankumba Peninsula and Cape Maclear.

ZOMBA

Malawi

The Zomba Plateau, forming the faulted edge of the Great Rift Valley and the Shire lowlands, is a magnificent massif largely forested with cypress, Mexican pine and Mulanje cedar. Its series of small waterfalls and rapids join to form the Mulunguzi.

This tranquil forest reserve, renowned for its temperate climate and natural splendour, is blanketed with wildflowers, ferns, thorn bushes and orchids. The summit is an impressive 1,800-m (5,906-ft) tower rising to over 2,080m (6,824ft) tall. The face of the southern edge, shadowing the colonial town of Zomba, is 750m (2,461ft) high.

IMPRESSIVE VIEWS
Queen's View, named after Queen Elizabeth following her visit in 1957, is said to offer 'the best view in the whole of the British Empire'.

DON'T MISS: The market here – one of the most colourful in Malawi, featuring an abundance of fresh fruits and vegetables set amid tinsmiths, second-hand clothes stalls, witch doctors and everything you can imagine in between.

MOZAMBIQUE

Mozambique

The idyllic coral paradise of the Island of Mozambique floats languorously in the Indian Ocean's crystalline waters near Madagascar. A study in architectural contrast, the island's port is resplendent in Arab, Indian and Portuguese influences, a reminder of its days as a major trading post on the sea route from Europe to the East Indies.

The town grew from the port outwards, with the land nearest the sea occupied by local business operations. Eventually the town spread, and villagers built homogeneous limestone, wood-beamed homes on winding, tangled streets surrounding a central square. The façades of the structures include cornices, high rectangular framed windows and rows of pilasters for decoration, while their flat roofs served to collect the rainwater vital on an island with no freshwater springs. The World Heritage Site, located in the north of Mozambique Island, includes a variety of attractions such as the Chapel of Nossa Senhora de Baluarte, considered the oldest European building in the southern hemisphere and dating back to 1522. Enjoy a walk here as the languid breezes rustle your hair and the dappled sunshine caresses your shadow. In the 30 minutes or so it will take you to traverse this small island, you will be touched by the quaint, rustic feel of the place as well as the friendliness of the locals, who will undoubtedly smile and tip their hat to you as you pass.

PARC NATIONAL DES VOLCANS

Rwanda

YOU SHOULD KNOW:
If you intend to make a gorilla visit, you will need to organize transport from Ruhengeri town to the park boundaries, where you will continue your guided trip on foot.

As you trek through evergreen and bamboo forest at the foothills of the scenic Virungas mountains, traversing rivers and streams that flow into the Nile, you walk up, up, up towards where the rainforest converges with the rest of this green, tropical paradise. It is here you will find yourself cloaked in the heart of the Parc National des Volcans. This is home to the rare mountain gorilla. As your guide leads you towards the gorillas, you will be surrounded by the sounds of bird calls – more than 670 species are found here – and the squawking and haunting noises of monkeys climbing above you, while getting an occasional peek of a buffalo or elephant if you're lucky. You will find yourself holding your breath as you walk silently on fallen leaves, hoping to catch an up-close glimpse of a silverback gorilla. Meeting these beautiful creatures is an incredible, unforgettable experience.

Right: One of the Parc National des Volcans' famous inhabitants

SILHOUETTE ISLAND

The Seychelles

Silhouette, the third-largest granite island in the Seychelles, is an unspoilt oasis of calm and tranquility. The lush, circular island is covered in dense, prehistoric rainforest. Accessible only by boat or helicopter and crossed only by unpaved tracks, this island remains virtually untouched by modern man. One of the amazing local draws is the giant tortoise, known to originate from only the Seychelles and the Galápagos Islands in the Pacific Ocean.

A designated National Marine Park, the island is surrounded by vast, colourful coral reefs that shelter exotic fish of all shapes and sizes, making it appealing to snorkelling and scuba fans. Other than relaxing on pristine beaches, enjoying the sunshine and exploring the rainforest and reefs, there is not much to do on Silhouette Island…heaven.

YOU SHOULD KNOW:
They have a cast-iron neoclassical mausoleum here that is supposedly the most remarkable piece of eccentricity in all of the Seychelles islands.

CONSERVATION
Today there is a large conservation drive to keep both Seychelles and Arnold's giant tortoises from extinction – the Seychelles Giant Tortoise Conservation Project. You can view these massive animals at the breeding farm near the old Dauban Coconut Plantation.

BAGAMOYO

Tanzania

WHEN SHOULD I GO?
During the dry season –
June–October and
January–February.
WHERE IS IT?
50km (31 miles) north of the
capital, Dar es Salaam.
ALSO KNOWN AS:
Bagamoyo means 'lay down
your heart' in Swahili.

Designated a UNESCO World Heritage Site, Bagamoyo is the oldest town in Tanzania and one of the most attractive, combining natural beauty with a significant, although sometimes grim, historical heritage – it was once a major slave-trading post.

The palm-studded, white sandy beaches of the area, with the crystalline blue waters of the Indian Ocean lapping on the shore, make for a relaxed atmosphere in Bagamoyo. Looking out towards the clear, blue sea, it is difficult to tell which century you are in as the traditional hand-built wooden dhows continue to ply the waters. The local fisherman sail in these Arabian-designed craft with their billowing triangular sails aloft, vying for space on the waves among the many dugout canoes. Women wade through the surf with impossibly large piles of laundry or fresh produce carried securely in baskets on their heads. Picture-postcard scenes from a bygone era.

MOUNT KILIMANJARO

Tanzania

Located in Mount Kilamanjaro National Park in the northeast of Tanzania, the famed Mount Kilamanjaro, Africa's highest peak, is a dormant volcano. It contains three cones: Kibo, Mawensi and Shira. Kibo is the highest and youngest peak, linked to Mawensi by an 11-km (7-mile) expanse at roughly 4,600m (15,000ft). Mawensi, the oldest cone, believed to have been the core of a former summit, is 5,400m (17,564ft) high. Shira rises to 3,800m (12,395 ft). The strenuous climb up the mountain is a very rewarding experience, and is a must for those seeking adventure. Experienced guides, accompanied by porters, lead visitors to the top of the mountain via various routes, passing through a variety of vegetation – forests, alpine vegetation, semi-desert and moorland – before reaching the icy top.

GREAT HEIGHTS
It's the highest mountain in Africa with an elevation 5,895m (19,340ft). The mountain extends for approximately 80km (50 miles) east to west and contains three cones.

YOU SHOULD KNOW: Visitors can arrange climbing tours from Moshi or Arusha and the climbs can take anywhere from five to eight days. The highlight is reaching the summit to view the vast expanse of Kenya and Tanzania below you at sunrise.

ZANZIBAR

Tanzania

A low-lying coral island, possibly part of the African continent at one time, Zanzibar is a jewel rising proudly out of the azure waters of the Indian Ocean. The island lures tourists with its coconut palms swaying in tropical breezes, its gently undulating hills still covered in some places with native forest and its stunning white sandy beaches. Another lure for visitors is the abundance of coral reefs surrounding the island. Dense with many types of marine life as well as different types of coral formations, Zanzibar is a scuba-diver and snorkeller's dream.

Stone Town is the old city and cultural heart of Zanzibar, little changed in the last 200 years. It is a place of winding alleys, bustling bazaars, mosques and grand Arab houses.

DON'T MISS:
Swimming with dolphins. Long-snouted spinner and bottlenose dolphins are favourites in these waters and monitored swims from the island can be arranged.

COMPETITIVE NEIGHBOURS

The original owners of the grand Arab houses found in Stone Town vied with each other over the extravagance of their dwellings. This one-upmanship is particularly reflected in the brass-studded, carved, wooden doors – there are more than 500 different examples of this handiwork.

SERENGETI

Tanzania

DID YOU KNOW?
Serengeti means 'endless plains' in the Masai language.

WORTH A SPLURGE:
This is the only park in Tanzania where you can take a hot-air balloon ride over the plains. If you do not treat yourself to this, you'll always wish that you had.

Serengeti National Park, established in 1951 as a wildlife refuge, occupies a vast expanse of land in Northern Tanzania. It is an appropriate description, as the park, the largest in Tanzania, rests on a high plateau with elevations ranging from 914-1,829m (3,000–6,000ft). Roughly the size of Northern Ireland, and considered to be the last great wildlife sanctuary, it comprises 14,763 sq km (5,700 sq miles) of rolling plains covered in savanna grasses. Home to more than 35 types of mammals including lion, cheetah, leopard, elephant, giraffe, hyena, hippopotamus, buffalo, rhino, baboon and antelope, as well as over 500 species of birds, the Serengeti is home to many plains animals that cannot be found anywhere else in the world. Its sparse vegetation allows for some of the best game viewing in Africa and it draws masses of visitors from across the globe.

The annual 800-km (497-mile) migration of wildebeest and zebras, driven by their search for food and water in the dry season around May, is one of the main attractions of the park. The unforgettable sight of a horde of one-to-two million of these animals stomping across the plains in organized chaos towards the western corridor is a spectacle not to be missed. The return pilgrimage generally takes place around December, depending on conditions.

NGORONGORO

Tanzania

DID YOU KNOW?
The area is often called 'The Eighth Wonder of the World' for its stunning beauty.

Nestled between the Serengeti and Lake Manyara National Parks, lies the stunning Ngorongoro Conservation Area. It is believed that millions of years ago Ngorongoro was roughly the same size as Mount Kilimanjaro. However, when the volcanic activity subsided it collapsed, forming a crater – the world's largest unbroken caldera. The crater is 610m (2,001ft) deep and covers an area of 260 sq km (162 sq miles). The park's diverse ecosystem includes active volcanoes, mountains, rolling plains, forests, lake dunes and the Olduvai Gorge. The area supports more than 550 species of birds and 115 species of mammals including elephant, cape buffalo, zebra, wildebeest and hippo. It is also the only place in Tanzania where you can more or less be guaranteed a sighting of the indigenous black rhino.

Another highlight of the park is the abundance on flamingoes of Lake Magadi on the crater's floor. The spectacle of a bubble-gum-coloured cloud of these magnificent birds against an emerald-green backdrop is unforgettable. The otherworldly scene is punctuated by the sight of Masai tribesmen in their traditional attire, herding cattle, sheep and goats. In the northern, and more remote, part of the conservation area are the Olmoti and Empakaai craters, Lake Natron and Oldoinyo Lengai, or the 'Mountain of God' as the Masai call it. On the eastern side of Empakaai are the Engakura ruins, which feature a terraced stone city.

HISTORICAL SIGNIFICANCE:

This is where Dr Mary Leakey found the fossil fragments of a distant human relative dating back 1.8 million years and the Laetoli footprints, proving that our ancestors walked upright 3.8 million years ago.

Right: The Ngorongoro Conservation Area

OLDUVAI GORGE

Tanzania

The home of the famous discoveries by Mary and Louis Leakey, Olduvai, or Oldupai, is the site where the fossil fragments of 'Nutcracker Man' or *Australopithecus boisei*, a 1.8 million-year-old fossil hominid, were discovered and is a must-see for archaeologist and anthropologist junkies. In 1976 Dr Mary Leakey invited Peter Jones to work with her at Olduvai. He helped assess the possible uses of the various stone tools and eventually uncovered the famous Laetoli footprints, which proved that our ancestors walked upright as long as 3.8 million years ago. The Olduvai Gorge contains a significant number of archaeological sites, with fossils, settlement remains and stone artefacts. Many of these can be seen in the museum. Olduvai is definitely worth adding to your itinerary for a day trip en route to either Serengeti National Park or the Ngorongoro Conservation Area.

LAKE MANYARA

Tanzania

WHAT IS THERE TO SEE?
Massive flocks of flamingoes
and lions sleeping in trees.

The lush, tropical oasis of Lake Manyara National Park, located at the foot of the Rift Valley, makes an excellent diversion on your visit to the Ngorongoro Crater and the Serengeti. Its shallow, alkaline waters are home to a variety of wildlife including huge flocks of flamingoes, lured by the crustaceans and algae that thrive in the high salt content of the lake.

The park, rich in acacia trees, attracts a number of giraffes, baboons, vervet and blue monkeys. There is also a healthy elephant population, although poaching means that the numbers are far below those that existed when Ian Douglas-Hamilton camped here in the 1970s, conducting extensive studies of these beasts that he subsequently published in his classic book *Among the Elephants*.

While you are here, you can watch the 350 species of birds that reside here, as well as a variety of mammals including gazelles, impalas, buffaloes, wildebeest, hyenas, hippos and the famous, tree-climbing lions. The best place for viewing lions and elephants, as well as many of the other larger mammals, is the Ndala River area. There are two hot springs, Maji Moto Ndogo and Maji Moto, that have large numbers of flamingo if the river waters are low.

RWENZORI MOUNTAINS

Tanzania

WHAT IS THERE TO SEE?
Luscious forest filled with a variety of trees, flowers, birds and small mammals.
WHERE IS IT?
25km (16 miles) from Kasese.
ALSO KNOWN AS:
'Rain maker'

Lying in the forested slopes of the Mubuku Valley, The Rwenzori National Park is an exotic paradise known for its lush afro-alpine vegetation and the plants and animals that thrive within it. The landscape here is a dense canopy of varying shades of green, and its textures make it resemble an enormous, leafy quilt. Symphonia trees, with their silver trunks and scarlet blooms, and podocarpus trees, with their fragrant evergreen scents, lend a soft, fresh, crispness to the air. Below these, adding to the tropical aromas, lie giant tree ferns, wild ginger, hisbiscus, begonias, balsams and aram lilies. Visitors can also view animals such as chimpanzees, black and white colobus monkeys, blue monkeys, elephants, bushbuck, giant forest hogs, hyraxes and leopards. You will not regret taking a trip to this African paradise.

MURCHISON FALLS

Uganda

WHERE IS IT?
97 km (60 miles) north
of Masindi, 354 km (220
miles) north of Kampala.
WORTH A SPLURGE:
Take a boat trip at the base
of the roaring falls
among the massive
hippo population.

Undoubtedly the highlight of the park is the roaring Murchison Falls, best enjoyed by boat. Here the Nile falls vertically 40m (131ft) through a 7-m (23-ft) gap crashing into the river below. From your river cruise you can watch, and listen to, hundreds of hippos wallowing along the shores, keeping the many Nile crocodiles company. If you prefer, the falls can be enjoyed from a path leading from above the falls to where the water crashes below.

Below the southern bank of the falls, thousands of bats can be seen roosting on the aptly named 'Bat Cliffs', swarming like large ravens at feeding time in the late evening. Giant kingfishers perch on low branches alongside Pel's fishing owls, and pennant-winged nightjars fly among herds of Uganda kobs and Jackson's hartebeests. Murchison Falls is certainly an adventure not to be missed.

LUANGWA

Zambia

The Luangwa Valley, at the western end of the Great Rift Valley opposite Lake Malawi, encompasses one of Africa's prime wildlife sanctuaries. Offering high concentrations and varieties of wildlife, the Luangwa National Park is framed by the Muchinga Mountain range where the valley floor lies 1,000 m (3,281 ft) beneath the surrounding plateau, bisected by the Luangwa River. The rugged beauty is made up of grass plains and woodlands dotted with thorn trees, with the the vegetation growing more densely the closer it gets to the river banks. Because of the vast number of streams and tributaries, the many-hued green forest beckons animals year-round. Game watching here is impressive with animals such as the rare black rhino, buffaloes, lions, leopards, spotted hyenas, roan antelopes and hartebeest. There is also a rich variety of birds.

DID YOU KNOW?
Luangwa is one of the best-known national parks in Africa for walking safaris.

WHEN SHOULD I GO? The park is open all year round, but between January and February the Luangwa River floods and turns the area into a rich, productive, beautiful ecosystem.

VICTORIA FALLS

Zambia

Described by the Kololo tribe living in the area in the 1800s as 'Mosi-oa-Tunya' – 'the Smoke that Thunders' – the vast columns of spray emanating from the majestic Victoria Falls can be seen from over 64km (40 miles) away as they plummet over a vertical drop of 100m (330ft) into a deep gorge below. In the height of the rainy season, over 546 million litres (2.5 million gallons) of water explodes through the nearly 2- km- (1.5-mile-) wide basalt fissure every minute, transforming the Zambezi from a tranquil, placid river into a tumultuous current of roaring water. Facing the falls, a twin sheer wall of basalt is capped by mist-soaked rainforest that has a path along its edge providing unparalleled views to the brave visitor who is not afraid to get soaked to the bone by the tremendous, smoke-like cloud of spray.

ROYAL CONNECTIONS

Dr David Livingstone, the first European known to discover Victoria Falls, named this natural phenomenon in honour of his queen.

WORTH A SPLURGE: To appreciate fully the incredible size of the falls, and the awesome power of the water as it carves into the deep gorges for 8km (5 miles), one must see it from the air. Pilots fly along the upper Zambezi and down into the gorge – making for an exhilarating and unforgettable experience.

ZIMBABWE RUINS
Zimbabwe

HOW TO GET HERE:
30km (19 miles) beyond the
south-eastern town
of Masvingo.
YOU SHOULD KNOW:
The ruins, although
extremely impressive in their
own right, mostly consist
of crumbling rock and
meandering pathways.

The Great Zimbabwe Ruins, a UNESCO World Heritage Site, are an architectural marvel covering nearly 730 hectares (1,800 acres), in an area stretching from eastern Zimbabwe into Botswana, across Mozambique and into South Africa. At its height, the capital of this wealthy Shona society was an important trading and religious centre, with upwards of 15,000 residents. The imposing structures, built by skilled masons on an open, wooded plain surrounded by hills, are made of regular, rectangular granite stones, carefully placed on one another in intricate patterns, without the use of mortar. The most impressive identified structure is the immense, elliptical Great Enclosure, which is thought to have been the royal compound. At nearly 100m (330ft) across and 255m (840ft) wide, it creates a vivid image of what this city may have looked like in its prime.

MATOBO NATIONAL PARK
Zimbabwe

The Matobo Hills, in Matobo National Park, are one of the world's most mythical places, their history dating back nearly four million years. The wind and rain have transformed the once flat area covered in sand and rock into giant granite boulders. The granite outcrops have been associated with human occupation since the middle Stone Age, providing natural shelter against the elements for the hunters and gatherers of the area. The boulders are home to hidden caves, sacred sites and one of the highest concentrations of rock art in Africa. The art is notable not only for its diversity, but also for its animation. The drawings depict men running, playing, hunting and dancing. Mammals are shown anatomically correctly and trees, birds, insects and reptiles are also accurately rendered, allowing ancient species to be identified.

WHAT'S IN A NAME
Mzilikazi, founder of the
Ndebele nation, named the area
'amaTobo', or 'the bald heads'
as the boulders reminded him of
his old ancestors.

YOU SHOULD KNOW: Some peaks, such as Shumba, Shaba and Shumba Sham, are considered sacred and locals believe that even to point at them will bring misfortune. Also, there are 39 species of snake here, most notably the deadly black mamba.

GRAND ERG OCCIDENTAL

Algeria

Algeria, nestled between Morocco and Tunisia, is the second-largest country in Africa. The northern portion, an area of mountains, valleys and plateaux between the Mediterranean Sea and the Sahara Desert, forms an integral part of the section of north Africa known as the Maghrib.

Contrary to popular belief, the majority of the Sahara is not soft, rolling sand dunes broken by a lush, green oasis complete with a blue lake in the centre. In reality, it's a vast expanse of rocks roughly the size of the United States. There is, however, an area where the Sahara turns into an endless sea of sand dunes that you may recognize from photographs, and this landscape phenomenon is known as an erg.

The Grand Erg Occidental is the second largest of the two dominating ergs of Algeria. The harsh conditions are such that no human life can be sustained here, so no villages are found within it and no roads cross through it. The endless dunes are experienced from the outside. You do not have to travel far into the erg before you experience a feeling of solitude and inferiority in this vast and majestic space.

DID YOU KNOW?
Most of the inhabitants of El Golea are Zenete Berbers and depend on agriculture for an income.

WHERE IS IT?
300km (186 miles) south of M'zab and 400km (249 miles) north of In Salah
CUTURAL ETIQUETTE:
This is a devoutly Islamic city and women should remain covered.

Right: The Grand Erg Occidental

EL GOLEA

Algeria

El Golea, also known as 'Little Eden', is a beautiful, lush oasis town in central Algeria and the gateway to the Sahara in the south. Situated 300km (186 miles) south of M'zab, and 400km (249 miles) north of In Salah, El Golea offers the best water in the country as well as a wide range of first-class agricultural products. Unlike most oases, which produce only dates, El Golea also offers plums, peaches, apricots, cherries, oranges and figs.

About 2km (1.2 miles) south of the oasis is the first Catholic church to be built in the Sahara, which was consecrated in 1938. Charles de Foucauld, a priest who wanted to bring Christianity to this part of Africa, is buried here.

DJEMILA

Algeria

Djemila is the modern name of ancient Cuicul and home to some of the greatest Roman ruins in northern Africa. The entrance to the site passes through the museum, which is bursting at the seams with its treasures. Its three rooms are loaded with mosaics, marble statues, oil lamps and traditional cookware.

Europe House, named after its most famous mosaic, is the best-known area of the ruins. Consisting of 18 rooms, it surrounds a courtyard dotted with decorative Ionic columns. The baptistery is ornamented by its original mosaics and the dome has been restored to its original glory. The Great Baths are in exceptionally good condition, and the pipes and double panels, where hot water once circulated, are visible in many places.

WHAT IS THERE TO SEE?
The ruins, the museum, Europe House, the baptistery and the Great Baths.
WHERE IS IT?
50km (31 miles) southwest of Setif and 150km (93 miles) east of Constantine.

UNESCO
'Situated 900 m above sea-level, Djemila, or Cuicul, with its forum, temples, basilicas, triumphal arches and houses, is an interesting example of Roman town planning adapted to a mountain location'

YOU SHOULD KNOW:
The central area of Tassili N'Ajjer can only be entered if you have an official guide with you, or you are travelling with an accredited tour group – most of which leave from Djanet.

TASSILI N'AJJER

Algeria

Tassili N'Ajjer, a vast mountainous plateau to the north of the Hoggar Mountains, is protected as a national park, biosphere reserve and World Heritage Site. Much of its wild landscape is characterized by deep chasms and dramatic cliffs. Composed largely of sandstone, erosion in the area has resulted in nearly 300 natural rock arches being formed, along with many other spectacular landforms. Because of the altitude and the water-holding properties of the sandstone, the vegetation is somewhat richer than the surrounding desert; it includes a very scattered woodland of the endangered endemic Saharan cypress and Saharan myrtle in the higher eastern half of the range. The range is also noted for its prehistoric rock paintings and other ancient archaeological sites, dating from the last Ice Age when the local climate was much wetter, with savannah rather than desert. The rock paintings, which are up to 8,000 years old, can be found in the central area of Tassili N'Ajjer Sahara.

HOGGAR

Algeria

The Hoggar Mountains, one of the true highlights of the Sahara, are too enormous and too scarcely populated for easy exploration, but it is worth the effort. If you have three days to explore the area, you can enjoy the journey known as the Hoggar Circuit. The first village of importance you will reach, after passing the Ermitage de Père Foucauld, is Hirafok, before Tazrouk. Tahifet, beyond the pass of Azrou, is a beautiful village set by a wide river. At Tamekrest, there are waterfalls even more impressive than those at Cascades de Imeleoulaouene. In the oasis of Abalassa, near the town of Tamanghasset, lies the tomb of Tin Hinan, the famous matriach believed to be the ancestor of the Tuareg of Ahaggar. According to legend, Tin Hinan originated from the Tafilalt region in the Atlas Mountains.

INHABITANTS
The Tuareg, one of the most mythical peoples of Africa, are famous for their blue garments and for having veiled men in contrast to the women, who enjoy a great deal of freedom.

WHEN SHOULD I GO? The climate is very hot in the summer but temperatures fall to below 0°C (32°F) in the winter.

HOW DO I GET THERE? There is no public transport to the Hoggar region, but it is easy to rent a 4x4 and a guide.

ASWAN

Egypt

DON'T MISS: Sharia el-Souq, a short way inland – a bustling outdoor market full of vivid colours and the aromas of exotic spices. Traditional food, Nubian jewellery and textiles can be bought here.

Aswan is the southernmost frontier town in Egypt, considered the 'gateway to Africa'. It lies at the first of seven cataracts, or Nile rapids, created by exposed granite that made the river impassable to boats, and thus created a thriving trade centre.

The relaxed atmosphere of this riverside town made it popular as a winter resort among wealthy Europeans enticed by the setting and the rumours that the dry heat provided a cure for various ailments. Because of the influx of foreigners, a Nile-side Corniche was created, providing moorings for the many steamers. The Aswan Corniche is the most attractive waterfront boulevard in Egypt and, with its lovely walkways and gorgeous views of palm-covered islands with a backdrop of sandy white hills, has been compared to the French Riviera. It is worth the cost of hiring a felucca and floating amidst the scenery as if in a dream.

At the southern end of the Corniche is the Old Cataract Hotel – famous as one of the locations for the film *Death on the Nile*. Built in 1899 on a rocky outcrop in the river, its grand, pink exterior and Moorish dining halls are a reminder of times past. Its large terrace has been enjoyed by such luminaries as Winston Churchill, Jimmy Carter and Diana, Princess of Wales.

VALLEY OF THE KINGS

Egypt

YOU SHOULD KNOW:
Tickets cannot be bought at the site and must be purchased at the West Bank Ticket Office – individual tickets are required for each tomb, temple or group of tombs.

Right: Ancient sculptures in the Mortuary Temple of Hatshepsut, Valley of the Kings

The Valley of the Kings lies in an unassuming, sun-scorched desert valley surrounded by steep, rocky hills on the west bank of Thebes. A total of 62 tombs has been discovered to date. The tombs were created to preserve the pharoah's mummies for eternity. Each of these, located deep within the ground, was designed to resemble the underworld with an descending corridor leading to an antechamber, or hall, and connected to a burial chamber. Mesmerizing floor-to-ceiling images decorate the chambers to offer a guide to the afterlife. Lavish jewels, papyrus scrolls, furniture, ritual objects, statues of various gods and effigies of the king filled the spaces as offerings to the gods. The most famous tomb in the valley is that of Tutankhamun, discovered nearly intact in 1922 by British archaeologist Howard Carter.

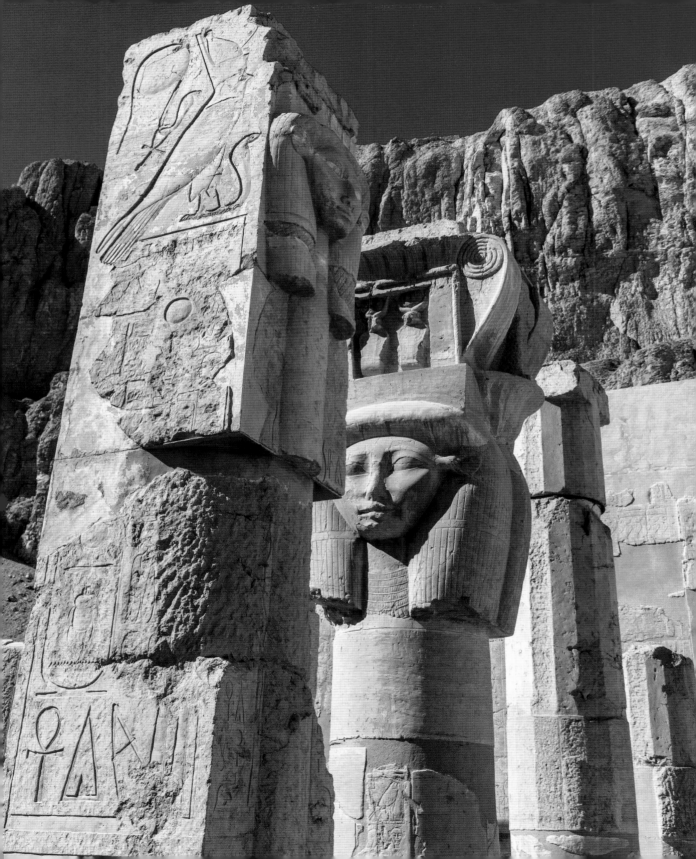

KARNAK

Egypt

DON'T MISS:
The sound and light show in the evenings – one of the best in the world.

Karnak, or Ipet-Isut as it was known to the ancient Egyptians, was built as the heart of Thebes, the thriving capital of Egypt, over a period of 1,500 years beginning during the Middle Kingdom (c. 1900 B C) with the erection of the Great Temple of Amun.

Surviving as the most stunning architectural example of the day, as well as the largest temple ever built, Karnak was known as the 'Most Perfect of Places'. Its enormous stature and ominous presence dwarfs anything else you will encounter in Egypt, and most probably the rest of the world.

The dizzying size and breadth of the legendary Great Hypostyle Hall is difficult to comprehend. It comprises 134 massive columns, measuring from 15m (50ft) up to an awe-inspiring 21m (69ft) in height. The columns are so wide, it takes six adults to reach around one, and it is estimated that at least 50 adults could comfortably stand on top of one. At one point the hall was covered, allowing minimal light among these dense columns – between each of which would have been large statues of the pharaohs – creating an incredibly imposing sight.

DID YOU KNOW?
The Great Pyramid at Giza is the only one of the Seven Ancient Wonders of the World still in existence.

PYRAMIDS OF GIZA

Egypt

TRAVELLERS' TIP:
Only 300 tickets are sold a day for each of the two entrances – it is first come, first served – and only two of the three pyramids are open at a time. Go early!

Right: The Sphinx and the Pyramids of Giza

The pyramids of Giza are the world's oldest tourist attraction and remain cloaked in mystery, continuing to amaze and confound archaeologists, physicists and astrologists alike. At first sight, the pyramids, not unlike the *Mona Lisa* at the Louvre, can be disappointing. After so many photographs of these hulking structures surrounded by nothing but desert, it is a bit disconcerting to see suburban Cairo virtually resting against the paws of the great Sphinx. Still, the enchanting half-lion (representing royalty), half-human figure (with a traditional headdress symbolizing power) casts an impressive image, particularly with the shadow of the Great Pyramid of Khufu looming in the near distance. Carved from a single outcrop of bedrock, it is the earliest example of colossal Egyptian sculpture.

MOUNT SINAI

Egypt

DON'T MISS: Spending the night on the mountain and watching the sun rise over the desert.

Mount Sinai, considered by many to be where Moses spent 40 days and received the Ten Commandments, continues to be one of the world's major pilgrimage sites. Whether you believe in the mountain's history or not, at a height of 2,285m (7,500ft), you certainly can't deny the spectacular desert views that can be seen from its peak at sunrise. Ask any of the hordes of visitors that make the trek daily!

Mount Sinai can be reached by various routes – the most direct, and challenging, one is via the 3,750 Steps of Repentance, named after the penitent monk who built them. The Camel Path – named after the Bedouin who wait here with their camels in case of an opportunity to help weary travellers – is slightly easier on the knees and takes on average three hours to reach the summit. The Camel Path joins up with the last 750 Steps of Repentance at Elijah's Basin, a hollow in the mountainside marked by a 500-year-old cypress tree where God is said to have spoken to Elijah as he hid from Jezebel. This is the spot where you're asked to sleep if you decide to spend the night here. On the actual summit is the Chapel of the Holy Trinity, a Greek Orthodox church built in 1934 on the ruins of a fourth-century church. The chapel once held beautiful paintings and ornaments, but usually remains locked now because of desecration by tourists.

SIWA OASIS

Egypt

ALSO WORTH A VISIT:
The town of Siwa – a 13th-century mud-brick settlement, surrounded by high walls created to protect against attack. In 1926, a series of violent rain storms caused the buildings to disintegrate, creating a Dali-esque appearance. These surreal buildings are fun to explore and afford an excellent view of the oasis and distant desert bluffs.

Siwa is the most remote of all Egypt's oases, lying some 18.3m (60ft) below sea level on an old date caravan route. It's a small life-sustaining area marooned in the middle of the Western desert, isolated from Cairo by 550km (342 miles) of nothing but desert..

Visitors can enjoy the dreamlike setting of dense green date palms, an abundance of olive trees, and more than 300 freshwater springs and streams. Also within the oasis is a small market, offering the highly valued and rare embroidered clothing and heavy, silver jewellery local to the area. Siwa is also known for its basketware woven from date palm fronds, as well as its highly coveted pottery.

WHITE DESERT

Egypt

The White Desert is one of the most frequently visited places in western Egypt. Its surreal rock formations and truly white sands offer a stunningly stark contrast to the yellow desert. The rocks take on tints of blue, pink and orange as the sun sets, and at night the sands resemble snow. Apart from the heat, it could easily be mistaken for an Arctic landscape.

HOW DO I GET THERE?
Trips into the desert can be arranged from either Bahariyya or Farafra – Farafra is recommended.
WHEN SHOULD I GO?
October to March is the most popular time to visit.

The formations, composed of a combination of chalk and limestone, were created by wind erosion. They consist of various organic shapes, sometimes defying the laws of nature and gravity, with enormous rocks perched precariously on particularly thin bases. The area is referred to by Bedouin as 'Wadi Gazar', or 'Valley of the Carrots', after the shape of some of the pinnacles found here. It has also been said that the rocks resemble white sphinxes, stone camels or mythological birds. One thing is for certain; the rock formations offer a stunning backdrop to an otherwordly desert experience. Also worth exploring are the springs found in the surrounding area. Unlike the rest of the desert, which lies in the 120-km (75-mile) Farafra Depression, the springs are marked by hillocks created when sand attaches itself to vegetation near water. The plants continue to grow despite their struggle to avoid being suffocated by sand, and eventually form dramatic hills.

TEMPLE OF EDFU

Egypt

The Temple of Edfu remains the best-preserved ancient temple in Egypt, as well as the second-largest temple after Karnak. It was built during the reigns of six Ptolemies in dedication to Horus, the falcon-headed god, with construction beginning in 237BC and ending in 57BC.

The temple was believed to have been built on the historic site of the great battle between Horus and Seth, so the current temple is only the last of many erected in this location. Legend has it that the original structure, home to a statue of Horus, was a prehistoric grass hut. The current ruins are built of sandstone, on top of a smaller New Kingdom temple pylon (doorway).

This masterpiece was found completely submerged underneath the desert sands, except the top of the entrance pylon. A small amount of stone had been removed from the exposed part, but upon excavation it was found to be in otherwise perfect condition.

The main building, including the great Hypostyle Hall, is impressive for both its size and its condition. Nearly every surface is covered in carvings, hieroglyphs and numerous reliefs.

DON'T MISS:
The Temple of Apollo, originally constructed in the seventh century BC, and rebuilt three centuries later. The Great Baths of the Temple of Apollo are in exceptional condition, with their pipes still visible. About 50m (165ft) from the temple lies the Fountain of Apollo, whose waters were once considered to be curing.

CYRENE

Libya

Cyrene is an important archaeological site near the village of Shahat. More than 76 Roman statues dating back to the 2nd century AD were found here in 2005. According to architects, so many of the statues remained undiscovered for such a long period because a supporting wall of the temple fell on its side during an earthquake in 365, burying them. The statues remained hidden under stone, rubble and earth for 1,600 years, protected from the elements.

The ruins, which are only partly excavated, are in incredible condition, the floor mosaics still clearly visible and the foundation structures largely intact.

LEPTIS MAGNA

Libya

DID YOU KNOW?

The prosperous Roman city was sacked by Berbers in 523AD and subsequently abandoned.

WHAT IS IT?
The home to Hadrian's baths and other significant ancient ruins.

WHERE IS IT?
On the Mediterranean coast of north Africa in the Tripolitana region of Libya.

Leptis Magna is a UNESCO World Heritage site on the Mediterranean coast of north Africa, in the Tripolitania region of Libya. Originally founded by the Phoenicians in the tenth century BC as a trading port, it survived colonization by Spartans, became a Punic city, and was eventually established as part of the new Roman province of Africa around 23BC. The spectacular city of Leptis Magna was built in traditional Roman architectural styles and was a hub for trade, culture and the arts.

The prosperous Roman city was sacked by Berbers in 523AD and subsequently abandoned. Various materials from the site have been recycled by pillagers throughout history, but during a series of excavations in the 1920s, the magnificent ruins, one of the best preserved Roman cities in the world, were uncovered. Despite the condition and range of the incredibly well-preserved ruins and its status as a World Heritage Site, Leptis Magna remains largely ignored, apart from some recent interest from a team of British archaeologists. Thankfully, the arid desert climate has preserved the ruins of Leptis Magna, which were covered in sand for at least half a century. These amazing structures provide an incredible insight into the life and times of the early Romans in Africa.

FÈS

Morocco

WHAT TO TASTE: *Harira*, a hearty bean-based soup with vegetables and meat, *tagines*, stewed vegetables, meat or fish cooked in earthernware cones, and cous cous.

Fès is the 'symbolic heart' of Morocco – its intellectual, historical and spiritual capital. As you wander through its labyrinthine shady streets, exotic smells of mint and spices waft through the air, dappled light falls on the whitewashed, crumbling grandeur of the old city and you can feel the tangible mystery and intrigue of this, the oldest of the four imperial cities.

Unlike many walled cities, Old Fès hasn't burst its banks, and its gates and walls remain intact. The *medina* of Fès el-Bali (Old Fès) is one of the largest living and working medieval cities in the world. Consisting of the 'traditional seven elements' – mosques, *medersas* (Koranic schools), *souks* (markets), *fondouks* (lodging and trading houses), fountains, a *hammam* (steam bath) and a bakery – it is a bustling combination of city, museum and workshop that has changed very little with the passing of time.

The streets are filled with artisans creating and selling their wares using traditional techniques. You can see baby-soft leathers being tanned, the sun glinting off copper pots as they are being soldered, brass plates being engraved, colourful ceramics, and embroidery, cedar, woodwork and carpets being hawked in hoarse voices that echo in the many courtyards.

WHAT TO DO:
Wander through the crumbling walls of the Kasbah, getting lost in the myriad streets of the *medina*, while taking in the exotic scents of cinnamon and tobacco floating on the coastal breeze. Stop in a local coffee shop and enjoy a cup of the traditional mint tea. When you want a break from the crowds, head to the rocky coast.

Right: Bou Inania Madrasa minaret, Fès

TANGIER

Morocco

As you arrive in Tangier, sailing on the turquoise Mediterranean, you will see a vast, rustic, yet developed coastline outlined by the Rif Mountains. Many visitors come to Tangier because of its easily accessible location – from Spanish day-trippers and those seeking sunshine on lovely beaches in modern resorts, to those wanting to experience a piece of history. Tangier is a melting pot with something for everyone. It has led a varied cultural existence through the years, and the city bears witness to Phonecian, Roman, Portugese, British and French influences. As you wander through the busy streets you are likely to rub shoulders with rural Rifi Berbers in their traditional striped *mehndis* (bright woven blankets), expats, tourists, diplomats, princes, poets and artists. Morocco has always been a land of free spirits, and Tangier is no exception.

MARRAKESH

Morocco

Marrakesh is the lively former capital of Morocco, famed for its markets and festivals, hippies and criminals, devout and destitute, debauched and intellectual – it is a study in dichotomies. As you wander down the crowded, maze-like, colourful, broad avenues you will pass crumbling architectural treasures, donkeys and mules carrying produce, woodwork and weaving workshops, steam-billowing hammams, ancient mosques and shiny, modern hotels.

The pulsating energy centre of Marrakesh is the Djemaa el-Fna. Follow the enticing aromas and deafening noise into the calamitous atmosphere of this enormous market in the midst of the *medina*. Part mystic zoo, part animalistic carnival, part Olympic village – this market has to be seen to be believed.

DON'T MISS: Sunset in the Djemaa when the surrounding buildings turn orange, blue and pink, after which the hundreds of gas lamps are lit, creating haunting shadows. The carnival-like atmosphere continues and grows in ferocity through the wee hours.

WHAT'S IN A NAME?
Marrakesh is also known as 'Assembly of the Dead' or 'Meeting Place at the End of the World', which is believed to refer to the practice of executing criminals here.

TAFRAOUTE

Morocco

DID YOU KNOW?

Trafraoute is known for its prehistoric rock carvings and the painted blue rocks of Belgian artist Jean Veran.

TRY TO CATCH:

The annual Almond Blossom Festival. The delicate blooms offer another dimension to this already spectacular landscape. During the festival, the otherwise sleepy town of Tafraoute is transformed by a carnival-like atmosphere when the *souk* (market), complete with dancers and musicians, springs up.

Tafraoute is a conglomeration of ochre-covered buildings set amid green trees, offering a spectacular contrast of colours against the surrounding pink rocks of the Anti-Atlas Mountains. The area is known for its dramatic geography, with its expanses of red desert, and is also the official almond capital of Morocco

While visiting Tafraoute, there are three attractions that should be on any traveller's list: Les Pierres Bleues – Jean Veran's famous Blue Rock; the palm groves southeast of Tafraoute; and the gazelle rock carving. Over a period of three months in 1984, the Belgian artist and a team of Morroccan firemen collaborated in the creation of one of the most unusual art installation pieces on Earth. They covered the small hills and granite boulders of the Anti-Atlas Mountains with 18 tonnes of blue, red, violet and white paint. Although now somewhat faded, the fusion of art and nature is still mesmerizing and the contrast of bright blue against the brilliant reds of the desert is unforgettable.

Also worth a full day's trip are the palm groves. Past 'Napoleon's Cap' with its massive boulders on your right, there is a winding, paved trail that leads you through the Anti-Atlas Mountains where you can enjoy scenic views of the Ammeln Valley from Ait Mansour, to Afella-n-Ighir and back to Tafraoute.

SIDI IFNI

Morocco

WHAT IS IT? A sleepy coastal town.
HISTORICAL SIGNIFICANCE: The last Spanish colonial outpost in Morocco.

The charming, sleepy coastal town of Sidi Ifni, the last Spanish colonial outpost in Morocco, offers impressive Art Deco architecture and a hospitable Spanish atmosphere to its guests. Its cliff-top location with Andalusian-style gardens and tiled fountains are a testament to its Spanish roots – they only left in 1969. The buildings are painted in whimsical pastel colours – in contrast to the surrounding French-influenced towns with their rich palette of dark hues – which lend a peaceful and relaxed air.

In the main square, Place Hassan II, you can wander among some modest private homes, the now-defunct Spanish Consulate, the law courts which were once a church, the town hall, the royal palace and the Hotel Bellevue which overlooks the beach and the port.

There is a Sunday souk, held at an abandoned airstrip near town, filled with storytellers and musicians. The beaches are pleasant, with camels wandering through the misty sea air, and quieter than the more established, but sometimes overrun, areas around Agadir.

DID YOU KNOW?
Chefchaouen is one of the largest producers of marijuana in Morocco.

CHEFCHAOUEN

Morocco

WHAT TO BUY:
Wool items and quality traditional crafts such as handmade bronze bowls, trays and plates.
YOU SHOULD KNOW:
Marijuana is sold in the open markets alongside the traditional vegetables, herbs and spices

A short drive from Tangier, nestled in the Rif mountain region, the picturesque medieval town of Chefchaouen was settled at the end of the 15th century as a mountain retreat for the Moors and Jews who had been expelled from Spain by the Catholic Monarchs. Its striking *medina* is one of the most charming in Morocco, with signature blue-washed, gabled houses and artisans on narrow streets selling traditional wares, including kaftans and embroidered jellabahs, carpets, leather goods, pottery and copper. The Plaza Uta El Hammam is dotted with elegant buildings and dominated by a 17th-century mosque with a delicate six-sided brick and plaster minaret, and is punctuated by mulberry trees shading welcoming cafés where you can sit and enjoy a refreshing mint tea.

TAROUDANT

Morocco

DON'T MISS:
Take a *calèche* (a horse-drawn carriage) around the city and watch the fading light of the setting sun highlight the olive trees surrounding the town.

An ideal base for the exploration of the Souss Valley and western High Atlas, Taroudant is known for its bustling market and fresh produce. A mixture of Arabic and Tashelhit Berber languages can be heard as you stroll through the town's recently restored salmon-coloured walls.

As you head towards the market you'll weave through crowds of men on bicycles with fresh bundles of coriander in their baskets, fishmongers and men tanning leather, shining brass pans or carving wood. The enticing smells of lavender, thyme, saffron and mint waft through the hazy sunshine, as you stop to admire the Grand Mosque with its yellow minaret and teal-green, houndstooth tiling. On a clear day, the snowy peaks of the Djebel Toubkal can be seen hovering in the distance past the gates of the Kasbah.

LIXUS

Morocco

Lixus is a wonderfully scenic site with incredible ruins of a Roman imperial outpost. Settled by the Phoenicians in the seventh century BC and later an important Carthaginian site, Lixus remains a most impressive ruin, for its relics as well as its stunning location.

Largely unexplored and unexcavated, Lixus is the site of an ampitheatre dating back to the first century AD, which would have held a few hundred people. Behind it are the baths, with spectacular mosaics that remain largely intact. If you can imagine back 2,000 years, it would be easy to realize that Lixus could quite easily have been one of the most beautiful Roman cities in existence.

LEGENDARY ASSOCIATIONS
The ancients believed this to be the site of the Garden of the Hesperides and a sanctuary of Hercules, where he gathered golden apples.

WHERE IS IT? North of the modern seaport of Larache, Morocco, on the right bank of the Wadi Loukkos, or Locus River.
WHAT IS THERE TO SEE? Remains of ancient baths, temples and other historical remnants.

AIT-BEN-HADDOU

Morocco

Ait-Ben-Haddou, a UNESCO World Heritage site at the crossroads of the southern oasis routes, is a striking example of the architecture of southern Morocco, with its earthen buildings surrounded by high walls on a hillside. The red *pise* (straw and mud) towers in this village fortress are said to resemble a melting sandcastle. The surrounding almond trees lend a sumptuous air to the village, which has beautiful views over the river valley. Among the dramatic terrain of the snowy Atlas mountains reaching to the Sahara desert, is a varied landscape encompassing large canyons, gorges and lunar steppes, making the province of Ouarzazate a preferred choice for filmmakers. Ait-Ben-Haddou is notable for Kasbah Taourirt, which is said to be the best-preserved kasbah in the country.

WORTH A SPLURGE:
Have dinner at Chez Dimitri, one of the best traditional restaurants in town.
WORTH A TASTE:
Mechoui – shoulder of lamb with fennel and peas.

IN THE MOVIES

Known as the 'Hollywood of Morocco', films such as *Soddom and Gomorrah*, *Lawrence of Arabia*, *The Last Temptation of Christ* and *Gladiator* were all filmed here.

VOLUBILIS

Morocco

BEST TIME TO VISIT:
Sunset, when the shadows on the monuments grow longer and you will have the place to yourself.
WHAT TO SEE:
Over 30 nearly perfect mosaics.

The Roman ruins of Volubilis, stretching out across 40 hectares (100 acres), are the best-preserved ruins in Morocco and well worth a visit. Located between Rabat and Fez near the Moroccan town of Meknes, Volubilis served as a central Roman administrative city in the third century BC. Built on top of a Carthaginian city, Volubilis, unlike most Roman outposts, was not abandoned after the Romans lost north Africa to the Arabs. The city remained inhabited until the 18th century when it was largely demolished to provide building materials for the palaces of Moulay Ismail, in nearby Meknes. Although much of the Roman architecture, mostly dating back to 217AD, was lost, there are still some well-preserved columns, a basilica, a triumphal arch and around 30 high-quality mosaics. It is truly a pleasure to witness such beautifully well-preserved artwork, whether or not you're an art-history buff.

THE SUDD

Sudan

More than half of the water flowing down the White Nile, or the Bahr al Jabal as the river is referred to in this region for its sluggish rate, is held in The Sudd, creating a massive floodplain called the toic. The Sudd is roughly 320km (200 miles) long and 240km (150 miles) wide. The dense aquatic vegetation making up The Sudd disperses the river into various channels.

The Sudd has created such an obstacle that passage was not managed until the Egyptians completed the first navigation in 1840. The first effort to create a channel took over four years and constant maintenance is required to keep the channel clear.

SIZE MATTERS
The Sudd is the world's largest swamp. It is about the size of England during the wet season.

DON'T MISS: The Zeraf Game Reserve which protects most of the central part of The Sudd wetland. The game reserve is important in protecting populations of Nile Lechwe antelope, Sitatunga antelope and Hippopotamus, not to mention the enourmous numbers of migrating birds.

TUNIS

Tunisia

Recognized by UNESCO as a World Heritage Site in 1979, the *medina* in Tunis remains the central artery to this diverse port city at the end of the Gulf of Tunis.

The lively, oval, walled city of the *medina* is made up of covered alleyways, hidden passages and tunnelled bazaars, all of which are active with traders and artisans hawking their wares and creating an enticing energy filled with exotic scents and vivid colours. There are 700 historical monuments to see, including palaces, mosques, mausoleums, *madrasas* and fountains dating back to the Almohad and Hafsid periods. The *medina* is characterized by its quirkiness, with various architectural and decorative styles including 400 Art Deco buildings.

WORTH A DIVERSION:
The pretty cliff-top resort town of Sidi Bou Said, with its whitewashed buildings and bright blue shutters.

HISTORY
Built in the seventh century AD, the *medina* lost its status as the heart of Tunis when the French built the new town around the turn of the 20th century.

EL DJEM

Tunisia

DID YOU KNOW?

El Djem is home to the world's second-largest coliseum.

HOW BIG IS THE COLISEUM?

It's an impressive 138m (453ft) long and 114m (374ft) wide. Its capacity is estimated to have been 30,000.

El Djem was once a thriving agricultural region known for its production of olive oil and wheat, as well as its grand coliseum, second only in size to the one in Rome, and the most impressive remaining Roman monument in Africa. The sight of this monument rising in the distance, surrounded by modest houses on the flat Sahel plain as you enter this small town, is both wonderful and slightly incongruous, its present surroundings lending no hint of its former glory.

Built around 200AD, it was the scene for often cruel and bloody gladiator circus 'games' modelled on those of ancient Rome. Today, the echoing cries of martyrs and large beasts have been replaced by classical Arabian music and haunting European concertos, as the coliseum now plays host to the world-famous orchestras that come to perform at its annual summer International Festival of Symphonic Music.

The craft of mosaic-making has been rediscovered and El Djem has been reborn as a centre for the art. Examples of a spectacular selection of original mosaics can be seen at the impressive archeological museum, which, in conjunction with the looming structure of the coliseum, makes this site well worth a visit.

DOUGGA

Tunisia

Dougga is an imposing site — some say the most dramatic in Tunisia. Once the seat of power for the Numidian King, Massinissa, it was a large and prosperous town and now stands as the best-preserved Roman monument in Northern Africa.

A welcome addition to the UNESCO World Heritage Site roster since 1997, Dougga is scenically positioned high on the side of a valley overlooking wheat fields. At one time more than 25,000 people lived here and the intact remains to be explored include 12 Roman temples (three of which were transformed into churches in the fourth century), three baths, numerous cisterns and fountains, two heavily restored theatres, a nymphaeum, an aqueduct, a market, a circus, several necropolises and a handful of mausoleums. The site is so well preserved that even the scars of chariot wheels on cobbled streets continue to bear witness to its history. The sheer number of buildings in such remarkable condition allow one to imagine the thriving metropolis's grand infrastructure.

The ruins of Dougga are a fantastic representation of a large Roman site, offering an interesting historical flashback for both the novice and the scholar.

DID YOU KNOW?
The island claims to be the Land of the Lotus Eaters, celebrated in Homer's *Odyssey.*

WHAT TO DRINK:
Boukha, the noxious local brew said to mimic the fabled response to imbibing lotus juice.
WHAT NOT TO DRINK:
The slightly saline tap water.

JERBA ISLAND

Tunisia

The island of Jerba claims to be the Land of the Lotus Eaters, celebrated in Homer's *Odyssey* as the perfect respite for relaxation and surrender. In the legendary tale, Odysseus and his crew stayed here enjoying the soothingly narcotic fruits of the lotus as they recovered from battle. Today there is a modern example of this fabled elixir, the locally brewed *boukha*, a fermented beverage made from dates or figs. This small, semi-arid, palm-fringed island of myth has pretty, but touristy, beaches on its shores and unique homes and mosques inland. The quaint interior of the island is divided into farms by date and olive groves. The whitewashed, fortified mosques, an anomaly in Tunisia, glow in the bright sunshine. A bicycle ride around the island is an excellent way to experience its charms.

KAIROUAN

Tunisia

TRAVELLERS' TIP:
The street names here change often, and usually have two names to begin with.
WORTH A SPLURGE:
Kairouan is well known for its beautiful knotted and woven carpets.

Tunisia's oldest city, and Islam's fourth holiest centre after Mecca, Medina and Jerusalem, Kairouan has been a religious pilgrimage site since 670 AD when it was chosen by Oqba Ibn Nafi because of divine inspiration. Several omens led him to the pronunciation of Kairouan as a holy site and capital city. First, upon leading his army to a stop, he looked down and spied a golden cup that he had last seen on a trip he had taken to Mecca long ago. Second, he discovered a spring connected to the holy well of Zem Zem in Mecca. Finally, he witnessed the appearance of 'noxious beasts and reptiles' that he had previously banished for eternity. The main attraction in Kairouan, a UNESCO World Heritage Site, is its Great Mosque, or the Mosque of Iqba, at the far northeastern section of the *medina*. The mosque is grand in its simplicity in comparison with the more delicate details seen in later examples of mosque architecture.

DAKHLA LAGOON

Tunisia

The Dakhla Lagoon in the western Sahara is an oasis of beauty between the desert and the sea, and offers a surprisingly prolific variety of wildlife. The natural habitat consisting of sea-grass beds, plains of algae and salt pans, hosts over 120 species of mollusc, including an endemic crustacean, the Cerapopsis takamado, and 41 species of fish. This is also the most northerly area to find Atlantic humpbacked dolphins, as well as the second-most important wintering site for migratory birds in Morocco. Here you are most likely to see Caspian terns, lesser black-backed gulls and great ringed plovers. It may be worth wandering down to the beach to see the traditional fisherman in their coloured boats, but otherwise head straight for the lagoon.

DID YOU KNOW?
This part of the Sahara is one of the least-populated areas on Earth.

DON'T MISS: The constant warm temperature, combined with regular wind, creates the ideal atmosphere for windsurfing, kitesurfing and wake boarding. The novelty of participating in watersports in the desert is reason enough to come and visit this fantastic Saharan outpost.

MATMATA

Tunisia

As you approach Matmata it is difficult to discern any life in this isolated and seemingly deserted, lunar-like outpost. Upon further examination, you'll discover the fascinating underground homes of the troglodytes. Made famous in the first *Star Wars* film, these traditional residences for the Berbers of the area have turned Matmata into one of the key tourist stops in Tunisia. The sandstone pit dwellings of the troglodytes are carved from the soft, sandstone hills of Matmata and boast a population of more than 5,000 Berbers. The pit dwellings are made using a design that is more than 400 years old. Rooms are dug around a vertical-walled circular pit, which is 7m (23ft) deep and 10m (33ft) in diameter. Often, smaller rooms are created on a second floor, and are reached by stairs.

TRAVELLERS' TIP:
While you are in the village, take advantage of viewing the traditional homes, but be sure to respect the privacy of the locals. Instead of peering through into their personal space, visit the museum, which was created by the local women, and stay overnight in one of the converted caves.

IN THE MOVIES
Hôtel Sidi Driss, one of the converted caves, has become one of the most famous filming locations of *Star Wars* and is nicknamed 'the *Star Wars* hotel'.

OKAVANGO DELTA

Botswana

WHERE IS IT?
Near the Moremi Game Reserve and Chobe National Park.
WHEN SHOULD I GO?
Mid-May to mid-September, when the water levels are neither too high nor too low.

The Okavango River, originating in the uplands of Angola, flows into, and then spreads over, the sandy spaces of the Kalahari forming an immense and wonderful inland delta It covers 15,000 sq km (932 sq miles), and its swamp waters are crystal clear and deliciously clean.

One of the best ways to explore is by *mokoro*, the traditional dugout canoe, paddled by one of the skillful local guides who can weave through the passages showing you some of the best wilderness that the country has to offer. Crocodiles, hippos, elephants, buffaloes and several rare species of antelope, in addition to other large game, can be found here, earning the Okavango its reputation as one of the world's premier wilderness areas. Why not sit back and listen to the tranquil sounds of the wild, the splashing of water buffaloes on the shore and the flapping of wings, or watch giraffes grazing in the distance, while date palms sway in the breeze.

THE SKELETON COAST

Namibia

The Skeleton Coast Park encompasses 2 million hectares (7,720 sq miles) of dramatic and surprising landscape including sand dunes, canyons and mountain ranges. The dunes come in a variety of guises, from hummock dunes to transverse dunes and crescent dunes, offering a loud whisper when a profusion of tiny, multi-coloured pebble granules, consisting of agates, lava and granites, slide down their steep surface. The windswept dunes and flat plains give way to rugged canyons and extensive mountain ranges with richly coloured walls of volcanic rock. If you're fortunate enough to be one of the visitors to the Skeleton Coast, you will not quickly forget the feeling of walking back through time and into a forgotten world.

SPOOKY SHORES

The aptly named coast is famed for the numerous ghostly shipwrecks located on its remote and inaccessible shores.

WHEN SHOULD I GO? Because of the fog-belt, temperatures at the coast vary considerably from 6–36°C (42–97°F), but never drop below freezing point. In the interior, although it is warm in the mornings, it cools off as the day progresses. A general lack of moisture gives rise to chilly nights.

CAPE CROSS SEAL RESERVE

Namibia

The Cape Fur Seal is the largest of the world's nine species of fur seals, and they are, in fact, a species of sea lion. Along the Namibian and South African coastline, there are as many as 650,000 fur seals in the 24 colonies. Cape Cross Seal Reserve in Namibia is the largest breeding area, with a population of between 80,000 and 100,000 seals.

The bulls, or males, arrive at the colony in October and, after marking their territories, will fiercely defend them. The pregnant cows, or females, usually arrive at the colony in November. Each will give birth to a single baby and become fertile again in a single week – this is when the rutting season begins.

The warm-blooded fur seals are able to withstand the waters of the frigid Benguela current because of their many layers of blubber and special double-layered fur coats. Although the fish they subsist on are not commercially caught species, many fishermen still consider the seals to be a threat to the fishing industry.

Witnessing the spectacle of such an enormous number of these beautiful creatures in their natural habitat is certainly worth the day trip from Henties Bay or Swakopmund.

DID YOU KNOW?
This granite mountain is 100 million years old. It is at its stunning best at sunset and sunrise.

YOU SHOULD KNOW:
Also found in this area are yellow butter trees and the poison tree, which leaks an extremely dangerous white juice that the Bushmen use to poison their arrows.

SPITZKOPPE

Namibia

Spitzkoppe, also known as the 'Matterthorn of Africa', is located between Usakos and Swakopmund in the Spitskop Nature Reserve. It is one of the most-photographed sites in Namibia, particularly during its stunning sunrise and sunset when the brown and grey granite turns striking saffron and ochre colours. Rising a majestic 1,829m (6,000ft) from the valley floor, the granite massif can often be seen dotted with experienced climbers of all nationalities. Part of the Erongo Mountains, Spitzkoppe was created by the collapse of a giant volcano, creating many interesting and sometimes bizarre rock formations. If you look carefully you may see Bushman paintings, particularly in the area called, appropriately enough, 'Bushman Paradise' underneath a large rock awning.

NAMIB DESERT

Namibia

WHAT IS THERE TO SEE?
Gigantic red and grey dunes in a barren, yet beautiful landscape.
MUST DO:
Camp overnight to see more stars than you ever thought existed.

The Namib Desert, the oldest desert on Earth, is located in the Namib Naukluft Park, the fourth largest conservation area in the world covering an astounding 49,768 sq km (19,215 sq miles). The desert occupies stretches along 1,600km (1,000 miles) of this seemingly endless barren land, with its enormous red and gray sand dunes, the highest in the world.

An unforgettable experience is to climb these dunes at sunrise or sunset, and look over the wind-sculpted rock formations, valleys and plains as the sun turns the dunes an array of yellows, pinks and purples. Climbing the 300-m (762-ft) dunes is no small feat – you may have to stop to catch your breath a few times. From the summit, you feel as though you are on the crest of one of thousands of waves in this sea of dunes, stretching as far as the eye can see.

DRAKENSBERG MOUNTAINS

South Africa

The Drakensberg Mountains are a spiky wall of bluish rock rising menacingly from the floor of the mountain kingdom of Lesotho, providing a natural defensive barrier. The highest range in South Africa, the Drakensberg, a World Heritage Site, is a hikers' paradise offering spectacular scenery and a variety of cultural attractions. The air surrounding the mountains is called 'champagne air' by the locals, because its sparkling breezes blow around the pinnacles of this unusual topography – an escarpment separating a high interior plateau from the Natal coastal lowlands. Many of the peaks exceed 3,000m (10,000 ft) and host streams and rivers that have carved out spectacular gorges.

LITERARY INSPIRATION
The Drakensberg are said to have inspired J.R.R. Tolkien's Middle Earth in his *Lord of the Rings* trilogy.

WHAT IS IT? The highest mountain range in South Africa.
WHAT IS THERE TO SEE? More than 40,000 ancient rock paintings from the San people.

THE BLYDE RIVER CANYON

South Africa

The Blyde River Canyon Nature Reserve offers one of the most spectacular views in South Africa. Home to gigantic rocks, deep gorges and high, grass-covered mountain peaks, the reserve stretches for 60km (37 miles) and includes The Blyde River Canyon, which is nearly 30km (19 miles) long.

The Blyde River Canyon is home to many remarkable natural wonders. Pinnacle is a 33-m (108-ft) needle made of quartzite rising dramatically from a fern-blanketed ravine. The river drops 450m (1,475ft) down the escarpment, creating a series of stunning waterfalls. At the Three Rondavels viewpoint you will discover an unforgettable view of three huge rock spirals rising out of the far wall of the Blyde River Canyon. Resembling the round, thatched African huts of the same name, these formations' red rocks create a magical contrast to the snaking, blue river below. Where the Blyde River, 'the river of joy', and the Treur River, 'the river of sorrow', meet, water erosion has formed one of the most remarkable geological phenomena in the country, known as 'Bourke's Luck Potholes'. Named after a gold prospector, the surreal cylindrical rock sculptures, created by whirlpools of emerald-green water, have formed a series of dark pools.

The descent from the nature reserve, down the escarpment to Abel Erasmus Pass is one of the most beautiful drives in the country and shouldn't be missed.

YOU SHOULD KNOW:
Despite its urban location, the mountain is home to a remarkably unspoiled wilderness and nature reserve. Wooden walkways and other designated paths allow you to wander around without damaging the 2,200 unique species of plant, while still affording you views of the grysboks, baboons and dassies.

Right: Table Mountain

TABLE MOUNTAIN

South Africa

Table Mountain is Cape Town's most famous landmark and one of the city's greatest attractions. There are many scenic routes that can be taken to climb the 1,086-m (3,500-ft) mountain, but most people take the revolving cable-car, which whisks them to the top in just a few minutes.

At the summit, the views in all directions are magnificent, especially on a clear day, although the fog can descend at any time from seemingly out of nowhere. Legend has it that an old Afrikaaner pirate, Jan van Hunks, who lived on Devil's Peak, challenged the devil to a pipe-smoking contest. The devil lost and the fabled 'tablecloth' cloud is said to serve as a reminder of his defeat.

CAPE POINT

South Africa

WHAT IS IT? The edge of Table Mountain, where the lighthouse sits.
WHAT IS THERE TO SEE? Historic shipwrecks and amazing views of the ocean.

Bartholomeu Dias, the Portuguese seafarer, was the first to sail around the Cape in 1488. On his particularly inclement return voyage, he stopped at the southwestern tip of Africa and named it Cabo Tormentoso, or 'Cape of Storms'. Later renamed Cabo da Boa Esperanca, or 'Cape of Good Hope' by King John of Portugal, it was rounded by Vasco da Gama in 1497 on a trip to India. The daring journeys of these Portuguese explorers led to the establishment of the Cape Sea Route, which led to more regular traffic around the Cape, but also a great number of casualties here because of the treacherous landscape and vicious fogs obscuring the coastline.

To try to minimize the shocking number of shipwrecks, the lighthouse at Cape Point was erected. The first lighthouse was built in 1857 on Cape Point Peak, 238m (781ft) above sea level, but because of its elevated position, clouds and fog obscured it for an alarming average of 900 hours per year. After the Portuguese liner Lusitania ran aground in 1911, the lighthouse was moved to its present location above Cape Point, only 87m (285ft) above sea level. This lighthouse is the most powerful lighthouse on the South African Coast. With a range of 63km (39 miles), the light beams out three flashes of ten million candlepower every 30 seconds.

DID YOU KNOW?
Juffureh is the birthplace of Kunta Kinte, made famous by the 1976 bestselling novel, *Roots*.

JUFFUREH

Gambia

WHERE IS IT?
Near Albreda and Banjul in The Gambia.
WHAT IS THERE TO SEE?
'The factory'; a fortified slave station built by the French in the late 17th century.

The small village of Juffureh, on the north bank of the River Gambia, was founded by the Taal family in 1455. It's a typical Mandinka settlement and has a long history of suffering prior to its rediscovery through the words of the 1979 television adaptation of the novel in which the family of Kunte Kinte was chronicled. The story of *Roots* tells of the days when Juffureh was a slaving centre and the Gambian population was at the mercy of the Portuguese, French, Spanish and English, who transported many of them from here to Europe, the West Indies, America and the rest of the world. The story of Kunta Kinte's 1767 capture and subsequent enslavement in America has created an interest in this otherwise rural town, because of its importance in the awareness of the racial injustice that took place.

BANDIAGARA PLATEAU

Mali

Amidst the stunning cliffs and sandy pleateaux of Mali in western Africa, the Cliffs of Bandiagara on the Bandiagara Plateau are home to one of the few remaining communities still practising many age-old traditions and rituals. A UNESCO World Heritage Site, the cliffs have been recognized for their natural beauty as well as their historical significance in understanding these ancient cultures through their surviving traditions.

WHAT IS IT?
A subtropical paradise with areas of historical and archeological importance.
WHAT IS THERE TO SEE?
Ancient rock-art sites, traditional masks and ritual ceremonies.

The Bandiagara Plateau, one of the main centres of Dogon culture, houses various small peripheral villages of the four Dogon tribes who migrated from the land of Mande centuries ago: the Dyon, Ono, Arou and Dommo. The village communities consist of desert-edge subsistence farmers divided into 'living men' and 'dead men', existing in symbiotic union with each other as well as having a symbolic attachment to their environment. Both of these relationships are represented in the ancient rock art that appears in and around the Bandiagara. The rock art, continually updated, works as an ongoing historical and social dialogue for these ancient peoples. Two main themes of rock art that have been identified are *bammi*, or ritual paintings, and *tonu*, or other, more mystical or practical paintings.

DJENNE

Mali

WHAT IS IT? The oldest existing city in sub-Saharan Africa.
WHERE IS IT? In the floodplain of the Niger and Bani rivers, 354km (220 miles) southwest of Timbuktu.

Djenne, the oldest known city in sub-Saharan Africa still in existence, has been recognized throughout history for its importance as a trade centre, as well as a centre of Islamic learning and pilgrimage. Established by merchants around 800AD, Djenne served as a meeting place between the Sudan and the Guinean tropical forests. During the 16th century it thrived as the most important trading centre because of its direct river connection to Timbuktu and its location on routes leading to the gold and salt mines. Following control by Moroccan kings, Tukulor emperors and the French, commercial activity moved to Mopti, at the confluence of the Niger and Bani rivers.

The Great Mosque, built in 1240 by the sultan Koi Kunboro, is one of the most stunning examples of Muslim architecture in Mali, dominating the large market square of Djenne. The mosque, formerly a palace, was deemed too sumptuous by Sheeikh Amadou, an early 19th-century ruler, so was replaced with a smaller, less flashy version in the 1830s. The current mosque, built between 1906 and 1907, is a UNESCO World Heritage Site and incorporates architectural elements found in mosques throughout the Islamic world. Using locally found mud and palm wood in the construction, senior masons coordinate and maintain the structure every spring. This event has turned into an annual festival.

WHY IS IT IMPORTANT?
It is the earliest iron industrial trade route and urban centre as well as home to great numbers of flora and fauna, including a large breeding ground for numerous species of waterfowl.
ALSO KNOWN AS:
Niger Inland Delta so that it is not confused with the Niger Delta in Nigeria.

NIGER DELTA

Mali

Mali's Niger Delta, between the Bani and Niger rivers in the southwest of the country, has provided the region with a fertile floodplain and a natural thoroughfare for trade, securing the area's position as a central economic, social and urban hub of the western Sudan. Comprising lakes and swamps channelled by the Erg Ouagadou sand dunes and located in the semi-arid Sahelian zone south of the Sahara Desert, the delta is home to Nile crocodiles and numerous mammals, such as the largest surviving population of west African manatees, hippos, antelope, reedbuck, warthogs and elephants. The southern half of the delta is low-lying floodplain, dense with grasses that are heavily grazed by large numbers of wetland birds including roughly 500,000 garganey and nearly 200,000 pintail.

SAINT-LOUIS

Senegal

WHY IS IT IMPORTANT?
The first French colonial city, it maintains much of its beautiful architecture.
ALSO KNOWN AS:
'Ndar' in the local Wolof language.

Saint-Louis, an island located between the mainland of Senegal and the 'Langue of Barbarie', is a narrow strip of land floating in the Atlantic Ocean, connected to the mainland by the 500-m (1,640-ft) Faidherbe steel bridge, which is a work of art in its own right. The district of Sor, a UNESCO World Heritage Site, is a lively fishing village that retains much of its charming French colonial architecture with wrought-iron balconies and verandas, a reminder of its early occupation. Although the centre of town is concentrated on the island of Saint-Louis itself, the urban sprawl continues in both directions on the mainland, the northern part occupying a long, sparse beach that stretches to the border of Mauritania as well as the nearby Parc des Oiseaux du Djoudj, famous for its bird life. Along with Gorée Island, Saint Louis remains the most characteristically French colonial destination in west Africa.

ISLE OF GORÉE

Senegal

First discovered by the Portuguese explorer Dias in 1444, the Isle of Gorée, off the coast of Senegal, was colonized by the Dutch in 1817 and later ruled by English and French powers. Gorée served as a way station for Dutch ships sailing the trade route between the Gold Coast of Ghana and the Indies. Between the 15th and 19th centuries Gorée was the largest centre of slave trade on the African coast. An estimated 40 million Africans were held here as they waited in anguish to be shipped to the Americas. Built by the Dutch in 1776, and preserved in its original state, the UNESCO World Heritage Site of the Slave House, or *Maison des Esclaves*, featuring the 'Door of No Return' is an emotional shrine and pilgrimage site for those wishing to reflect upon the horrors of the period.

WHAT'S IN A NAME
The name Gorée comes from the Dutch *goeree* meaning 'island' or possibly *goode Reede* meaning 'good harbour' for its sheltered bay

WHAT IS IT? A former French colonial-occupied island.
WHERE IS IT? 3km (1.8 miles) from the capital of Dakar by ferry.
WHY IS IT IMPORTANT? It was once home to the largest slave trade in western Africa.

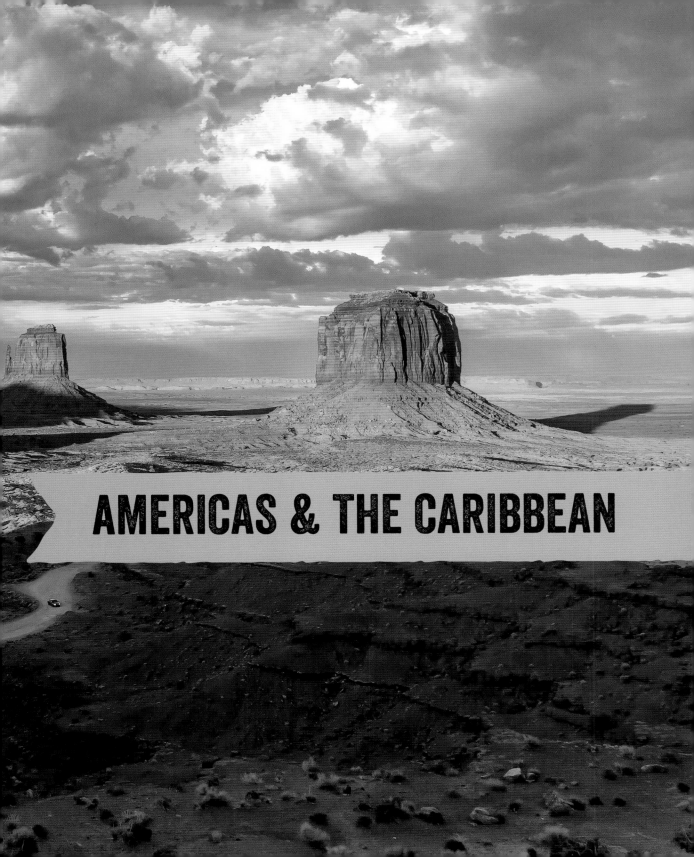

AMERICAS & THE CARIBBEAN

CAT ISLAND

FAMOUS CONNECTIONS: Sidney Poitier, the internationally acclaimed actor, spent his boyhood days on the island, and later returned to settle here.

The Bahamas

Cat Island, home to Mount Alvernia, the highest point in the Bahamas at an astounding 63m (206ft) above sea level, is the sixth largest island in the Bahamian island chain. It is rumoured to have been named after Arthur Catt, the famous British sea captain, or from the hordes of wild cats that the English encountered here upon their arrival in the 1600s, depending on who you listen to. The cats were said to be descendants of those orphaned by the early Spanish colonists who left them behind in their rush to find the gold of South America. Cat Island stretches out into the Atlantic Ocean and is said to be the original landing site of Christopher Columbus in the New World.

Cat Island is approximately 77km (48 miles) long and averages between 1.6–6km (1–4 miles) in width. It is located southeast of Eleuthera and northeast of Long Island.

This boot-shaped, untamed island is one of the most beautiful and fertile in the Bahamas. From its high cliffs there's an uninterrupted view of the densely forested foothills and the 97km (60 miles) of deserted pink- and white-sand beaches. You will not want to leave.

DID YOU KNOW?
Anegada is home to the 29-km (18-mile) long Horseshoe Reef, the largest barrier reef in the Caribbean.

ANEGADA

British Virgin Islands

HOW DO I GET THERE?
Access to the island is via the small Auguste George Airport, thrice-weekly ferries, and private boat.
WHY IS IT IMPORTANT?
It is the only island formed from coral and limestone rather than volcanic rock.

Right: One of Anegada's perfect white sandy beaches

At about 38 sq km (15 sq miles), Anegada is one of the larger British Virgin Islands, but it is also the most sparsely populated of the main islands (with a population of roughly 200, including the tourists). Most of the inhabitants live in The Settlement, the main town on the island.

It is known for its picture-postcard white sandy beaches and the large salt ponds that cover the west end of the island. In the 1830s, thousands of roseate flamingoes lived in these ponds. Hunted for food and their feathers throughout the 19th and early 20th centuries, they had all but disappeared by 1950. The flamingoes are currently being reintroduced into the ponds, creating a draw for tourism that officials are monitoring to ensure the birds can flourish.

ARENAL

Costa Rica

WHAT IS IT?
The fourth-most active volcano in the world set amidst the incredible beauty of Costa Rica.

Soaking in the bubbling thermal hot waters of the Tabacon Hot Springs, surrounded by lush, tropical greenery, the sound of thunder rumbles in the distance. To the uninitiated this may sound like the forewarning of an upcoming storm, but it is actually the eruption of the nearby Arenal Volcano, in the northern central area of Costa Rica, located next to the friendly town of La Fortuna. Currently ranked as the world's fourth-most active volcano, the awe-inspiring Arenal Volcano and its stunningly beautiful surroundings of pristine ancient rainforest will leave you enchanted. Located next to the large, gorgeous, man-made Lake Arenal, this experience is a highlight of any trip to Costa Rica.

Driving on the winding roads with lush verdant hillsides and farmlands fading to low-lying, monkey-filled jungle, the landscape, flora and fauna of this incredible landscape are captivating. Many visitors come here for the world-class windsurfing or to fish the abundant machaca and rainbow bass, but the most enjoyable spectacle of all is watching a live volcano erupt before you, as the lava creeps down the sides of the steep cone, and fire hisses from its mouth. Charming La Fortuna, the small town next to Arenal Volcano National Park and Cano Negro Reserve, is the starting point for many of the varied outdoor activities available in the region.

DID YOU KNOW?
Carriacou has a mix of Scottish and African ancestry.

CARRIACOU

Grenada

WORTH A TASTE:
The local Maroon food of rolled rice and corn with stewed meats and peas cooked over an open wood fire.
WHEN SHOULD I GO?
For the annual Carriacou Regatta, held in July and August.

Known as the Land of Reefs, Carriacou is the largest of Grenada's sister islands, even through it is a mere 33 sq km (13 sq miles). Despite its size, Carriacou is filled with activities to satisfy your thirst for adventure, or to fill your day with the relaxing rhythms of local flavour.

Dive into the crystal-clear waters and take advantage of the world-class snorkelling and diving on some of the Caribbean's most pristine reefs, or enjoy a day simply lounging on the stunning beaches of Anse La Roche, Paradise Beach or Sandy Island. With a restaurant or bar on every corner, you are sure to satisfy your appetite as well. With its wealth of historical attractions and cultural festivals, there is something for everyone on beautiful Carriacou.

HAVANA

Cuba

DID YOU KNOW?
Havana's official nickname is *Ciudad de las Columnas* or 'City of Columns.'

WHY IS IT IMPORTANT?
It is one of the last remaining bastions of Communism.
WHAT IS THERE TO SEE?
Spanish colonial architecture and stunning beaches.

There is nowhere in the world like the magical Caribbean island of Cuba or its capital, Havana. From the spectacular dilapidation of Havana Centro to the UNESCO World Heritage Site of Havana Vieja, with its Spanish colonial buildings, Cuba is a city of survivors, artists, masterful musicians and an endless stream of colourful characters. Bereft of the consumer trappings of other cities, Havana is full of character and packed with interesting museums, history and beaches. One of the last bastions of Communism, its political isolation has prevented it from being overrun by tourists, although those who make it to the island will not be disappointed with the amenities or the welcoming locals. Cuba is rich in culture, music, food and art. There is nothing better than sitting in a café with a mojito in hand, watching the locals go about their day, as the beat of a Cuban samba floats through the air. If you are fortunate, one of the locals, who by nature are incredibly generous and warm, will invite you into their home. They will offer you anything and everything they have available to share and may even cook you a wonderful homemade meal consisting of plantains, rice, beans, pork and freshly squeezed mango juice, followed by many cups of strong Cuban coffee. Even though the people are very poor here, there is a sense that they would give you the shirts off their backs to ensure that you enjoy your stay in their homeland.

SABA

The Leeward Islands

WORTH A TASTE: The local Saba Island rum, Saba Spice, is masterfully blended with Canadian rum to achieve a smooth, distinctive, complex taste – truly a national treasure.

The Leeward Islands, lying in the northern area of the Lesser Antilles, are part of the greater West Indies. Just over 1,000 people populate this small 13-sq km (5-sq mile) Dutch island paradise.

The rugged island is the cone of an extinct volcano, rising skyward 850m (2,800ft) to Mount Scenery, the highest peak in the 'Kingdom of the Netherlands'. The peak can be climbed via a series of more than 1,000 steps. Alternatively, you can drive up the single spiral road that winds its way up the steep cliffs through lush greenery. The road connects the quaint villages of Hell's Gate, Windwardside, St John's and The Bottom.

These four small villages on this largely unspoiled island are as quaint and charming as the gentle, friendly Saban people. A trip to Saba is like wandering back in time. The emerald forests, punctuated by their crimson cottage roofs, offer a stunning contrast to the still, clear-blue sea with all of its underwater delights. Dive tourism began slowly here. In the early days, most of the visitors came for a one-day visit from St Maarten, but as word of Saba's underwater riches spread, the number of tourists increased. Realizing the tourist potential, the local fishermen made a pact with the local dive shop to avoid fishing on the favoured diving reefs. This makes Saba an anomaly in that the reefs were protected before any damage could be done.

BARBUDA

The Leeward Islands

HISTORY:
Barbuda was unsuccessfully settled by the British and the French until 1680 when Christopher Codrington began cultivating sugar on the island after establishing a British colony large enough to survive the ravages of nature and the local Carib population.

Barbuda is one part of a three-island state with Antigua and Redonda, located in the northeastern Caribbean. An unspoiled paradise of seemingly endless stretches of white- and pink-sandy beaches, Barbuda is surrounded by the deep blue Atlantic Ocean on one side, with its driftwood and sea-shell-strewn wild beaches, and the calm, clear waters of the Caribbean Sea on the other.

Undeveloped except for a small number of boutique resorts, Barbuda is perfect for swimming and snorkelling, with plenty of opportunities to see turtles and tropical fish as well as some interesting shipwrecks that lie undisturbed in the turquoise water.

Right: Endless stretches of sandy beaches await you in Barbuda

PORT ANTONIO

Jamaica

Port Antonio was described by American poetess Ella Wheeler Wilcox as, 'The most exquisite port on Earth'. The town's twin harbours, azure sea and verdant hillsides still ensnare visitors to this day. The story of this old port town is the story of men who came, saw and were conquered by its beauty and character. All of them, from Captain Lorenzo Dow Baker to film star Errol Flynn and billionaire Garfield Weston, sought to develop the town and all of them failed. Like Montego Bay, Port Antonio claims to be the hub of the tourist trade, but unlike other resort areas on the island, its potential remains underdeveloped.

During the town's golden age, a Yankee skipper, Lorenzo Dow Baker, planted and harvested large banana plantations and subsequently sold his fruits through the United Fruit Company to North America. It was said that on Banana Day, whenever the cargo ships were being loaded at the port, the farmers would light their cigars with five-dollar bills. This age of prosperity ended with the onset of Panama disease, which crippled the industry. The banana trade and Port Antonio have never quite recovered. The island continues slowly to regain its prosperity, with the redevelopment of the harbours, and is sure to become the height of fashion once again.

DID YOU KNOW?
This is where Brooke Shields and Christopher Atkins swam together in the film *The Blue Lagoon*.

BLUE LAGOON

Jamaica

This is an unspoiled oasis where you will feel as though you are the only remaining person on Earth. Here the magnificent turquoise-blue and emerald-green waters are an astonishing 56m (185ft) deep. Created by underground mineral springs fed from the Blue Mountains, it is one of the last remaining truly tropical paradises on the island. The spectacular cove is surrounded by lush, steep hills, which complete the dreamlike setting. While swimming in the Blue Lagoon you will feel streams of warm water at times, and streams of cold water at others. There are parts where the water is shallow enough to walk right in, but other areas are steeply sloped. You can even watch as the mineral water bubbles through the ground. Heaven on earth.

WHAT IS IT?
A large, deep, stunningly beautiful cove.
WHERE IS IT?
Near Port Antonio.
WHAT IS IT KNOWN FOR?
Its emerald-green and azure crystalline waters.

PERITO MORENO

Argentina

DID YOU KNOW?
The glacier stretches
5km (3 miles) across and
soars to a height of more
than 60m (197ft).

WORTH A TASTE:
Collect some of the pure
waters to use later in a
celebratory drink as you
and your companions
talk over your amazing
adventures in this
prehistoric Arctic.

Patagonia encapsulates many things: vast, wildflower-strewn valleys, daunting snow-capped craggy Andean peaks, gorgeous lakes surrounded by lush, pine-dotted, emerald hillsides and dramatic glacial environments – most notably in the Los Glaciares National Park. Declared a World Heritage Site by UNESCO in 1981, the park holds many glaciers that belong (or used to belong) to southern Patagonia's ice cap. Among them, the most impressive is the Perito Moreno glacier, one of the few in Argentina that is not retreating.

The small town of El Calafate, where the Santa Cruz plateau meets the Andes, is the gateway to the Perito Moreno glacier. The western end of the Lago Argentino gives access to the glacier, which periodically advances across the lake, blocking it until the weight of water upstream ruptures the ice in one of nature's most spectacular events. It is a humbling and awe-inspiring experience to watch the simultaneous creation and destruction of the continent through a completely natural process. In this neverending display of nature, visitors can watch and listen to the roar as ice calves from the enormous glacier, crashes into the waters below, and is renewed as brilliant turquoise and milky-white icebergs.

PATAGONIA

Argentina

Few places in the world have captivated the imagination of explorers and travellers like Patagonia. Since Ferdinand Magellan sailed here many have settled, and yet this vast, remote region is still, for the most part, unexplored and largely uninhabited. Patagonia's beautiful, untamed landscape consists of narrow straits and steep-sided fjords rich in marine life, rugged mountains, harsh, windswept plateaux and glacial valleys. It is home to some of the most beautiful natural attractions in the world, from the granite towers of Torres del Paine and Los Glaciares National Park to the northern and southern ice fields with their enormous glaciers, and the flat pampas broken only by bluffs of multi-coloured sedimentary rocks and stunning emerald lakes and rivers.

WHAT IS THERE TO DO?
Trek, raft, ride, ski, drink wine, eat gourmet food and experience lovely hospitality and even lovelier scenery.

LAND OF CONTRASTS
From dense woods and petrified forest to deserts and shoreline, Patagonia offers something for everyone, from the literal heights of the Andes, down to what many consider to be the southernmost city in the world, Ushuaia.

IGUAZÚ FALLS
Argentina

WHAT IS IT?
Nearly 300 waterfalls of unbelievable scope and width.
NOTABLE QUOTE:
Upon her first sight of the Falls, Eleanor Roosevelt is said to have exclaimed, 'Poor Niagara!'

The pounding impact of nearly 300 waterfalls, with heights averaging up to 70m (230ft), spanning a verdant, jungle-clad stretch of 2.7km (1.7 miles) is not quickly forgotten. The Iguazú Falls, of the Iguazú River on the border of the South Region of Brazil and the Argentine province of Misiones, is one of the great natural wonders of the world. Taller than Niagara Falls, and more than twice as wide, Iguazú Falls makes its smaller cousin appear to be a mere gentle overflow. Part of the Iguazú National Park on the Argentine side and Iguaçu National Park on the Brazilian side, the Iguazú Falls have been recognized as a UNESCO World Heritage Site for their ferocious beauty.

The majority of the falls lie in Argentina, but panoramic views are also available from the Brazilian side. That being said, the view from a boat en route to Isla San Martin, in Argentina, is hard to beat.

SANTA CRUZ CARNIVAL

Bolivia

Among the most famous carnivals in the world are those of Rio de Janeiro, New Orleans and Venice, but in different countries carnivals take on their own local character, and the tropical fiesta that is carnival in Santa Cruz, Bolivia is one not to be missed. Part religious procession, part dance party and part paintball game, the carnival in Santa Cruz is a riot of colour, sound and movement that is often compared to that of Rio for its sheer exuberance. For the two weeks before Ash Wednesday, the streets come alive with troupes of jewellery- and costume-clad locals and foreigners dancing in wild abandon to the beats of salsa, samba or anything else that is being played. The Santa Cruz carnival is a fantastic experience – a heady mix of dancing, parades, floats and fun-loving crowds that will ensure you'll still be tapping your feet to the samba beat long after the celebrations are over.

DID YOU KNOW?
A feature almost unique to Bolivia is the way that revellers throw ink-filled *globos* at each other.

WHAT IS THERE TO SEE? Traditional and non-traditional dress, dancers, parades, floats and crowds.
WHAT IS THERE TO DO? Dance, dress up, sing and celebrate.
WHEN IS IT? Carnival season is in February/March for the two weeks before the traditional Christian fast of Lent.

TRANCOSO

Brazil

Trancoso is a rustic fishing village situated on the wild, jungle-like shores of Bahia, the northeastern part of the vast Brazilian coast, which has become a haven for those seeking solitude with a touch of glamour. Surrounded by untouched tropical forests, turquoise bays and white, sandy beaches, Trancoso was one of the earliest Portuguese settlements in Brazil.

During the day, laughing children play football in the town square, the elderly stroll beneath the vast rows of palm trees and sarong-clad visitors, loaded with sunscreen and cameras, head for some of the most beautiful beaches in Brazil.

At sunset, people ride horses and enjoy a glass of wine or a cocktail, gearing up for the magic to begin. At nightfall, the entire Quadrado (square) is lit up by hundreds of candles, musicians play drums and guitars and the dancing begins, in a truly dreamlike setting underneath the starry skies.

Despite its status as an upmarket resort, Trancoso has remained a charming village with strong threads linking it to its past – the weathered fishermen still haul in their fresh catch from their brightly coloured schooners in the shallow waters of the bay.

DID YOU KNOW?
Ilha Grande translates as 'Long Island'.

WHAT IS THERE TO DO?
Sail among the pristine beaches.
WHAT IS THERE TO SEE?
The biological reserve and beautiful beaches.
WHEN SHOULD I GO?
March to June.

ILHA GRANDE

Brazil

Ilha Grande is a mountain ridge emerging from an emerald sea, blanketed in tropical forest and fringed with some of the world's most stunning and pristine beaches. The bay of Ilha Grande is dotted with more than 360 idyllic, hardly developed islands. Much of Ilha Grande is designated as the Ilha Grande State Park and Praia do Sul is now a Biological Reserve. Abraão, the unofficial capital of Ilha Grande, is a peaceful, quaint village with whitewashed churches and low, colourful buildings in pretty hues of yellow, blue and pink with tiled roofs. The village of Abraão consists of inns, restaurants, bars and handicraft shops. Walking tracks through the forest lead to the beaches, waterfalls and historical monuments such as the aqueduct and the old lazaretto of the Black Beach.

RIO DE JANEIRO

Brazil

DID YOU KNOW?
According to Brazilians, God made the world in six days and the seventh he devoted to Rio.

WHAT IS THERE TO SEE?
Ipanema, Sugar Loaf Mountain, the statue of Christ on Corcovado.

WHAT IS THERE TO DO?
Dance, shop, bake in the sun and experience the unique culture of this fantastic and sinfully beautiful city.

A large city on the South Atlantic coast, Rio is famous for its glorious backdrop of tumbling wooded mountains, stark rocky crags and a deep blue sea studded with islands. From the statue of Cristo Redentor (Christ the Redeemer) on the hunchbacked peak of Corcovado, or the conical Päo de Açúcar (Sugar Loaf Mountain), you can get an aerial view of this lush, dynamic beach playground sweeping 220km (137 miles) along the southwestern shore of the Baia de Guanabara. From the stunning, curved Copacabana beach with its scantily clad beauties to Ipanema, land of the world's most striking sunsets, and the boisterous, Bacchanalian carnival, Rio is one of the world's most dynamic cities, bursting with charm, culture, art and colour.

Still the greatest reason for visiting Rio seems to be the carnival. The most advertised party in the world lasts for nearly two weeks, when the city is taken over by people adorned in feathers, beads, headdresses, thongs and little else. The streets teem with parades of samba groups gathering thousands of people at every corner, noisily revelling to the exotic beats. Carnival time in Rio is an experience not to be forgotten.

BARRA GRANDE

Brazil

Located on the south coast of Bahia, in northeast Brazil, the Maraú Peninsula is an area of pristine beaches, tropical forest, rivers and waterfalls. Barra Grande, the main village on Camamu Bay, the third-largest bay in Brazil, is a great base from which to explore this paradise.

With the atmosphere of a traditional fishermen's village and an unspoiled landscape, Barra Grande is a charming and peaceful haven for those who want to get away from it all. There are virtually no cars and the streets are unpaved, as the locals prefer to live to the rhythms of the lapping tide. The simple architecture is punctuated by lush gardens with the vivid hues of purple, orange, yellow and red exotic flowers.

This quaint village, surrounded by coconut palms and mango trees, has a surprisingly vast cultural diversity, apparent through its range of bars and restaurants, which treat the visitor to a multitude of tastes. The real lure of the area, however, is its beaches. Mangueiras Beach, the main beach of the village, boasts fine, white sand and calm, azure waters. It is an excellent spot to relax over a caipirinha and take in the brilliant sunsets.

The snorkelling and diving here are both rewarding, with a diversity of underwater life including an abundance of fish species and rich, colourful corals.

FERNANDO DE NORONHA

Brazil

WHAT IS THERE TO DO?
It is known as the best dive spot in Brazil.
WHAT IS THERE TO SEE?
Spinner dolphins, turtles, sharks and other marine life.

Right: The idyllic Fernando de Noronha

Calling the archipelago of 21 islands that includes Fernando de Noronha an idyllic paradise is an understatement. This area is one of the most important ecological sanctuaries in the world and in 2001, together with Rocas Atoll, it became a UNESCO World Heritage Site. Seemingly abandoned amidst the clear blue waters of the Atlantic Ocean, the verdant mountains and sheer cliffs of Fernando de Noronha, a National Marine Reserve, jut out from the sea in all their lush, tropical glory. A beacon to divers from around the world, the waters surrounding the islands are home to a multitude of fish, manta rays, lemon sharks and spinner dolphins. Every morning in the aptly named Baia dos Golfinhos (Bay of Dolphins), more than 1,000 spinner dolphins gather to frolic and dance in the early sunshine.

FLORIANOPOLIS

Brazil

WHEN SHOULD I GO? From June to November you have a fairly good chance of seeing small pods of right whales migrating along the coast.

Brazilians love their beaches and the Ilha de Santa Catarina, also known as Florianopolis, is famed throughout the country for its endless stretches of sand, excellent seafood and traditional Azorean fishing villages. Tropical weather, beautiful coastline, exotic landscapes, attractive inhabitants and a laidback lifestyle are characteristic of this hot spot, which is particularly favoured by Brazilians. The island itself can be divided into five areas – north, east, central, south and west. The beaches of Canasvieiras, Jururê and Praia dos Ingleses on the northern part of the island are largely urbanized and packed with tourists, particularly in the high summer months of December to February. Jururê is popular with Brazilian celebrities, many of whom own homes in the area's exclusive neighbourhoods. Just to the east are the beautiful, wide, sandy beaches of Galheta, Mole and Joaquina. Surrounded by lush green hills and big, surfable waves, this area is a magnet to many of those looking for that perfect ride. In the centre of the island, near Lagoa da Conceição, a large lagoon, partially surrounded by large sand dunes, is where some of the best restaurants and nightlife in the region can be found. The southern end of the island is divided into two areas – on the east side towards the rugged, deserted beaches of Campeche, Armaçao, Lagoinha do Leste and Naufragados, which look out towards the clear Atlantic waters; and on the west side, Ribeirão da Ilha, which features beautifully preserved Acorean and Portuguese fishing villages with colourful architecture and friendly inhabitants.

DID YOU KNOW?
Brigette Bardot helped to make this area popular when she visited in 1964.

BÚZIOS

Brazil

WHAT IS IT?
An idyllic island rated as one of the ten most beautiful areas in the world.
WHERE IS IT?
169km (105 miles) or two hours from Rio de Janeiro.

Compared by many to St Tropez for its glorious beaches, picturesque setting and tropical sophistication, the town of Búzios on the peninsula of the same name is where those seeking year-round elegance and amenities, combined with a charming, traditional fishing atmosphere, come to play. Only a two-hour drive from Rio de Janeiro, this is the perfect place to recover from the excesses of that famed party town. Or not. Búzio offers a vast array of dining, shopping, golf, watersports and nightlife options for the visitor wanting a respite, but not a total break from the Brazilian *joie de vivre*. However, the town has managed to retain a certain degree of the charm of its fishing-village past. Búzios boasts more than 20 magnificent beaches, forming a striking contrast to the sculpted landscape inland with its lush, exotic vegetation.

JERICOACOARA
Brazil

YOU SHOULD KNOW:
The beach here has been voted as one of the ten most beautiful in the world.
WHAT IS THERE TO SEE?
Watch sunrise, moonrise sunset and moonset over water.

Jericoacoara, a former fishing village in the northeast of Brazil, in the state of Ceará and close to the equator, was until recently an isolated area with little contact with modern civilization and no modern amenities such as electricity, telephones, roads, television or even newspapers, and with an economy based on bartering fish for goods. The government declared this extraordinarily beautiful place an Environmental Protection Area in 1994, and it has finally been reached by tourism, but its peaceful and unhurried atmosphere and its pristine natural environment are carefully maintained. To this end, hunting and building paved roads are forbidden, as is anything that might cause pollution. No buildings may be constructed outside the village, and all new homes must conform to the traditional architectural style. The number of tourists is limited by the number of amenities here and, despite the numbers of visitors who would like to travel to this paradise, no new hotels can be built.

MONTE VERDE

Brazil

The charming mountain village of Monte Verde is situated on top of Mantiqueira Ridge, in the Brazilian Highlands of southeast Brazil. The quaint and scenic town is surrounded by gorgeous peaks of up to 2,000m (6,562ft) and dotted with European-style architecture.

Monte Verde boasts green grassland and tall, strong trees as far as the eye can see. The bushy woodland belongs to the remains of the Mata Atlântica, the relic of what was once an extensive Atlantic rainforest. With the scent of fresh pine and eucalyptus in the air, the dense trees, some of which date back 500 years, provide a haven for many animal species, including a large variety of tropical birds.

BRAZIL'S ALPS
The quaint and scenic town is dotted with European-style architecture, which has gained the area a comparison to the Swiss Alps.

WHAT IS THERE TO DO? Hike around the hills and mountains or just enjoy a beer at the local watering hole.
WHAT IS THERE TO SEE? Gorgeous alpine scenery and European-style architecture.

SALVADOR

Brazil

Salvador is the third largest city in Brazil and capital of the state of Bahia. Salvador, sometimes referred to simply as Bahia, is home to colonial architecture and stunning beaches. Perched on the magnificent Bahia de Todos os Santos, the biggest bay on the Brazilian coast, its emerald waters are punctuated by 38 lush islands. A dominating cliff rises 71 m (233 ft) above the eastern side of the bay, where the older city districts, with buildings dating back to the seventeenth and eighteenth centuries, can be found. In the upper city lies the historic centre, a UNESCO World Heritage Site and national monument. Here, the Portuguese erected their fortified city, including some of the most important examples of colonial architecture in the Americas. The pastel colours are a striking contrast to the azure skies.

WORTH A TASTE:
One local delicacy is *acaraje*, or black-bean cakes, deep-fried and slathered with a spicy *vatapa*, or shrimp paste.

MULTI-CULTURAL
Salvador is dubbed 'Africa in exile' for its cultural mix of African and Brazilian population and influences.

EASTER ISLAND

Chile

Easter Island, or Rapa Nui, is a remote, roughly triangular island with an extinct volcano at each corner. The chief reason to visit is to see the 600 or so giant carved stone statues (*moai*) gazing out to sea from the shoreline. The origin of the statues, and the islanders who created them, has provoked controversy ever since the first Europeans set foot on its shores.

The early settlers called the island 'Te Pito O Te Henua', or 'The Navel of The World'. It was rediscovered by the Dutch Admiral Jacob Roggeveen, and its name was unofficially changed to Easter Island, as it was on this day in 1722 that he landed here. Located more than 3,219km (2,000 miles) from the nearest area of any significant population, roughly halfway between Tahiti and coastal Chile in the South Pacific, Rapa Nui is one of the most isolated places on Earth. A UNESCO World Heritage Site, it is a unique and starkly beautiful landscape with volcanic craters, lava formations, brilliant blue water, beaches, low rolling hills, cattle farms and a vast array of archeological sites, most notably, the hulking *moai* figures. These are an imposing 9m (30ft) in height and very broad. One of them, on Anakena beach, was restored to its near-original state along with a plaque commemorating the visit of Thor Heyerdahl in 1955. The remaining figures are scattered about the island.

DID YOU KNOW?
Easter Island is one of the most isolated places on Earth.

WORTH A TASTE (IF YOU DARE):
Pisco, originally from Peru, a spirit made from fermented grapes, is the unofficial drink of the island. Try a pisco sour, which is pisco mixed with lemon juice.

TAYRONA NATIONAL PARK

Colombia

North from Taganga, the Tayrona National Park stretches for 85km (53 miles), a largely unspoiled and beautiful coastline where you can see monkeys, iguanas and snakes in their natural habitat. Here the main objective is relaxation and swimming in these azure, protected waters. If you are feeling inspired, you can always visit the archeological site of Pueblito and its indigenous peoples.

Visitors to the park hike the scenic trails to the mouth of the Piedras River and to the beautiful beaches of Cabo San Juan de Guia, Arrecifes, Shell Bay or the Cove of Chengue. The park is ideal for exploring and consists of a tropical dry forest, marine-grass prairies and an exciting array of coral reefs with an abundance of undersea life. More than 100 species of land mammals and birds, from the common deer to the elusive white eagle, also call the park home.

Camping and ecotourism are the only options for overnight accommodation as the importance of environmental conservation is taken very seriously. The ecohabs, or ecologically-friendly structures, are characteristic of the local Tayrona architecture, adding another element of charm to this already special place. If you prefer staying out of doors, El Cabo where you can hang your hammock and sway to the sea breezes, is one of the most popular campsites.

DID YOU KNOW?
The statues share a common feature of blank eyes staring into the distance.

SAN AUGUSTÍN

Colombia

San Augustín Archaeological Park is a UNESCO World Heritage Site known for its large number of ancient carved statues, the relics of a civilization that flourished and died between the sixth century BC and twelfth century AD. Thought to be a cultural centre for various indigenous groups before the Incas arrived, the site at San Augustín, hosts a variety of pre-Colombian artefacts.

WHAT IS THERE TO SEE?
More than 500 pre-Colombian statues, monuments, tombs and carvings.
WHAT IS THERE TO DO?
Wander through the idyllic scenery and gaze at these ancient antiquities.

The park sprawls across an area of 800 sq km (300 sq miles) and is considered the largest pre-Colombian site in South America. The archaeological remains represent an amalgam of cultural influences from peoples of the Andean, Amazonian and Caribbean groups.

GALÁPAGOS ISLANDS

Ecuador

WHAT IS THERE TO DO?
Watch the blue-footed boobies dance, snorkel with sea otters or swim with penguins.
WHEN SHOULD I GO?
The peak season lasts from mid-June to early September and from mid-December to mid-January.

The Galapágos Islands, a small archipelago of islands belonging to Ecuador in the remote waters of the eastern Pacific Ocean, are remarkable for their untouched variety of unique and fearless wildlife, providing the inspiration for Charles Darwin's theory of evolution though natural selection. Lying roughly 1,000km (620 miles) west of the South American continent, the Galápagos archipelago consists of 13 main islands and six smaller isles, together covering more than 50,000 sq km (19,500 sq miles). The largely barren and volcanic islands are home to some of the best wildlife in the world including giant tortoises, the indigenous Galápagos sea lions, penguins, marine iguanas, Galápagos flamingoes, magnificent frigatebirds, otters, Darwin's famous finches and blue- and red-footed boobies to name just a few.

CORO

Venezuela

Founded in 1527 by Juan de Ampies, the lovely and relaxed city of Coro is home to many beautiful colonial buildings including Los Arcaya, one of the best examples of 18th-century architecture. Founded by Spanish colonists, Coro is the capital of the Falcon State and the oldest city in western Venezuela.

Recognized as a UNESCO World Heritage Site, the port, with its cobbled streets and hundreds of historic buildings, reflects a variety of cultures including the Spanish Islamic style and the Dutch influence with its colony of Curaçao. Surrounded by the massive sand dunes of Los Médanos de Coro National Park, the only desert in Venezuela, Coro has something for every visitor to enjoy.

UNDER THREAT
Vulnerable to rain damage, the heavy storms in recent years have damaged some of the city's buildings, one factor in its current UNESCO 'at risk' status.

WHAT IS IT? A charming colonial city, the oldest in western Venezuela.
WHAT IS THERE TO SEE? Enchanting architecture and excellent museums.

MACHU PICCHU

Peru

WHAT IS IT?
A complete Incan city in the Sacred Valley of the Incas.
WHERE IS IT?
Near Cuzco, Peru.
WHAT IS THERE TO SEE?
The most impressive Incan ruins in the world.
WHEN SHOULD I GO?
April–May and October–November.

As it appears dramatically from the verdant, jungle-clad peaks and steep, terraced slopes that fall to the valley below, with the Urubamba River snaking through its emerald floor, Macchu Picchu takes your breath away when you first catch sight of it.

If you decide to trek to these monumental ruins, you will take the arduous but awe-inspiring Inca Trail, a pilgrimage route for centuries, winding from the Sacred Valley near Ollantaytambo through exotic vegetation and magnificent mountains that afford unforgettable views. The exceptional towering Huayna Picchu and its surrounding ruins are well worth the effort, although the train is a quicker alternative.

A complete Incan city, Macchu Picchu, a UNESCO World Heritage Site, was uncovered in 1911 by American archaeologist Hiram Bingham. Perched dramatically 305m (1,000ft) above the valley, the site comprises staircases, terraces, temples, palaces, towers and fountains. From the top of Funerary Rock you will be able to take in the picture-postcard view – this is the ideal spot to watch the sunrise if you do not mind the crowds, including the herds of llamas grazing nearby. From here, the layout of the ancient city, with its clearly defined agricultural and urban zones separated by a long, dry moat, is clearly laid out in front of you.

One of the most famous edifices is the Temple of the Sun, or Torreon, with its extraordinary masonry and rounded, tapering tower with windows that are perfectly aligned for the sun to illuminate the central temple during the winter solstice in June. Below the temple is the Royal Tomb, carved inside the rocks, complete with an altar, and the Royal Sector, a series of dwellings around a still-functioning water canal and interconnecting fountains. The Temple of the Moon is a less-visited ruin encompassing mysterious caverns, niches and portals as well as carved thrones and an altar – its purpose has not been determined.

However much of this stunning landscape you chose to explore, a trip to Machu Picchu is an unforgettable experience.

VANCOUVER

British Columbia, Canada

Vancouver is a magical city, full of contradictions. The gateway to the Pacific, it is a multicultural city with an easy-going air, filled with cosmopolitan restaurants and boutiques, and offering visitors the opportunity to sail and ski in the same day. Gastown is a charming Victorian cobbled area, complete with mews, antique shops, boutiques and art galleries housed in historic buildings. At the entrance to Gastown, you can enjoy the sweeping 360-degree views from the Lookout Tower, a 33-floor observation deck above Harbour Centre. From here, awe-inspiring vistas greet you at every turn.

From trendy Robson Street to timeworn Hastings Street, Vancouver is a paradise for those seeking thrills in the wilderness, on their palate, on the stage or in their wardrobe.

DON'T MISS:
The 410 hectare (1,000 acre) Stanley Park. One of the largest urban parks in North America, it is the city's most famous landmark and boasts woodland trails, secluded lakes and the largest aquarium in Canada.

IN THE MOVIES

Vancouver is the third-largest film production centre in North America outside of Hollywood and New York.

VANCOUVER ISLAND

British Columbia, Canada

DID YOU KNOW?
'The island' is considered paradise for the opportunity to ski and play golf in the same day.

WHERE IS IT?
90 minutes from Vancouver by ferry across the Strait of Georgia.
WHAT IS THERE TO DO?
Enjoy spectacular scenery and take advantage of the wealth of outdoor activities.

Vancouver Island, known for its laidback artistic culture, stunning coastal scenery and year-round blanket of flowers, is separated from the western mainland of British Columbia by the Strait of Georgia. This region is a paradise of pristine beaches and lush emerald rainforests, pounded by the Pacific Ocean. It is home to various plants and animals, the majestic snow-capped Olympic mountains and glistening bays, rivers and lakes. The varied ecosystem includes farmland, vineyards and wildflower-strewn meadows – allowing its visitors the luxury, variety and adventure of having the opportunity to ski and play golf in the same day.

The picturesque capital, Victoria, at the southern tip of the island, offers a snapshot of Britain with its historic parliament, narrow streets dotted with cafés, pubs and colourful gardens, and boats floating lazily in the sparkling harbour.

The fishing village of Tofino, located on Clayoquot Sound, is a centre for ecotourism. The sandy beaches south of the town are the main attraction of the area, along with whale watching and surfing. Vancouver Island is truly a remarkable place, with plenty to keep you occupied and entranced.

RAFT COVE

British Columbia, Canada

DID YOU KNOW?
You may be lucky enough to catch a glimpse of migrating whales from the shoreline.

On the northwest coast of Vancouver Island is Cape Scott Park. At the southern end of the park you will discover Raft Cove, a provincial park consisting of an isolated, forested coastline at the mouth of the meandering Macjack River. Cutting through an unpaved, twisting trail, among ancient towering hemlock, western red cedar and Sitka spruce, you will come upon the rugged shoreline, notable for its unobstructed majestic views of the pounding Pacific. From here you might be lucky enough to see migrating whales. At the end of the beach is a wild sandy bay, accessible at low tide, which is home to the dilapidated trapper's cabin of Willie Hecht, an early Cape Scott settler. Abandoned and crumbling, the remnants of Hecht's home lie on the southern bank, opposite the tip of the wooded peninsula. The best fresh water is available from the nearby stream. Camping on the beach, or in wilderness campsites amongst the canopy of trees, is popular, as are surfing, swimming, fishing and hiking. Black bears, cougars and wolves live in the park so caution should be exercised when staying overnight.

This is the land of pioneers, virtually untouched by man. Hiking here, you will feel as though you are discovering your own secret wilderness.

WHISTLER MOUNTAIN

British Columbia, Canada

HISTORICAL TRIVIA:
The mountain was named Whistler by early settlers after the shrill sound made by the local western hoary marmots living among the rocks.

Right: Alta Lake in the resort of Whistler Blackcomb

Located in the mountains of British Columbia, the spectacularly scenic mountains of Whistler and Blackcomb are home to the internationally known ski and snowboard resort of Whistler Blackcomb. Nestled in a cosy, scenic river valley, it is reached by a spectacular two-hour drive from Vancouver along the 'Sea to Sky Highway', one of Canada's most breathtaking corridors.

The scenic splendour of the glorious mountain tops soaring high above are reflected in Lake Alta as you enter the resort. Whistler, (highest lift 2,182m/7,160ft) and Blackcomb (2,284 m/7,494 ft) have the largest vertical drop and the largest area – more than 28,000 hectares (7,000 acres) – of ski and snowboard terrain on the continent.

OKANAGAN VALLEY

British Columbia, Canada

The Okanagan Valley, stretching from the arid Osoyoos at the United States' border north to lush Vernon in British Columbia, interspersed with blankets of orchards and vineyards, makes an excellent place to stop and experience the various fruits of the earth. The warmest region in Canada, the Okanagan Valley offers a veritable feast of flavours. The vast Osoyoos and Oliver regions are nearly arid enough to warrant being called a desert, but farther north cherries, peaches, pears, apricots, plums, apples and grapes all grow in abundance. The fruit trees blossom in spring, making this a particularly pleasant time to visit.

Autumn is also beautiful, as this is when the grapes are plump on the vines. Winemaking is serious business in Okanagan. British Columbians have long taken pride in their wines, and Kelowna in the Okanagan Valley is the centre of this burgeoning industry. Home to large producers as well as estate and boutique wineries, there is a taste of France in this beautiful valley. No visit is complete without a vineyard tour and a wine-tasting session. In Kelowna, if you happen to visit from mid-September to mid-October, you might catch the astonishing sight of wild salmon spawning in Lion's Park. In summer, there are countless sandy beaches where you can loll in the sunshine, swim, fish and dive in the scenic Lake Okanagan.

DID YOU KNOW?
Local folklore says that the islands are haunted by spirits, as well as a Sasquatch-like creature.

GOD'S POCKET

British Columbia, Canada

God's Pocket, on the north side of the Goletas Channel, is a provincial marine park set on group of small islands at the entrance to the Queen Charlotte Strait. The largest islands are Hurst, Bell, Boyle and Crane islands. Bald eagles and whales are common in the area, and there is a seabird breeding colony as well as various archaeological sites. Above all, God's Pocket is known for the quality of scuba diving on offer. The clean, clear waters here are alive with marine life. Most diving takes place in nearby Browning Pass, an area that Jacques Cousteau, the great underwater explorer, considered one of the best dive sites in the world. Experienced divers can witness orcas, harbour seals, Pacific white-sided dolphins, Steller sea lions and, somewhat less often, humpback and grey whales.

WHAT IS IT KNOWN FOR?
Jacques Cousteau rated God's Pocket as one of the best dive sites in the world.
WHERE IS IT?
20km (12.5 miles) northwest of Port Hardy on Northern Vancouver Island.

QUEEN CHARLOTTE ISLANDS

British Columbia, Canada

Arguably one of the most beautiful and diverse landscapes in the world, the scenery of the 1,884 islands of this archipelago is stunning. The seven largest islands, peaks of a submerged mountain chain, are Langara, Graham, Moresby, Louise, Lyell, Burnaby and Kunghit islands. Just 2–3 km (1.2–2 miles) offshore, the continental shelf falls away dramatically to the immense depths of the Pacific Ocean, making this the most active earthquake area in Canada and landslides are common.

Haida Gwaii has been home to the Haida people for at least 7,000 years. In 1774, Juan Perez was the first European to reach this isolated paradise. Fur traders followed, creating a major impact on the Haida as Europeans arrived en masse to exploit the abundant resources. In 1787, the islands were renamed after Lord Howe's flagship, HMS *Queen Charlotte*, in honour of Queen Charlotte, wife of King George III.

The islands retain their wild peace and have a rich cultural history. The Haida earn their living traditionally, the main industries being mining, logging and commercial fishing. Tourist activities include sport fishing, hiking, camping, kayaking and whale-watching.

DID YOU KNOW?
The islands are sometimes called the 'Galápagos of the north'.

WHAT IS THERE TO DO?
There are countless beaches, streams, fishing holes, coves and abandoned Indian villages to explore. Many unique subspecies of flora and fauna share these islands with the residents.

GASPE

Quebec, Canada

WHERE IS IT?
On the eastern tip of the province of Quebec, north of New Brunswick, surrounded by the St Lawrence estuary and gulf.

The Gaspe Peninsula, or Gaspesie, on the eastern tip of Quebec, north of New Brunswick, is a largely coastal region surrounded by the St Lawrence estuary and gulf as well as by the Bay of Chaleur. First claimed for the king of France by Jacques Cartier in 1534, today Gaspe is known for its deep-water port and the three salmon rivers that empty into it.

Far from the crowds, Gaspe offers an abundance of attractions worth seeing. Heaped with woodland-covered hills whose slopes drop into the sea and low rolling pastures with sleepy cattle grazing, the peninsula is dotted with small fishing villages populated with friendly locals, offering guests an intimate and relaxing experience. Camping, hiking, biking and fishing attract people far away from the bright lights of the big city.

One of the highlights of the north shore near Grand Métis is the Jardins de Métis, a horticultural spectacle offering more than 2,500 varieties of plants in a British-style garden. The 100,000 plants attract an array of colourful butterflies with their fragrant aromas, whilst singing birds flit from branch to branch. Also of interest is the UNESCO World Heritage Site of the Listuguj Indian Reserve, Miguasha Park, near the Bay of Chaleur, the most temperate area on this stunning peninsula.

DID YOU KNOW?
This is where *Brokeback Mountain* was filmed.

CALGERY

Alberta, Canada

DRESS CODE:
Do not forget your jeans, cowboy boots and your stetson.
YOU SHOULD KNOW:
The Stampede is so popular that hotels get booked up a year in advance, so plan ahead if you want to get rowdy with these cowboys.

The territory of Alberta, Canada is a modern take on the old wild west. Its cities, Calgary and Edmonton, are hospitable and friendly, surrounded by vast stretches of lush, unspoiled prairies and grassy cattle-rich ranges from Montana to the south, the Rocky Mountains to the west and Saskatchewan in the east. Calgary is known largely for some of the finest mountainous scenery in Canada, as well as the largest, rowdiest and most prestigious annual rodeo in North America, The Calgary Stampede. Every year, at Stampede Park, locals and fans from around the globe don their best cowboy gear and whoop it up at this outrageously riotous occasion. Not just a rodeo, this event has everything you can imagine to keep your boots moving and your spurs jingling.

ALGONQUIN

Ontario, Canada

DID YOU KNOW?
The area inspired the famous Group of Seven Artists.

WHAT IS THERE TO DO?
You can canoe in the 1,610km (1,000 miles) or so of canoe routes, hike among the 6–88km (4–55 miles) of backpacking trails, ride a mountain bike, cross-country ski, fish or birdwatch.

Algonquin's Provincial Park in Ontario encompasses 7,725 sq km (4,800 sq miles) of forests, lakes and rivers, reminiscent of wilderness from a vanishing past. The park is set in a transition zone amid both deciduous and coniferous forests, with a lush landscape of maples, spruce bogs, beaver ponds, lakes and wildflower-strewn cliffs, each of which provides ample opportunities to see a wide array of plants and wildlife not commonly found together.

Within the park's boundaries you will find 53 species of mammals, 272 species of birds, 31 species of reptiles and amphibians, 54 species of fish and roughly 7,000 species of insects. More than 1,000 species of plants, as well as more than 1,000 species of fungi, are also found here.

Algonquin Provincial Park was established in 1893 as a wildlife sanctuary to protect the headwaters of the five major rivers that flow from the park. Eventually this area of majestic beauty was 'discovered' by adventurous fishermen, then by Tom Thomson and the famous Canadian landscape painters, the Group of Seven, and a host of other visitors. People travel from around the world to hear the howls of wolves echoing in this beautiful area, as well as to catch sight of the moose that inhabit the park in large numbers.

QUEBEC WINTER CARNIVAL

Quebec, Canada

In the winter wonderland that is the annual Quebec City Winter Carnival, everyone in the city flocks into the streets to celebrate the bitter cold while the rest of the population, if they are not skiing, are wishing it to end. This is the most celebrated global winter event, and the largest carnival in the world after Rio de Janeiro and New Orleans' Mardi Gras.

A variety of activities is available for every age range, from the snowboard park, snow 'rafting', a multitude of fabulous parades and horse-drawn sleigh rides and Bonhomme's Ball. You can visit a traditional Aboriginal igloo village, and stay in one overnight if you wish. In the International Snow Sculpture Event, artisans from around the world create dazzling examples of enormous ice art.

WORTH A TASTE:

Guaranteed to warm your chilly bones, *caribou* is a potent but tasty concoction of red wine, white rum and maple syrup.

ICY NIGHTS

After admiring the sculptures and enjoying the spectacle of the snow sports why not really enter into the winter carnival spirit and rent an igloo instead of a hotel room for a night.

HISTORIC QUEBEC

Quebec, Canada

DID YOU KNOW?

Vieux-Quebec was Canada's first settlement.

WORTH A SPLURGE: Treat yourself to a night in the magical Château Frontenac, or at the very least to a drink in one of its bars overlooking Terrasse Dufferin.

The first significant settlement in Canada, the French-inspired historic district of Quebec is a UNESCO World Heritage Site. Slate-roofed granite houses surround the fabulous, romantic Château Frontenac, with sweeping views of the scenic St Lawrence River below. Vieux-Quebec, the old walled city, comprises two areas, Basse-Ville and Haute-Ville. Both are almost entirely French-speaking, and very proud of their French culture. Basse-Ville, the original colony, located at the foot of Cap Diamant, is a burgeoning area of cafés and boutiques, once the home to merchants, traders and boatmen. Haute-Ville, fortified by walls and connected to Basse-Ville by funicular, is particularly European in architecture and style. Pavement cafés, horse-drawn carriages and cobbled streets prevail here. As you wander through the gas-lit lanes of compact Haute-Ville, you may come across an ancient convent and museum, and the nearly hidden, partially star-shaped Citadelle – the largest group of fortified buildings in North America, despite no shot having been fired here. Dufferin promenade at the height of the city affords majestic river and mountain views.

The majestic Château Frontenac, on Cap Diamant, is the city's iconic landmark. A large-scale model of a Loire valley château, it can be seen from nearly every quarter of the city.

THE LAURENTIANS

Quebec, Canada

WHAT ARE THEY?
Mountains of awe-inspiring beauty dotted with the charming European-style villages of Mont-Tremblant and Saint-Jovite.

WHERE ARE THEY?
145km (90 miles) north of Montreal.

ALSO KNOWN AS:
Little Switzerland.

WHAT CAN I DO THERE?
Every imaginable outdoor activity throughout the year is available here, or you can just sit back and enjoy the spectacular scenery.

SPECTACULAR SIGHT
In the autumn, the Laurentians put on a brilliant display of colourful autumn foliage. The annual Tremblant 'Symphony of Colours' festival allows visitors to enjoy the spectacular natural canvas from a gondola.

The village of Mont-Tremblant, now merged with the village of Saint-Jovite, is a spectacular, all-season paradise in the heart of the Laurentian Mountains

A famous scenic European-style resort just north of Montreal, the area was colonized in the late 19th century by Father Antoine Labelle, in reaction to the threat of Protestant expansion. He chose the Laurentian Mountains for their rich, fertile soil, access to waterways, and their potential contact with Quebec. These initial pioneers of the area fought poverty and struggled in the undeveloped landscape. Eventually, through the father's generosity and vision, they thrived in this lush, majestic scenery.

Father Labelle sensed that tourism would provide a key resource for the region and arduously petitioned for the installation of the Montreal–Saint-Jérôme railway line, which was completed in 1892, enabling the development and growth of the settlement.

In 1938, Joseph Bondurant Ryan, a wealthy American from Philadelphia, came north to prospect for gold. He was immediately taken with the pristine beauty of the 'mountain of the spirits'. He scaled it, and upon seeing the breathtaking view of the snow-blanketed landscape, vowed to transform the wilderness into a world-class alpine village. In February 1939, his dream was realized when the Mont-Tremblant Lodge, its architecture reminiscent of Old Quebec, was opened for business. In 1991, the Swiss-style pedestrian village was created.

The beauty of the landscape has been luring visitors since the Native Americans, although rather than hunting and gathering food, the hordes now come to ski, hike, fish, bike, golf, raft or simply enjoy a respite from the nearby urban chaos. Maintaining the beauty of the area remains a priority for the people who live here.

MONTREAL

Quebec, Canada

Montreal, Quebec's largest city, offers an exciting mix of French and English history and culture dating back to its European settlement in 1642. More than half of the population is French and all residents are bilingual, adding a European charm to this vibrant, cosmopolitan hub.

Whether sipping a cappuccino at an outdoor café in Little Italy, gambling at the massive Casino de Montreal complex or exploring historic Old Montreal, you will find the energy of this urban playground contagious. The international flavour of the city pervades all aspects of daily life, from the award-winning cuisine to the jazz festival and music scene, large gay community, fashionable shops and edgy arts scene.

WHAT IS THERE TO DO?
A veritable feast for the senses, whether enjoying the urban sights and sounds above ground, or in the underground city.
DON'T MISS:
The Summer International Jazz Festival.

PARISIAN CULTURE
Veux-Montreal is filled with Parisian-style outdoor cafés, artists, street performers and florist stands. St Denis is a convivial area dense with cafés, bistros, quirky boutiques and art galleries. It has been compared to St Germain des Pres in Paris, for this is the heart of French Montreal.

NIAGARA FALLS

Ontario, Canada

SCIENTIFIC IMPORTANCE:
Water from the falls drives large hydroelectric turbines producing electricity for southern Ontario and western New York State.
ALSO KNOWN AS:
'The honeymoon capital of the world'.

Niagara Falls was formed when melting glaciers created the five Great Lakes, one of which, Lake Erie, ran downhill towards another, Lake Ontario. The rushing waters carved out a river during their descent, passing the Niagara escarpment and causing the water to back up into the river. The path left from this phenomenon, created roughly 12,000 years ago, is known as the Niagara Gorge. Its current rate of wear is roughly 30cm (12in) a year. The falls at Niagara consist of the cataract of Niagara Falls on the New York side of the bridge, and the Horseshoe, or Canadian Falls across the border. The crescent-shaped Canadian Falls are 54m (177ft) high and carry nine times more water than their American counterpart, flowing at roughly 56.3kph (35mph). The combination of height and water flow is what makes the falls so incredibly beautiful and dramatic. Every minute, the Canadian Falls spew 168,000 cubic m (6,000,000 cubic ft) of water over their lip.

CHURCHILL

Manitoba, Canada

The area around Churchill, Manitoba has many sights to offer, but it is best known for its status as the 'Polar Bear Capital of the World'. Polar bears have been here since 1771 when the town was founded. From October to early December, these magnificent creatures gather where the Churchill River runs into Hudson's Bay, waiting until the bay freezes over to resume seal-hunting. At this time, the population of Churchill swells from 900 permanent residents to more than 10,000 visitors, and upwards of 1,200 polar bears. It is not unusual to see 20 polar bears in one day, particularly since some of the more curious ones actually wander into town!

BEAR FACTS
Polar bears are the largest land carnivores in the world, an average adult male weighing 350–680kg (775–1,500lb), reaching maximum size by the age of ten.

WHAT IS IT? The world's polar bear capital.
WHEN SHOULD I VISIT? The Northern Manitoba Trappers' Festival in February hosts the world championship dog-sled races, a moose-calling contest, ice fishing and beer fests, but October to early December is when you will see polar bears.

BANFF NATIONAL PARK

Alberta, Canada

Designated Canada's first national park in 1885, Banff's jagged, majestic outlines set against vast blue skies epitomize the Canadian Rocky Mountains. Declared a UNESCO World Heritage Site for its world-renowned rugged, scenic splendour, the park attracts more than four million guests from around the world every year. Banff National Park encompasses 6,641 sq km (2,564 sq miles) of grassy meadows, lush fir, pine, aspen and spruce forests as well as limestone and shale mountains dating as far back as 45–120 million years. There is so much to see and do here. Particularly wonderful is the sensation of being surrounded by ten snow-clad peaks towering more than 3,030m (10,000ft) above you, as you paddle a canoe through the turquoise waters of Moraine Lake.

WHAT IS THERE TO SEE?

Gorgeous mountain landscapes, large varieties of plants and mammals and the highest town in Canada.

DON'T MISS:

The views from Moraine Lake.

WHAT'S IN A NAME?

'Banff' is derived from Banffshire in Scotland, the birthplace of two of the original directors of the Canadian Pacific Railway.

BAY OF FUNDY

New Brunswick & Nova Scotia, Canada

ECOLOGICAL IMPORTANCE:
The Bay of Fundy serves as the summer home to many northern right whales – the most endangered whale in the world.

The Bay of Fundy lies to the southeast of Canada, off New Brunswick and Nova Scotia, and touches on the US state of Maine. It is best known for its huge tidal range. Twice a day, 100 billion tonnes of water ebb and flow, creating the highest tides in the world. The strength of the tides has differentially eroded the red sandstone and volcanic rock surrounding the water, resulting in the creation of dramatic cliffs, caves and sandstone sea stacks, the most famous of which are the Flower Pot Rocks on Hopewell Cape. Another result of the tides that sweep here is 'Old Sow', the second-largest whirlpool in the world after Norway's maelstrom.

The area's most famous visitors are the whales and dolphins. Each summer, many endangered northern right whales come to the Bay of Fundy to mate. They are spectacularly graceful creatures, and seeing them swimming effortlessly at the surface will make any whale-watching trip here worthwhile.

THE GREAT LAKES

Ontario, Canada

Illinois, Indiana, Michigan, Minnesota, New York, Ohio, Pennsylvania & Wisconsin, United States

The five Great Lakes of North America make up the largest group of freshwater lakes on Earth. They are known both for their contribution to the Earth's ecology and for their diversity and beauty. Lying on or near the Canadian/US border, the Great Lakes consist of Lake Superior, Lake Michigan, Lake Huron, Lake Erie and Lake Ontario. They formed at the end of the last ice age, roughly 10,000 years ago when the Laurentide ice sheet retreated and the meltwater filled the valley that had been gouged out by glaciers. As the glaciers melted and began receding, their leading edges left behind high ridges, some of which can be seen today in the cliffs of Door County, Wisconsin, and the Bruce Peninsula in Ontario, as well as at Niagara Falls.

WATERWORKS

The largest group of freshwater lakes on Earth. They account for 20 per cent of the world's freshwater resources.

WHAT CAN I DO THERE? As well as water-based activities such as yachting, canoeing and kayaking, fishing and scuba diving, the land surrounding Lake Ontario is great for biking, birding, hiking and camping. The remote wilderness areas contain black bears, grey wolves, elk and the highly endangered Canada lynx.

LOS CABOS

Mexico

The two towns at the tip of the rugged Baja Peninsula are commonly referred to together as Los Cabos, although they could not be more different. San José del Cabo and Cabo San Lucas are separated not just by 30km (20 miles), but also by their attitudes and personalities. Cabo San Lucas focuses mostly on sports and fiestas, whereas San José del Cabo remains a tranquil Mexican town. The latter offers the best of traditional Mexico: graceful, tree-lined pavements, small cafés, smiling locals and an unhurried pace of life. It has a beautiful, fairytale town hall in its centre with murals of old Baja decorating its inner corridors and a two-storey courtyard shaded by a large Mexican laurel. As you stroll through the streets you can enjoy art exhibitions and live concerts by traditional Mexican bands in the tiled plaza. There are plastered and columned old colonial buildings with their *paseos*, or inner courtyards, full of shops.

Since its regentrification in the past decade, Cabo San Lucas has become host to some of the best resorts in the world. The beaches here are magnificent, coloured a variety of pinks, yellows and oranges as the sun sets. It is also a place where nature lovers can watch turtles lay their eggs, hike in the estuary, birdwatch or just collect shells on the seafront. This gorgeous landscape, a mix of unspoiled desert, white sandy beaches and dramatic rock outcroppings, including the distinctive 'El Arco' at the tip of Land's End – the most famous geographic landmark of the area where the Pacific Ocean meets the Sea of Cortez – will blow you away.

DID YOU KNOW?
In the 19th century this port town experienced a boom, shipping coffee and wood from its harbour.

WORTH A VISIT:
Nearby sights include the lagoon of Ventanilla where birds and crocodiles are in abundance, the Los Reyes waterfall and the tropical spring-fed El Paraiso. The surrounding caves can be accessed for diving and snorkelling trips as well.

PUERTO ANGEL

Mexico

Puerto Angel, a rural fishing village on the Pacific coast of Oaxaca, lies in a picturesque bay surrounded by craggy peaks and sandy beaches between Puerto Escondido and Bahias de Huatulco. The two beaches in the area, Playa Principal and Playa del Panteon, are in the centre of the village. The main beach, Playa Principal, is largely used by fishing boats and has strong waves, whereas Playa del Panteon is surrounded by rocks that host some interesting marine life. This sleepy town with its dusty, largely unpaved roads is not for the adventurous, but rather those seeking solitude in a peaceful environment. A good starting point for day trips to various ruins, Puerto Angel is a wonderful place to put your feet up, breathe in the salty air and listen to the sounds of the waves lapping on the shoreline.

DON'T MISS:
Visit during one of the spectacular festivals such as *Dia de los Muertos* ('Day of the Dead') in early November or the Guelaguetza festival in July.

OAXACA
Mexico

Most people visit Oaxaca for its white sandy beaches with clear aquamarine waters that form an area of spectacular natural beauty. Some of the most attractive beaches are Zicatela, which is ideal for surfing; Escobilla, a turtle beach; Zipolite, a nudist beach; and Puerto Angel and Puerto Escondido, two bays with a truly Oaxacan environment.

The city of Oaxaca itself is a lovely place with colonial architecture and numerous plazas, courtyards and narrow streets. High above the city on a mountaintop lies the magnificent ceremonial centre of Monte Alban. An impressive collection of buildings, ball courts and plazas, its design varies from the Mayan ruins most commonly visited in the eastern part of the country.

TEOTIHUACÁN

Mexico

The ruins of Teotihuacán are among the most important in the world. The fate of its civilization remains unclear, but we do know that this was once the centre of an advanced society with a population of more than 200,000. Occupation began about 500BC, but it was only after 100BC that building of the Pyramid of the Sun began. The magnificent pyramids and palaces once covered 31 sq km (12 sq miles) but were abandoned in about 700AD and little is known about the people. Today, the rough stone structures of three pyramids, sacrificial altars and some grand houses, all of which were once covered in stucco and painted with brilliant crimson frescoes, remain.

BEST VIEW
The Pyramid of the Moon is surrounded by small temples and the Palace of Quetzalpapalotl and its straight perspective down the Avenue of the Dead is breathtaking.

TRAVELLERS' TIP: There will be a lot of walking, especially if you choose to climb the pyramids, at an alitude over 2,120m (7,000ft) so take it slowly and bring sunscreen and water.

PYRAMID OF KUKULCÁN

Mexico

The famed pyramids and temples of Chichén Itzá are the Yucatán Peninsula's best-known ancient monuments. Walking among these stone platforms, pyramids and ball courts helps you to better understand and appreciate this ancient advanced civilization.

Led by Quetzalcoatl (who the Mayans called Kukulcán), the Toltec came here from their capital, Tula, in north-central Mexico in roughly 987AD. Along with Putún Maya coastal traders, they built a magnificent metropolis, Chichén Itzá, constructing it using Puuc Maya methods and embellishing it with Toltec motifs including feathered serpents, warriors, eagles and jaguars. Chichén Itzá was to become the most powerful place in the whole of the Yucatán peninsula.

WHAT IS IT?
The most impressive ruin of Chichén Itzá, the best known of Yucatán's ancient monuments.
WHY IS IT IMPORTANT?
They are some of the largest, most grand and best-restored monuments of this age.

IMPRESSIVE DISCOVERY
Overgrown with jungle and slowly decaying, the massive structures of Chichén Itzá were first seriously explored by archaeologists in the 1920s. Many of the ancient structures have been restored, including the temple known as El Castillo, or the Pyramid of Kukulcán.

POPOCATEPETL

Mexico

Popocatepetl, an active volcano and the second-highest peak in Mexico, is host to 14 monasteries, standing on its slopes. The monasteries are well-preserved examples of the architectural style adopted by the first missionaries – Franciscans, Dominicans and Augustinians – who converted the indigenous populations to Christianity in the early 16th century after the Spanish conquest of Mexico.

The first monastery, at Huejotzingo at the foot of the volcano, was dedicated to the Archangel Michael. Perched on an ancient mound in the bustling town centre, its walled courtyard is secluded from the noise of the outside streets. It is chiefly famous for its extraordinary 16th-century art and architecture, including the elaborately carved corner chapels of the churchyard, medieval Moorish arches emblazoned with Franciscan escutcheons and stunning murals lining the walls of the church and cloister.

All of the churches host a great number of treasured antiquities and religious artefacts, and all are recognized by UNESCO as World Heritage Sites.

WHAT IS IT?
An active volcano and the second-highest peak in Mexico.
WHERE IS IT?
70km (43.5 miles) southeast of Mexico City.
WHAT IS THERE TO SEE?
The 14 monasteries on the slopes of the volcano.

MOUNT RUSHMORE

South Dakota, United States

Carved into the southeast face of a mountain in South Dakota, at a height of 1,737m (5,700ft) above sea level, are the faces of presidents George Washington, Thomas Jefferson, Theodore Roosevelt and Abraham Lincoln. Looking down from its position high above the Black Hills, this majestic memorial to American history is spectacular to behold. It was conceived by Doane Robinson in 1923 as a way to attract more people to the Black Hills of South Dakota, and lies in the former Harney National Forest Preserve.

A sculptor, Gutzon Borglum, was contracted to undertake the job of carving the Needles area into a tall granite figure, but instead chose Mount Rushmore for the work because it was the highest peak in the area and its southeastern-facing site meant it would receive sunlight for most of the day. He then selected the subjects of national focus that would be highlighted in his work – the four presidents mentioned above.

Borglum continued working on the final details of the sculptures for a further two years. In 1941 he died suddenly and his son Lincoln took over on the project until funding ran out a few months later. The studio was shut and the presidential faces were left as they were. Mount Rushmore continues to be a reminder of these four important figures in American history, and the original goal of increasing traffic to the Black Hills has been met with resounding success.

CUSTER STATE PARK

South Dakota, United States

WHAT IS IT?
A national park that is home to spectacular landscapes and historical monuments.
WHERE IS IT?
Between Mount Rushmore and Wind Cave National Park.

Custer State Park in the Black Hills of South Dakota is home to a selection of historical monuments, spectacular parkland and abundant wildlife. Covering an area of roughly 29,000 hectares (72,000 acres), the park boasts gently undulating meadows, rolling foothills, pine forests, large lakes and the giant, finger-like granite spires of the Needles. The scenic drive on the Needles Highway (SD 87) highlights the towering rock formations, including the awe-inspiring 'Needles Eye', an impressive granite spire jutting 9–12m (30–40ft) into the air, with an 'eye' just 90–120cm (3–4ft) in width. Don't be surprised if you encounter bison on your drive. A 1,500-strong herd – one of the largest in the world – roams freely throughout the park, and often stops traffic along the Wildlife Loop Road.

BADLANDS

South Dakota, United States

DID YOU KNOW?
Also known as *les mauvaises terres a traverser* or 'bad lands to cross'.

WHAT IS IT?
A desolate moonscape of saw-toothed spires, eroded buttes and ragged ridges.

HOW DO I GET THERE?
There are airports in Rapid City and Sioux Falls. There are various routes to drive into the park, including Highway 240, 'Badlands Loop Road', which is a scenic drive.

The Badlands National Park in southwest South Dakota is an eerie place of startlingly beautiful desolation. From the ragged ridges and saw-toothed spires, to the sharply eroded buttes and pinnacles and the wind-ravaged moonscape of the Sage Creek Wilderness Area, Badlands National Park is an unsettling yet awe-inspiring experience. The Sioux Indians named this land *mako sica* or 'land bad' and early French-Canadian trappers labelled it *les mauvaises terres a traverser* or 'bad lands to cross' because of its inhospitable terrain, the result of deposition and partial erosion of sedimentary rocks. The serrated ridges and deep canyons of the Badlands were formed about 500,000 years ago, when water began to cut through the rock layers, carving fantastic shapes in the flat floodplain. Ancient rocks, buried for millions of years, became exposed. Erosion averages around 2.5cm (1in) a year, so the buttes will be gone in 500,000 years.

The Badlands are one of the richest Oligocene fossil beds known. Fossils of 25–35 million-year-old three-toed horses, dog-sized camels, sabretooth tigers, giant pigs and other species have been found. Some 11,000 years of human history are here, too, including the sites of the Sioux Ghost Dances (protests at government land-grabs) of 1890. A walk through the Badlands visualizing its human history and the geological processes that have taken place here is truly a must.

NEW ENGLAND

Connecticut, Maine, Massachusetts, New Hampshire, Rhode Island & Vermont, United States

Every October, the leaves in New England burst into a spectacular symphony of vibrant colours before they fall to the ground as the trees become dormant for winter, and 'tree peeping' is a common pastime here during the autumn. Once you see the joyous explosion of colours bursting over the picturesque landscape, you will understand why this is the most popular season for visiting the area.

So why do leaves change colour in autumn? At this time of year the production of chlorophyll in leaves stops and so they lose their vibrant green colours, revealing the underlying tones caused by the presence of other pigments, such as carotenoids which provide yellow, orange and brown colours, and anthocyanins which give red and purple colours.

The range and intensity of autumn colours are greatly influenced by the weather, and the brightest autumn colours are produced when dry, sunny days are followed by cool, dry nights. Regardless of timing, if you are fortunate enough to see the stunning autumn colours that cover vast swathes of New England, you will understand why there is even a foliage hotline offering hourly reports on the best places to go.

DID YOU KNOW?
This is the site of the last major clash between American Indians and US troops in North America.

WHAT IS IT?
A battlefield in Wounded Knee, South Dakota.
WHAT IS THERE TO SEE?
The battleground and cemetery for those killed in the fight.

Right: Stunning fall foliage in Vermont, New England

WOUNDED KNEE

South Dakota, United States

Wounded Knee, South Dakota represents the last major clash between American Indians and white US troops in North America. On the morning of 29 December 1890, the Sioux chief Big Foot and 350 of his followers camped on the banks of Wounded Knee Creek, surrounded by US troops with orders to arrest him and disarm his warriors. This tense moment had been building for years, as the once proud Sioux, a nomadic people, had found their way of life destroyed, as they were confined to reservations and dependent on Indian agents for their existence. Approximately 200 Sioux were killed that day, including Big Foot, as well as 25 US soldiers. Many others on both sides were wounded. The site of the Wounded Knee battleground includes the cemetery containing the graves of the Indians who died that day.

MOMA

New York, United States

WHAT IS IT? One of the world's premier collections of modern art and design.
WHERE IS IT? New York City

Founded in 1929 as an educational institution, the Museum of Modern Art, or MoMA, in New York City is dedicated to being the foremost museum of modern art in the world.

Considered by many to have the best collection of modern masterpieces in the world, MoMA's holdings include such notable works as Vincent Van Gogh's *Starry Night*, Pablo Picasso's *Les Demoiselles d'Avignon*, Salvador Dali's *The Persistence of Memory,* Piet Mondrian's *Broadway Boogie Woogie*, a triptych of *Water Lilies* by Claude Monet, Henri Matisse's *Dance*, Paul Cezanne's *The Bather* and Frida Kahlo's *Self Portrait with Cropped Hair*. MoMA also holds works by leading American artists such as Jackson Pollock, Jasper Johns, Edward Hopper, Andy Warhol, Chuck Close and Ralph Bakshi. The museum's design collection includes works from Paul Laszlo, the Eameses, Isamu Noguchi and George Nelson as well as many industrial pieces ranging from a self-aligning ball-bearing to an entire Bell 47D1 helicopter.

The Museum of Modern Art seeks to create a dialogue between the established and the experimental and the past and the present, in an environment that is responsive to the issues of modern and contemporary art, while being accessible to all visitors to this beautiful space.

THE STATUE OF LIBERTY

New York, United States

Two famous New York City landmarks are the Statue of Liberty and Ellis Island, making up the Statue of Liberty National Monument. With their historical and symbolic significance, these two icons of America stand as a reminder of the American ideals of freedom, liberty and justice for all.

WHERE IS IT?
New York harbor.
WHY IS IT IMPORTANT?
They are symbols of the American ideal of freedom, liberty and democratic justice for all.

The people of France gave the Statue of Liberty to the people of the United States more than a century ago in recognition of the friendship established during the American Revolution. Declared a UNESCO World Heritage Site after its refurbishment in 1986, the Statue of Liberty represents the pillars on which the American constitution was established, including life, liberty and the pursuit of happiness.

WHAT IS IT?
A famous architectural masterpiece by Frank Lloyd Wright.
WHY SHOULD I GO?
Fallingwater is the most acclaimed American architectural work, promoting harmony between man and nature.

FALLINGWATER

Pennsylvania, United States

Frank Lloyd Wright, internationally recognized as one of the leading modern architects of his day, is best known for creating a new form of American housing, the prairie house, as well as the award-winning single family home, Fallingwater. Frank Lloyd Wright was commissioned by the wealthy Pittsburgh businessman Edgar Kaufman Sr to build a weekend home in the rural Bear Run area near Pittsburgh, Pennsylvania. Kaufman requested a simple structure overlooking the waterfall and its attendant cabins. Instead Wright proceeded to build one of his most acclaimed works, which was voted 'the best all-time work of American architecture' by the American Institute of Architects. A spectacular example of organic architecture, a harmonious blend of man and nature through design, Wright used every modern construction tool available in 1935 to create this naturally integrated home, seemingly part of the underlying rock bed and waterfall.

WASHINGTON DC

District of Columbia, United States

Washington DC (District of Columbia) is the capital of the United States. Nestled between Maryland and Virginia on the eastern seaboard, the district covers an area of 108 sq km (67 sq miles) centering on the US Capitol. As one of the most historically significant and charming areas in the United States, Washington is well worth a visit. Tourist highlights include the US Capitol, the many monuments and museums of 'the mall', the White House, Georgetown and Adams Morgan. Tours of the Capitol, where senators and representatives meet to shape legislative policy, are available. These include the stunning Rotunda, the Statuary Hall, the original Supreme Court chamber and the Crypt, intended burial place of George and Martha Washington.

BEST VIEW
The Washington Monument, a 169-m (555-ft) granite spire with 893 steps (or a lift ride) to the top, affords amazing 360-degree views of Washington's metropolitan area.

WHEN SHOULD I GO? The city is alive with activity throughout the year but highlights include the Cherry Blossom Festival in early spring, the Fourth of July celebrations and the lighting of the national Christmas tree. Winters are cold and summers are hot and humid.

VIETNAM VETERANS MEMORIAL

District of Columbia, United States

The Vietnam Veterans Memorial in Washington DC recognizes and honours the men and women who served and sacrificed their lives in one of America's most divisive wars. Sometimes referred to simply as 'The Wall', the memorial was born from a need to heal the nation's wounds. Conceived and designed to make no political statement, it is a place where people can come together and remember their loved ones. It is made of three elements: the Wall of Names, the Three Servicemen Statue and Flagpole and the Vietnam Women's Memorial. Set in Constitution Gardens, the long, black granite wall is not prominent, grand or imposing, but is simple, thoughtful, powerful and profound. Etched into the granite are the names of the 58,249 men and women who died and 1,200 who went missing in the Vietnam War. The two panels of the wall extend from a central point at a wide angle, with one side pointing towards the Washington Monument and the other towards the Lincoln Memorial. The descent to the centre of the wall reveals a towering 3-m (10-ft) looming shape surrounded by grassy slopes, which is oddly ominous in its serenity. The names appear in a seemingly endless stream, in chronological order from 1959 to 1975. Many family and friends leave mementos or flowers.

This memorial is impressive and powerful in every way, and it is worth visiting to share a moment of silence for those who fought in the Vietnam War.

THE NATIONAL AIR AND SPACE MUSEUM

District of Columbia, United States

The Smithsonian Institution's National Air and Space Museum maintains the largest collection of historic air- and spacecraft in the world. A vital centre for research into the history, science and technology of aviation and spaceflight, as well as planetary science, terrestrial geology and geophysics, its treasures are kept in two buildings; one on the National Mall and the other in the Steven F. Udvar-Hazy Center located near Dulles Airport. A shuttle-bus service runs between the two sites.

WHAT CAN I SEE?
Orville and Wilbur Wright's original 1903 *Wright Flyer*, the *Enola Gay,* which dropped the atomic bomb on Hiroshima, the Space Shuttle *Enterprise* and the Apollo 11 command module, to name just a few exhibits.

The mall building in Washington, DC has hundreds of artefacts on display including the original 1903 *Wright Flyer*, the *Spirit of St Louis*, the Apollo 11 command module and a touchable lunar rock sample.

THE SMOKY MOUNTAINS

Tennessee & North Carolina, United States

DID YOU KNOW?
The name of the area comes from the natural haze that often hangs over it.

WHAT IS IT?
The most-visited national park in the Eastern United States.
WHERE IS IT?
On the border of Tennessee and North Carolina.
WHAT IS THERE TO DO?
Hike the Appalachian Trail.

A major mountain range in the southern part of the Appalachians, the Smoky Mountains straddle the border between Tennessee and North Carolina. The name comes from the natural haze that often hovers above it. As in the neighbouring Blue Ridge Mountains just to the east, hydrocarbons produced by trees and other vegetation, together with higher humidity, give the sky a bluish cast, even over short distances.

The most-visited national park in the eastern United States, the Great Smoky Mountains National Park is home to Clingmans Dome, the highest point on the Appalacian Trail at an elevation of 2,030m (6,643ft). A paved road leads to within 91m (300ft) of the summit, from where visitors can walk to the top for a view over Tennessee, North Carolina, South Carolina and Georgia. It also holds significant numbers of the Smokies' symbol – the black bear – and other important wildlife. The Appalachian National Scenic Trail, is the main attraction here. A 3,500-km (2,174-mile) marked hiking trail, the AT extends between Springer Mountain in Georgia and Mount Katahdin in Maine. Along the way, the trail passes through North Carolina, Tennessee, Virginia, West Virginia, Maryland, Pennsylvania, New Jersey, New York, Connecticut, Massachusetts, Vermont and New Hampshire.

CHARLESTON

South Carolina, United States

Charleston is located on a narrow peninsula between the Ashley and Cooper Rivers where they flow into the Atlantic Ocean. Originally known as 'Charles Town' after King Charles II of England, the town was established in 1670 and settled a decade later. Downtown Charleston serves as the central business district of Greater Charleston and is home to many historic and cultural sites and buildings of architectural interest. 'Old Charleston' — with its homes with wrought-iron gates, courtyard gardens and oak- and palm-lined streets — is a fine example of southern colonial charm. It is like stepping back in time as you sniff the clean, salty air and listen to the horse-drawn carriages clop past the grand homes of this beautiful historic city, one of the most elegant places in America.

WHAT IS IT?
A lovely historic town in South Carolina.
DON'T MISS:
Charming 'Old Charleston'.
WHEN SHOULD I VISIT?
The best time to visit is March to November.

LITERARY INSPIRATION
Charleston has inspired many novels including Pat Conroy's *Prince of Tides, South of Broad* and *The Lords of Discipline*.

SAVANNAH

Georgia, United States

DID YOU KNOW?
Midnight in the Garden of Good and Evil, based on a true story, was filmed here.

WHAT IS IT?
A stunning, historically significant southern town, the first planned city in America.

WHAT IS THERE TO SEE?
Exceptionally preserved and restored architecture dating back to the early 1800s.

In 1733, General James Edward Oglethorpe and 120 travellers landed on a bluff high along the Savannah River, naming the 13th and final American colony, Georgia, after England's King George II. Savannah became its first city.

As the economy grew and cotton regained its importance, Savannah entered the new century re-establishing herself as the 'Belle of Georgia'. The Historic District was designated a National Historic Landmark, and remains one of the largest historic landmarks in the country.

Many restored old buildings survive, including: the Pirates' House, built in 1754; the Herb House, dating back to 1734 and the oldest existing building in Georgia, and the Pink House, built in 1789 as the site of Georgia's first bank. There are also several restored churches. The fourth-largest city in Georgia, Savannah is known not only for its historical architecture and famed cemeteries, but also for its jazz and blues, tranquil and pristine beaches, excellent golf courses, deep-sea fishing and exceptional museums.

ST AUGUSTINE

Florida, United States

WHAT IS IT?
The oldest city in the United States.

St Augustine, Florida, also known as the 'Ancient City', is the oldest city in the United States as well as the longest continually occupied European settlement in the continental United States. First discovered by the Spanish admiral Pedro Menendez de Aviles in 1565, it was founded as San Agustín.

The Castillo de San Marcos, built from 1672 to 1695, served as an outpost of the Spanish Empire, guarding the town and protecting the sea route for treasure ships returning to Spain. Although the castillo has served a number of nations throughout its history, it has never been taken by military force. During the 18th century, the castillo went from Spanish control to British and back to the Spanish, as a result of a series of treaties.

The town of St Augustine retains some of its original European charms. Strategically located among the intercoastal waterway, the Matanzas River and the Atlantic, the area's historic district has quaint cobbled streets lined with charming cafés, bars, boutiques and guesthouses. The area is home to 69km (43miles) of lovely beaches offering visitors the opportunity to take advantage of the fishing, diving, surfing, parasailing and many other watersports that are on offer. In addition to its historical importance, St Augustine is simply a lovely town to visit.

FLORIDA KEYS

Florida, United States

WHAT IS IT?
An archipelago of 1,700 islands
WORTH A SPLURGE:
Stay in one of the lovely guesthouses with their wrap-around porches in Key West, and enjoy the tropical hospitality of Jimmy Buffet's famed 'Margaritaville'.
WORTH A TASTE:
You cannot leave without a taste of conch fritters followed by key lime pie.

The Florida Keys are a subtropical archipelago consisting of 1,700 islands off the southeastern tip of the Florida peninsula, the farthest of which is Key West, its southern tip only 145km (90 miles) from Cuba. They are accessed via the scenic Overseas Highway, an extension of Route 1, the largely two-lane road consisting mostly of bridges that connects the islands, each of which has its own laidback character.

The Subtropical Keys are closer in nature to the Caribbean than the rest of Florida, although unlike the Caribbean's volcanic islands, the Upper Keys are remnants of large coral reefs, fossilized and exposed as sea levels declined. The Lower Keys are composed of sandy limestone grains produced by plants and marine organisms.

SOUTH BEACH, MIAMI

Florida, United States

DID YOU KNOW?
South Beach has replaced Los Angeles and New York City as the United States' most popular nightlife spot.

South Beach, or 'SOBE', the lower section of Miami Beach, Florida, originally developed in the early 1900s, has stunning Art Deco architecture. Although many of the Art Deco buildings are either crumbling or have been demolished, South Beach retains the world's largest collection of Streamline Moderne Art Deco architecture, and a recent resurgence in the popularity of the area has caused a lot of regeneration and restoration of this lovely destination.

WORTH A SPLURGE:
Stay overnight in one of the fashionable art deco hotels and sip an expertly prepared mojito (quite possibly surrounded by supermodels) by the stunning poolside at the Delano Hotel.

A longstanding spring-break favourite, the long stretches of white sand and crystalline waters of South Beach are separated from 'the strip' by Ocean Drive. The pastel cityscape of boutique hotels, mixed with expensive high-rise blocks of modern flats, nightclubs, cafés, restaurants and bars shows evidence of the rampant tourism, but if you sit back and enjoy the show, you are guaranteed to get into the swing of things – there's something for everyone in South Beach.

A major location for photoshoots and high fashion, South Beach's palm-studded promenade is a well-recognized backdrop for events ranging from the *Sports Illustrated* swimsuit issue to the National Women's Volleyball Championship. Here, people pride themselves on their physique and fashionable appearance, whatever it may be, and they are not afraid to show it off. Viva South Beach!

FLORIDA EVERGLADES

Florida, United States

Everglades National Park, a World Heritage Site, encompasses the largest designated wilderness east of the Rocky Mountains. This subtropical preserve, comprised of both temperate and tropical plants, includes sawgrass prairies, mangrove and cypress swamps, pinelands and hardwood stands. It is also known for its marine and estuary environments, with its rich bird life, numerous manatees and noteworthy existence of alligators and crocodiles living side by side. As you approach the park via 'Alligator Alley', you immediately begin to get the sense of history here. It is easy to visualize the indigenous Indians plying the waterways in their hand-hewn canoes. Here there are no peaks, no mountains and no hills to shelter you – it is just swampland and grasses as far as the eye can see.

WHAT IS IT?
The third largest National Park in the United States.
WHERE IS IT?
Southern Florida.
WHEN SHOULD I VISIT?
November to March is the best time.

DID YOU KNOW?
This is the only place on earth where alligators and crocodiles cohabit.

SAN ANTONIO

Texas, United States

WHERE IS IT?
The city is on the northern edge of the South Texas region and south-east of the Texas Hill Country.
WHAT IS THERE TO SEE?
The historic Alamo Mission, the River Walk and an eclectic blend of multicultural architecture.

San Antonio, the only major city in Texas founded before it won independence from Mexico, was once populated by Spanish missionaries and militiamen, German merchants, southern plantation owners, western cattle ranchers and eastern architects. Their existence is still felt in the city's downtown area and is evident in the current culture and cuisine. San Antonio is largely known for three things: its parties, its eclectic architecture and the Alamo.

San Antonio hosts many celebrations, some comparable to Mardi Gras. Here they might break confetti eggs called *cascarones*, listen to oompah bands, and cheer rodeo bull-riders in festivals that mingle all the area's cultural backgrounds. It is also America's capital for Tejano music, a unique blend of Mexican and German sounds. The city's architecture also reflects its multi-ethnic history in an eclectic mixture of different styles.

SANTA FE

New Mexico, United States

Nestled in the picturesque Sangre de Cristo Mountains, Santa Fe was planned around a central plaza, according to Philip II of Spain's 'Laws of the Indies' in 1573. The north side of the plaza is home to the Governor's Palace, to the east is the church, now the Cathedral Basilica of Saint Francis of Assisi. In 1912, in an effort to establish tourism, it was decreed that a single style of architecture should be used across the city to promote a unification of the varied styles that had been built through the town's history. Local officials decided on the Spanish Pueblo Revival look, inspired by the defining features of local architecture: *vigas* (wooden beams) and *canales* (water spouts on the roof) from the old adobe homes, the churches found in the *pueblos* (villages) and the earth-toned, adobe-coloured exteriors.

LOCAL CULTURE
Visit during the annual autumn fiesta to celebrate the 'reconquering' of New Mexico by Don Diego De Vargas.

WHAT IS IT? The capital of New Mexico.
WHAT IS THERE TO DO? The city is a mecca for artists, it is not far from scenic Taos and there's also a local ski area.

TAOS

New Mexico, United States

WHAT IS THERE TO DO?
Ski, sightsee, shop, fish, explore and enjoy the scenic wonders of this beautiful artistic village.

Taos, a scenic New Mexican community, is famous for many things, including skiing, art, architecture and historical sites. A mix of Native American, Spanish and Anglo-American cultures is represented in art and architecture, music, dance, food and festivals. Historic Taos Plaza and its side streets have old adobe buildings, once the homes of some of Taos' leading citizens such as Kit Carson. Renovated into galleries, stores and boutiques it offers a pleasant stroll with many hidden treasures.

Taos Pueblo (or Pueblo de Taos) is the ancient town of the northern Tiwa-speaking tribe of the Pueblo American Indians. Lying 1.6km (1 mile) north of modern Taos on the Rio Pueblo, it has been home to this tribe for more than 1,000 years. The Pueblo's reddish-brown adobe housing, built between 1000 and 1450AD, is a National Historic Landmark and a World Heritage Site and it remains occupied to this day.

Home to the ski resorts of Taos, Red River, Sipapu and Angel Fire, Taos offers uncrowded skiing on wonderfully diverse terrain, feather-light powder and an intimate alpine village for skiers of all levels.

Taos is a natural wonderland. Whether you want skiing, horseriding, biking, hiking, rafting or kayaking, the stunning mountains and the Rio Grande Gorge offer a number of fantastic outdoor pursuits.

DID YOU KNOW?
Large parts of *Jurrassic Park*, *Raider's of the Lost Ark* and the original *King Kong* were filmed here.

WHAT IS IT?
One of the most stunning islands in the Hawaiian archipelago.
WHAT IS THERE TO DO?
Tour the 'Grand Canyon of the West' or kayak along the beautiful Na Pali coast.

Right: The striking coastline of Kauai

KAUAI

Hawaii, United States

Formed over six million years ago, Kauai, the oldest and most northerly of the main Hawaiian islands, is roughly 550 sq miles (1,430 sq km) in area. The Na Pali coast has spectacular scenery. Emerald valleys, jagged 1,219-m (4,000-ft) cliffs towering above the blue Pacific, caves, lava tubes and pristine beaches make this one of the most stunning and unspoiled areas on the entire island. West Kauai is full of spectacular natural wonders and Hawaiian cultural landmarks. Awe-inspiring Waimea Canyon is the main draw. A vast 16km (10 miles) long and 1,098m (3,600ft) deep, its scale and scope, and the rainbow colours streaking it, are incredible. The view into Kalalau Valley is one of the most beautiful sights on the island: at sunset the walls reflect pink, orange, red and grey.

SEDONA

Arizona, United States

WHAT IS IT? A stunning city made of red sandstone formations.
TRIVIA: Sedona is home to the world's only McDonald's with turquoise arches. Town planners resisted the usual yellow.

Founded in 1902, Sedona has become a gathering place for mystics who believe that the Earth's energy flows around the area's famed red rocks, concentrating into power spots, called vortices. Believers in Vortex Healing cite the Sedona area as home to several of these vortices, which allows them to access a 'healing realm' of divine consciousness, empowering them to cure both physical and emotional conditions. In addition to the spas that have arisen from this belief, Sedona is also home to many yoga, art and literary societies, as well as a number of luxury resorts catering to visitors who want to visit the stunning array of red sandstone, mudstone and limestone formations that glow brilliant orange and red when lit by the rising or setting sun.

Named after Sedona Schnebly, the wife of the city's first postmaster, Sedona is a popular stopover for visitors. Its location at the base of the Mogollon Rim, surrounded by fascinating natural crimson sandstone monoliths, inspired *Weekend Travel Report* to name Sedona, Arizona as 'The Most Beautiful Place in America'.

Here you can bike, fish, go birdwatching, take a pottery or art class, go on a narrated star-gazing trip or a Native American-led hike or play golf on any of the first-class resort courses. There's even a natural water slide at Slide Rock State Park.

THE PAINTED DESERT

Arizona, United States

WHAT IS THERE TO SEE?
A stunning, ever-changing landscape offering spectacular views.
YOU SHOULD KNOW:
Stick to marked trails in the Petrified Forest as the plants are very fragile. It is illegal to remove the petrified wood.

The Painted Desert is an area of breathtaking beauty, stretching along the Little Colorado River from the Grand Canyon to the Petrified Forest National Park in northern Arizona. The desert, named *el Desierto Pintura* by the Spaniards, because of its brightly coloured land forms, consists of badland hills and Chinle formation rocks as well as spectacular mesas and buttes rising from the desert floor.

The Painted Desert's rocks and soils have various combinations of minerals and decayed plant and animal matter that contribute to the many colours, particularly the red rocks, throughout the formations. At sunrise and sunset, the crimson formations are especially beautiful when they turn shades of violet, blue and burnt orange.

MONUMENT VALLEY

Utah, United States

DID YOU KNOW?
Etiquette dictates that you should not take pictures of the Native Americans or their property without permission.

WHAT IS IT?
The quintessential desert landscape defining the American West.
WHAT SHOULD I KNOW?
Monument Valley is a Navajo Indian Tribal Park, not a national park, and an entrance fee is payable.

Monument Valley is an area of sandstone rock formations rising majestically up to 300m (1,000ft) from the desert floor, providing one of the most enduring images of the American West. These isolated red mesas and buttes, surrounded by vast, empty desert, have been filmed and photographed countless times, giving the visitor a sense of familiarity, but once in the valley you cannot fail to be amazed at the vivid, deep, rich colour palette of this otherworldly landscape.

The view from the visitor centre is spectacular enough, but the majority of the park can only be seen from the Valley Drive, a 27-km (17-mile) road. Winding among the magical towering cliffs and mesas including the Totem Pole, a stunning 91-m (300-ft) rock spire only a few metres wide. As well as eroded rocks, this area is also home to a series of ancient cave and cliff dwellings, natural arches and petroglyphs.

Not a valley in the conventional sense, Monument Valley is actually a wide, flat, desolate landscape, interrupted by the crumbling formations, the final remnants of the sandstone layers that once covered the entire region. Monument Valley is the quintessential, spectacular, breathtaking Wild West.

GRAND CANYON

Arizona, United States

The Grand Canyon, cut by the Colorado River, is one of the United State's most famous landmarks and stretches an incredible 322km (200 miles) across the desert highlands of northern Arizona. Named as one of the seven natural wonders of the world, the Grand Canyon was designated a National Park in 1919. Here you will find a breathtaking chasm of unimaginable scope in a palette of crimson, gold and orange cliffs, purple abysses and clear rushing waters, making it one of the most astonishing landscapes on Earth. The southern rim of the Grand Canyon is the most popular area – it allows easy access from the main road that parallels the canyon edge for a substantial distance and has many scenic overlooks, as well as a selection of hiking trails.

WHAT IS IT?
One of the seven natural wonders of the world.
WHERE IS IT?
The desert highlands of Arizona.

POETIC INSPIRATION

Upon seeing the drama of a Grand Canyon sunset, the poet Carl Sandburg remarked, 'There goes God with an army of banners'.

MESA VERDE

Colorado, United States

DID YOU KNOW?
Mesa Verde is Spanish for 'green table', named after the tree-covered flat geological formations.

WHAT IS IT?
The largest archaeological site in the United States.
WHERE IS IT?
The park entrance is located on US 160, 16km (10 miles) east of Cortez in Colorado.

Mesa Verde is a large archaeological area in the United States, with more than 4,000 sites dating from 600 to 1300AD, including the most impressive cliff dwellings in the southwest. The inhabitants of the Four Corners region of Mesa Verde were the Anasazi (ancestral Puebloans), who in the 13th century built houses in the shallow caves but abandoned them less than 100 years later.

The caves were discovered in 1888 by ranchers Charles Mason and his brother-in-law Richard Wetherill, but many artefacts were looted before a Denver newspaper aroused national interest in the site's protection and it was declared a national park in 1906. The Chapin Mesa Archaeological Museum provides information about the Anasazi civilization and displays findings and artwork from the dwellings. Spruce Tree House, Balcony House and Cliff Palace are open to the public, and mesa-top ruins include the Far View Complex, Cedar Tree Tower and the Sun Temple.

SAN DIEGO

California, United States

Set around a graceful curving bay, free from the smog and the crowded, sprawling freeways of Los Angeles, sits the beautiful city of San Diego. The site of the first mission in California, it was not until the arrival of the Santa Fe Railroad in the 1880s that the city became a significant trading port. The second-largest city in California, it has farms, state parks and forests, desert areas and mountains rising above the snow line, as well as kilometres of stunning Pacific-coast beaches. It has an eclectic mix of architectural styles from Spanish Colonial Renaissance to neo-Gothic and Moorish and offers a wide array of art and culture.

Mission Beach Boardwalk is a highlight, with rollercoasters, an arcade, restaurants and surf shops. You can hire bikes, surfboards, roller skates and roller blades or just enjoy the white sandy coastline. Another lovely beach is Pacific Beach. Known as the 'PB' by local residents, it is also home to one of San Diego's larger nightlife areas, with dozens of bars and cafés lining Garnet, the main street. A golden beach stretches for miles from the Mission Bay jetty up to the stunning cliffs of ritzy La Jolla. For a different atmosphere, try the historic Gaslamp Quarter, where many of the buildings are Victorian-inspired. San Diego also has many naval bases, including Miramar, where *Top Gun* was filmed. Silver Strand Beach National Park and Mount Soledad are other highlights. San Diego is a city with something for everyone.

DID YOU KNOW?
The Luxor, a black glass pyramid, boasts the world's most powerful beam of light.

WHAT IS THERE TO DO?
Gamble, watch live entertainment, eat at gourmet restaurants, play golf, shop, stay in luxurious resorts or just hang out by the pool.

Right: The bright lights of Vegas

LAS VEGAS

Nevada, United States

Las Vegas is known for many things: glitz, glamour, ostentation, gambling, entertainment, debauchery, shopping and excess. The most populous city in the state of Nevada, it is the largest founded in the 20th century, and is the centre of gambling in the United States. Beginning as a stopover en route to the pioneer trails to the west, Las Vegas became a popular railway town in the early 20th century, serving as a staging point for the mines in the surrounding area that shipped their goods out to the country from its station. With the growth of the railway, Las Vegas became less important, but the construction of the Hoover Dam injected a new vitality into Las Vegas and the city has never looked back. The increase in tourism caused by the dam and the legalization of gambling led to the advent of the casino-hotels for which Las Vegas is famous.

HOLLYWOOD

California, United States

WHAT IS IT?
The quintessential tinsel town, known for its cinematic glamour.

Hollywood is a region west of downtown Los Angeles, known around the world as the home of the American film industry. It is all about celebrity here. You can visit your favourite celebrity grave, take a tour of celebrity homes, walk down Sunset Strip, Hollywood Boulevard and Sunset Boulevard, shop along the celebrity-studded Rodeo Drive and Wilshire Boulevard in Beverly Hills or take a stroll down the Walk of Fame. No trip is complete without a visit to the Hollywood Entertainment Museum or a tour of the Hollywood Studios. Venice Beach is still quintessential California, with street performers, outdoor cafés and lots of life. Hire a bike and ride the cycle path south to Redondo Beach. Take a trip to Santa Monica's pier or stop by Zuma Beach up the Pacific Coast Highway from Malibu. Catalina Island in Anaheim is where the Angelenos go to scuba dive. Skip the tourist-ridden Avalon and explore the wild side of the island with its excellent hiking, camping, fishing and kayaking.

There are many other excellent ways to pass the time in Los Angeles, such as the LA County Museum of Art and the Museum of Contemporary Art. This relatively small museum is devoted to postwar art and has a permanent collection of 5,000 works. If you like great art, stunning architecture, peaceful gardens and wonderful views (smog permitting), then the Getty Center is not to be missed.

DID YOU KNOW?
Clint Eastwood was once mayor of this beautiful seaside town.

CARMEL

California, United States

WHAT IS THERE TO SEE?
Gorgeous coastline, world-class golf and the magical '17 mile drive'.
WHAT IS IT KNOWN FOR?
Stunning scenery, extraordinary golf, beautiful homes and artistic history.

Carmel is a charming small town on the Pacific Coast of the Monterey Peninsula in central California. Predominantly a residential community, it is also celebrated as having one of the best, and certainly most scenic, golf courses in the United States at Pebble Beach, as well as a lively arts scene. Built as a seaside artists' colony, attracting such people as Robinson Jeffers, Sinclair Lewis, Robert Louis Stevenson and Ansel Adams, Carmel was created as a peaceful and intellectually inspiring enclave. It was built largely of cottage-style homes with a fairytale twist, including rambling gables, shutters, trellises and large front and rear gardens. These homes were planned to retain the town's character as a 'village in a forest'.

BIG SUR

California, United States

DID YOU KNOW?
Big Sur, by Jack Kerouac, was inspired by this lovely coastline.

WHAT IS THERE TO SEE?
Stretches of scenic beauty along the winding Route 1.
WHAT IS THERE TO DO?
Hike, kayak, dine, camp or just enjoy the view.

Big Sur is derived from the Spanish *el sur grande*, meaning 'the big south'. Named by early Monterey settlers, the southern coastal area is imposing but treacherous to ships.

Although the region includes many state parks, the Big Sur region covers a much larger area of central California, occupying roughly 143km (89 miles) of the Pacific coastline.

The magnificent coastal scenery of jagged cliffs, pristine beaches, precarious bridges, lofty emerald hills, forests and hot springs has been a beloved landmark for Californians since it was discovered in 1872. In addition to the many stunning hikes, cycle trails and other abundant outdoor facilities available here, there are also beautiful cliff-side hotels and restaurants. Famous actors have found solace here, as have hippies, naturalists, authors, artists and dot-com millionaires.

SAN FRANCISCO

California, United States

San Francisco is consistently rated one of the top tourist destinations in the United States and is also one of the most recognizable. One visit and you will understand the famed lyrics, 'I left my heart in San Francisco'.

A relatively compact city, the fourth largest in California, San Francisco is only 18 sq km (7 sq miles) in area – making it the second-most densely populated American city after New York. However, its largely waterfront location, its rolling hills and its many parks ensure that it never seems more than a large town. Whether you are searching for the best in sightseeing, dining, culture, history, sports, outdoor activities or splendid scenery, San Francisco has something to offer everyone.

The best way to get a full view of the city is to take the scenic '49-mile drive', which will lead you through the parks and beaches as well as the various historical and scenic spots of interest. Also a must is a trip on one of the cable-cars. The two routes will take you from Fisherman's Wharf, through Russian and Nob Hills and down to Union Square – do not forget your camera!

DID YOU KNOW?
Named for the 'little willow' trees, or saucelito, found growing along its streams.

WHAT IS IT?
A scenic coastal town on the San Francisco Bay.
WHAT IS THERE TO SEE?
Stunning bay views and an attractive waterfront promenade.

Right: Alamo Square in San Francisco

SAUSALITO

California, United States

Sausalito is the gateway to the beautiful coastal Highway 1 that twists and winds among the rugged and spectacular Pacific Ocean cliffs. With only 7,500 residents, and best known for its waterfront views, peaceful Sausalito is said to resemble the Mediterranean. With a slower pace than its bigger neighbour, San Francisco, and friendly atmosphere, Sausalito has a scenic waterfront with galleries, boutiques, cafés and restaurants, bars and souvenir shops. Tourists flock here for the seafood and sometimes spend the night in one of the lovely hotels overlooking the bay. Home to outdoor concerts such as Jazz/Blues by the Bay and Arias in the Afternoon, there are also autumn festivities such as the Floating Homes Showcase Tour, Doggy Day and the Winterland Festival.

LAKE TAHOE

California, United States

DID YOU KNOW?
Indian Love Call, The Godfather and *The Bodyguard* were all filmed here.

One of the United State's most beautiful landmarks, Lake Tahoe's shimmering waters span 19 x 35 sq km (12 x 22 sq miles). With nearly 300 days of sunshine a year, and the majestic Sierra Nevada Mountains surrounding it, Lake Tahoe offers stunning scenery and a multitude of year-round activities. North and South Lake Tahoe are where you will find the majority of the world-class ski resorts. North Lake Tahoe is home to some of the ritzier and more upmarket neighbourhoods and resorts including Alpine Meadows and Squaw Valley USA, home to the 1960 Winter Olympics; South Lake Tahoe is the most populated area, with larger high-rise resorts, some excellent skiing areas such as Heavenly, and many casinos.

One of the most scenic areas to explore in the southwest is Emerald Bay, one of the most photographed natural locations in the United States. It has amazing views of the mountains, the lake, and Tahoe's only island, Fannette Island.

Whether you are interested in hiking or camping, skiing or snowmobiling, being pampered at a spa, eating gourmet cuisine or picnicking while watching live Shakespeare, there is something to fulfil everyone in this area of incredible beauty.

GIANT REDWOODS

California, United States

DID YOU KNOW?
The Giant Redwoods are the tallest trees in existence.

HOW DO I GET THERE?
The Avenue of the Giants parallels Highway 101 and the Eel River for 50km (31 miles), and can be accessed from a number of signposted exits. The Avenue can be reached from Eureka in just over 30 minutes.

There are three species of Giant Redwood trees in the world, two of which can be seen in California; the coastal redwood and the giant sequoia. Standing near them is a humbling and surreal experience. Tourists come every year to drive along the Avenue of the Giants, a 50-km (31-mile) stretch of the scenic old Highway 101 in Humboldt Redwood State Park. Here you will be surrounded by a dense 20,730-hectare (51,222-acre) forest of the largest remaining stand of virgin redwood groves in the world. Stretching through the mist, over 91m (300 ft) into the air, these 3,000-year-old trees, protected as part of an international biosphere reserve and noted as a UNESCO World Heritage Site, are known to weigh up to 2,000 tonnes: this is truly an experience not to be missed.

YELLOWSTONE NATIONAL PARK

Wyoming, United States

DID YOU KNOW?
Yellowstone was designated as the world's first national park by Ulysses S Grant in 1872.

WHERE IS IT?
Largely in Wyoming, but extending into Montana and Idaho.
WHAT IS IT KNOWN FOR?
Fantastically diverse geological features and stunning scenery.

Yellowstone National Park, designated as the world's first national park by Ulysses S. Grant in 1872, is also a biosphere reserve and World Heritage Site for its spectacular topography. Lying mostly in Wyoming, its 8,987 sq km (3,472 sq miles) extend into Montana and Idaho. Elevations range from a maximum height of 3,462m (11,358ft) at Eagle Peak to 1,610m (5,282ft) at Reese Creek. Most of the park is covered by forest interspersed with grassland and water. The park is also home to the planet's most diverse collection of geysers, hot springs, mudpots and fumaroles. Two-thirds of the Earth's geysers — more than 300 — are here — and combined with over 10,000 other thermal features, you have a place like no other. There is also an active volcano, roughly 2,000 earthquakes a year, one of the world's largest petrified forests, one of the world's largest calderas — measuring 72 by 48km (45 by 30 miles), and some 290 sizeable waterfalls, the highest of which is the 94-m (308-ft) Lower Falls of the Yellowstone River. The most popular attraction of the Park, located in the Upper Geyser Basin, is Old Faithful. Named for its punctuality, Old Faithful, although not the largest or most spectacular of the geysers, erupts more frequently than any of the others, on average every 80 minutes, spraying water up to 57m (184ft) into the air.

YOSEMITE NATIONAL PARK

California, United States

Yosemite National Park, famously known as the focus of the American photographer Ansel Adams, is a spectacular combination of awe-inspiring mountain-and-valley scenery in the Sierra Nevada Mountains, named a national park in 1890. The park encompasses a grand collection of waterfalls, meadows and forest land including massive groves of giant sequoias, the world's largest living trees. If there is one remarkable landmark that stands out here, it is probably Half Dome. Rising 1,219m (4,000ft) from the valley floor, it is the most photographed mountain in the park, with its shaved surface offering a stunning contrast to the surrounding jagged peaks. Those who dare can choose to either hike it or climb it, but be prepared for sore muscles the next day. Another of the park's natural highlights is Yosemite Falls with its roaring runoff from a height of 740m (2,425ft). One of the world's tallest, Yosemite Falls is actually made up of three separate falls: Upper Yosemite Falls measuring 436m (1,430ft), the middle cascades at 206m (675ft), and Lower Yosemite Falls at 98m (320ft). It is a very short walk to Lower Yosemite Falls, but it is a strenuous, all-day trip to reach the towering Upper Yosemite Falls. Glacier Point's views of Yosemite Valley, with its high cliffs and waterfalls, are what dreams are made of. The Mariposa Grove, containing hundreds of ancient giant sequoias, is something not to be missed and Tuolumne Meadows, a large subalpine meadow surrounded by mountain peaks, will leave you breathless.

DID YOU KNOW?
It was once known as 'the Fuji of America' for its symmetrical beauty.

MOUNT ST HELENS

Washington, United States

WHAT IS IT?
A remarkable volcano that erupted and caused the largest avalanche ever recorded.
WHAT IS THERE TO SEE?
The crater, lava dome and blast zone of the volcano.

Right: The stunning Yosemite Falls

On 18 May, 1980 at 8:32 am, the north face of Mount St Helens collapsed in the largest debris avalanche ever recorded, caused by an underlying earthquake that measured 5.1 on the Richter scale. The volcano's height was reduced from 9,677 ft (2,950 m) to 8,364 ft (2,550m). Today, visitors come to Mt St Helens to marvel at the destruction and devastation caused by this natural disaster as well as to gaze in awe at nature's remarkable ability to recover. Over a quarter of a century later, the signs of healing are evident. The pre-eruption landscape, once dominated by dense coniferous forests and clear streams and lakes has begun to re-establish itself. The lower forests once dominated by Douglas fir and western hemlock have started to regrow, and tourism has returned to this area of scenic beauty.

ASIA

GUILIN

China

WHAT IS THERE TO SEE?
Natural karst formations, temples, palaces and spectacular rural Chinese scenery.

Guilin's scenic splendour is difficult to comprehend. Large emerald-green limestone karsts seemingly float on the Li River, whose natural beauty and historic treasures combine to create a magical landscape. Situated majestically southeast of Guilin city and on the west bank of the Li River, Elephant Trunk Hill is regarded as the main symbol of Guilin's landscape. Originally named 'Li Hill', 'Yi Hill' or 'Chenshui Hill', it has a history of 360 million years. The large karst formation resembles a mammoth elephant leisurely sipping water from the river with its long trunk.

Towering 55m (180ft) above the water, 108m (354ft) long and 100m (328ft) wide, the elephant has a cave between its trunk and legs in the shape of a full moon, which penetrates through the hill. Locals refer to this as 'Moon-over-Water Cave'. When the waves lap and the moonlight gleams, the scene is particularly enchanting. On the walls in and around the cave, there are more than 70 inscriptions from the Tang and Song dynasties (618–907 and 960–1279AD respectively) praising the beauty of hills and waters nearby. Halfway up the hill lies another cave, which goes through the hill and serves as the eyes of the elephant, through which visitors can admire the beauty of Guilin city.

DID YOU KNOW?
Lijang has been called 'Venice of the Orient'.

LIJIANG

China

WHAT IS IT?
A beautiful ancient town with meandering slate lanes threaded by rivers.
WHERE IS IT?
Northwest of Yunnan province.

The Old Town of Lijiang, built on a plateau 2,400m (7,874ft) above sea level, is surrounded by mountains to the north and west, and vast fertile fields to the southeast. The only old city built without a wall, Lijiang became a multicultural place, with architecture incorporating styles from Han, Bai and Tibet into a unique Naxi form. Now a World Heritage Site, it has narrow, meandering lanes, timber and tile homes with engraved figures on their windows and doors and vibrant gardens decorating their fronts. Water is the soul and blood of Old Lijiang, and Black Dragon Pool (Heilongtan) is the main artery. The water is fed into streams so every family and every street has access. The aqueducts feed the abundant willow trees that shade the nearly 350 pretty bridges, some of which were built during the Ming Dynasty.

HUANG LONG
China

WHAT IS IT?
A stunning valley that resembles a yellow dragon surging down from the snowcapped peaks of Mount Minshan.
WHERE IS IT?
About 250 km (155 miles) away from Chengdu, the capital of Sichuan.

Bordered by the Tibetan Plateau, the Three Gorges, the Yangtze River and lofty mountains, Sichuan is known as the 'Land of Abundance', boasting three places on the World Cultural and Natural Heritage List: Jiuzhaigou Scenic and Historic Interest Area, Huanglong Valley and Mount Emei Scenic area including Leshan Giant Buddha Scenic Area.

A UNESCO World Heritage Site, the Huang Long Valley is one of the most stunning areas of the province, covering an area of roughly 700 sq km (270 sq miles) and consisting of Huanglong and Muni Gorge. Huanglong has unique scenery, rich natural resources and a primeval forest. The majestic and unrivalled emerald lakes, layered waterfalls, colourful forests, snow-capped peaks and Tibetan folk villages blend harmoniously into the mountains sparkling like jewels, giving it the nickname of 'mountain fairyland'.

SHANGHAI

China

Shanghai, on the estuary of the Yangtze River, is the largest industrial city in China. Originally a seaside fishing village, it is now a multicultural metropolis combining the best of modern and traditional China. An important seaport and China's largest commercial, industrial and financial centre, Shanghai is also great for tourists. Sightseeing, business and shopping are centred around People's Square and along the Huangpu River. Shanghai is a shopper's paradise. Nanjing Road and Huaihai Road are perfect for those seeking the lastest fashions, while Xujiahui Shopping Centre, Yuyuan Shopping City, and the Jiali Sleepless City are popular destinations for those looking for a memento of their visit. Huaihai Road is also known for its cafés, antique shops and the marvellous old French Concession.

CITY STATUS
Shanghai is the largest industrial city in China, the hipper cousin of Hong Kong and the more alluring sister of Beijing.

WHAT SHALL I DO THERE? Eat dim sum, shop for souvenirs in the Dongtai Road antiques market, join the crowds on the Bund, then recover with a classic martini at the roof terrace of M on the Bund, located in one of the 1920s-era buildings that still line the riverfront.

IMPERIAL PALACES, BEIJING

China

Beijing, China's capital city, is rich in history having been inhabited for more than 3,000 years and serving as the capital for the last 800 years through the Yuan, Ming and Qing Dynasties. It is a stunning combination of ancient splendours and modern delights. Thirty-four emperors lived and ruled here and their Imperial Palaces stand as a reminder of the strength of this vibrant country's past. The Forbidden City (Gu Gong) is the most grand and best-preserved imperial palace complex in the world. Lying at the centre of Beijing, it served as the imperial palace during both the Ming and Qing dynasties. Now called the Palace Museum, it covers the northern half of Tiananmen Square. It is an incredible sight that has to be seen to be believed.

YOU SHOULD KNOW:
Locals do not tend to speak English and getting around can be tricky without the help of an English-speaking Chinese guide.

REMARKABLE ACOUSTICS
Enclosing the Imperial Vault of Heaven, Echo Wall has a perimeter of 193m (633ft). If you whisper facing the vault while standing on one side of the wall, you will be heard on the opposite side.

THE GREAT WALL

China

The Great Wall of China, a UNESCO World Heritage Site and one of the great man-made wonders of the world, lies like a gigantic dragon, stretching up and down across deserts, grasslands, mountains and plateaux covering an area of approximately 6,700km (4,163 miles) from east to west. At more than 2,000 years old, some sections of the Great Wall are understandably in ruins or have disappeared, but it remains one of the most incredible feats of man and its architectural grandeur and historical significance are breathtaking.

The construction of the Great Wall was started by the Qin dynasty between the seventh and eighth centuries BC and took more than 1,800 years to complete. It is believed that it was originally intended as military fortification against intrusion from the north, but over time grew to become not only a symbol of defence, but also of the great power of the emperor. When taking the strenuous hike through the various sections, it is difficult to comprehend how many men it must have taken to build this massive structure, nearly 8m (26ft) across and how the enormous quantities of stones must have been transported here. Looking out over the spectacular emerald hills and valleys, you can sense the history and understand what effort and sacrifice must have taken place to enable the construction of such a massive undertaking. It is truly one of the most memorable experiences that you will ever have.

DID YOU KNOW?
The wall covers more than 6,700km (4,163 miles) from east to west China.

TRAVELLERS' TIP:
Head 60km (37 miles) north of Beijing to the Huanghua (Yellow Flower Fortress) section of the wall where there are fewer tourists.

PINGYAO

China

WHAT IS IT? A fantastic example of Ming Dynasty walls surrounding a quaint and historic city, as well as the famed compounds of the Wang and Qiao families.

Ancient Pingyao, a UNESCO World Heritage Site, is a small city about 90km (56 miles) away from Taiyuan, the capital city of Shanxi Province, and is known for its well-preserved city wall as well as the nearby Wang and Qiao family compounds. At the southern edge of the Taiyuan Basin and next to the Loess Plateau in the south, its location on the banks of the Yellow River enabled it to serve as an important communications and commercial hub.

The ancient walls surrounding Pingyao are one of the best examples of Ming Dynasty building, being an unbroken rectangle that features a rammed-earth and brick structure 6.2km (3.85 miles) around. The wall is said to resemble a tortoise, the sacred symbol of longevity in Chinese. The south and north gates count as the head and tails with the pairs of east and west gates as the four feet. Two wells, resembling the eyes of the tortoise, stand just outside the south gate, and the criss-crossing streets inside the city are taken to be the markings on the shell.

There are some 4,000 old buildings and family compounds in the city and in the surrounding region. Two particularly grand family compounds outside the city are the Wang and the Qiao mansions. Consisting of 54 courtyards and 1,052 rooms, the Wang compound is the epitome of Oriental domestic architecture.

DID YOU KNOW?
The Mogao Caves are also known as the 'Caves of 1,000 Buddhas'.

MOGAO CAVES

China

WHAT ARE THEY?
492 caves famous for their statues and wall paintings.
YOU SHOULD KNOW:
Photography is forbidden anywhere in the complex.

Listed as a UNESCO World Heritage Site in 1987, the Mogao Caves in Gansu Province contain more than 1,000 years of Buddhist art. According to legend, in 366AD a monk called Lo-tsun had a vision of 1,000 Buddhas, and began to carve out the first cave. The site is strategically placed on the Silk Road – one of the most important east–west trade routes – and he sought funding from passing merchants. As Buddhism spread, the caves became a pilgrimage site. The caves were carved out of the soft sandstone, and 492 of them survive: the largest is 40m (130ft) high and the smallest under 1m (39in). Known as the 'Caves of 1,000 Buddhas', they contain 2,415 painted clay statues of the Buddha, holy men, bodhisattvas and the Buddhist faithful, ranging in size from 10cm (4in) to 33m (108ft).

LUSHAN NATIONAL PARK

China

WHAT IS IT KNOWN FOR?
Its stunning scenery and sites, and for being the birthpace of Pure Land Buddhism.

Lushan National Park is a UNESCO World Heritage Site and Geopark in the north of Jiangxi Province, centred around Mount Lushan. Covering 302 sq km (117 sq miles) and set within a larger protected area, this 2.5-million-year-old landscape contains 100 scenic peaks, the highest of which, Dahanyang Peak, soars to 1,474m (4,836ft). Mount Lushan's spectacular landscape of mist-shrouded peaks and roaring waterfalls is also home to many Pure Land Buddist, Taoist and Confucian sites. At the base of Mount Lushan the Five Elderly Men Peaks (Wulaofeng) can be seen reflected in the clear waters of Poyang Lake, a well-known summer resort for locals and tourists alike. Other scenic lakes in the area that have inspired Chinese poets for centuries include Small Heavenly Lake (Xiaotianchi) and Big Heavenly Lake (Daitianchi), which is said to have been hand-dug from the rocks by an immortal.

WOLONG NATURE RESERVE

China

The Wolong Nature Reserve is best known for its tremendous efforts in the protection and reintroduction of the endangered giant panda. Located in Wenchuan County, Sichuan Province, 136km (85 miles) from Chengdu, the reserve covers nearly 200,000 hectares (494,000 acres) at the eastern foot of the Qionglai Mountains. The Sichuan Giant Panda Sanctuary, of which it forms a part, gained UNESCO World Heritage Site status in 2006. The reserve lies on the transition zone between Qinghai, the Tibetan Plateau and the Sichuan Basin, hosting over 4,000 species of plants, 50 mammal varieties, 300 bird species and 29 rare and endangered species including the giant panda and the lesser panda, which is also called the red panda or small panda, and snow leopards.

CONSERVATION
The snow-capped peaks of the reserve have been home to the Panda Breeding Centre since it was established by the Chinese government in the early 1980s.

HOW DO I GET THERE? It is a four-hour drive from Chengdu at the eastern foot of the Qionglai Mountains.
WHEN SHOULD I GO? April and May are the best months to visit.

HONG KONG

China

Hong Kong is a dynamic city, a kaleidoscope of cultures, a sophisticated fusion of East and West. Standing at the railing of the Star Ferry as it glides across the harbour past junks, with a vast skyline of towering buildings in the distance, it is hard not to marvel at this city of striking contrasts, with its eclectic mixture of the exotic and technically advanced, the modern and the ancient, the past and the present. Modern skyscrapers and five-star hotels are covered with bamboo scaffolding, Cantonese and Mandarin food stalls are surrounded by gourmet French bistros, Rolls Royces pass old men pushing wheelbarrows, hawkers selling chicken feet and dried squid talk on mobile phones and the largest shopping centres in the world jostle for your attention with lively street markets selling traditional wares.

WHAT IS THERE TO DO?

Wander the streets and secret alleys and take the tram (and your camera) to Victoria Peak for a panoramic view of this incredible skyline and one of the world's best harbours.

EAST MEETS WEST

Much of Hong Kong's Western fabric comes from its legacy as a former British colony. British influence remains evident, from the school system to the free-market economy, from rugby teams to double-decker buses and from English pubs to afternoon tea.

KAILASA AND LAKE MANSAROVAR

Tibet

DID YOU KNOW?

According to Buddhists, this is the birthplace of the world.

According to Hindu belief, Shiva, the god of destruction and regeneration, resides at the summit of the legendary mountain Kailasa, regarded by many religions as the centre and spiritual birthplace of the entire world. Tibetan Buddhists refer to the mountain as Khang Ripoche, 'the Precious One of Glacial Snow'. The three hills in the distance are believed to be the residence of the Bodhisattvas: Manjushri, Vajrapani and Avalokiteshvara, who help humans achieve enlightenment. The ultimate destination of souls, the sacred peak of Kailasa is an ancient pilgrimage site, difficult to get to and even more difficult to walk around. Pilgrims must take the 52-km (32-mile) route around the mountain – clockwise for Buddhists, anticlockwise for Bons. The journey takes from one day to three weeks, depending upon the devotee's stamina. It is believed that a pilgrim who completes 108 circuits of the mountain is assured enlightenment.

LHASA

Tibet

Lhasa, the traditional capital of Tibet and now capital of the Tibet Autonomous Region of the People's Republic of China, as well as the traditional seat of the Dalai Lama, literally means 'place of the gods'. The city rose to prominence more than 1,300 years ago when the original Jokhang Temple and the first Potala Palace were built in the seventh century. Three large Gelugpa monasteries – Ganden, Sera and Drepung – were built by Je Tsongkhapa and his disciples in the 15th century.

Lhasa is a mystical, mysterious and remote city with an impressive heritage and spiritual history that defines Tibetan culture. Surrounded by the majestic Himalayas, Lhasa is punctuated by the snaking Kyi Chu River, a tributary of the Brahmaputra, which runs through the city.

GREAT HEIGHTS

Lhasa is one of the highest cities in the world at an elevation of 3,650m (12,000ft).

WHERE IS IT? In the south of the Tibet Autonomous Region of the People's Republic of China, high in the Himalayas.
WHAT IS THERE TO SEE? Stunning landscapes and architecture including the breathtaking Potala Palace.

SHIRETOKO NATIONAL PARK

Japan

WHAT IS THERE TO SEE?
The spectacular landscape
and varied wildlife.
WHAT IS THERE TO DO?
Climb up the river to see the
natural hot pools.
HOW DO I GET THERE?
By air from Tokyo to Kushiro,
by train from Kushiro to
Shari, then by bus.
WHEN SHOULD I GO?
Between June and
September for the
best weather.
YOU SHOULD KNOW:
If hiking, avoid the
brown bears.

Shiretoko National Park lies on the peninsula of the same name on the island of Hokkaido. The landscape here is wild and dramatic, and the active volcanoes that march up the centre of the island have thrown out vast black rocks that litter the coastline.

The main port in the area is Uturo, which is 10km (6 miles) from the wonderful Shiretoko Go-ko. Here you will find five perfectly beautiful lakes all joined by paths and wooden walkways. The complete circuit takes over an hour to walk, although it is no more that 2.5km (1.5 miles). The landscape is glorious and you can spend longer than you would imagine admiring the reflections of the mountains in the water.

A little further along the peninsula and you come to Kamuiwakka-no-taki, a strong reminder that this is volcano country. Iozan volcano produces hot water for this river and its waterfalls and there are natural hot pools at three different levels. To reach the pools, which become warmer the closer they are to the top, you have first to climb up the river, which is quite tricky, but the water is warm. Iozan volcano can be climbed, but the most popular hike is up Rausu-dake, the highest peak on the peninsula. Even if you stick to the lower trails, the scenery is splendid and you will probably spot deer, foxes and other wildlife. During summer you can take a boat from Uturo to the lighthouse that stands on the end of the peninsula.

REBUN AND RISHIRI

Japan

These two beautiful and isolated islands lie off the northwest coast of Hokkaido, about as far north as it is possible to go in Japan. They form the main area of a national park, together with Sarobetsu and other areas on Hokkaido itself.

Rebun is a narrow, low-lying island that is rightly famous for its wildflowers. More than 300 different species of alpine plants grow here, and the island is perfect for hiking. The most popular route is the Hachi-jikan, which runs down the whole of the west coast from Sukoton Misaki (cape) in the north, through woods and across green slopes covered with flowers, to Motochi in the south. There are several other, less lengthy and arduous hikes to be enjoyed, including the Momoiwa route, a cliff-top trail that takes you to the lighthouse (Motochi Todai) at the southern tip of the island.

Rishiri Island is formed by the almost circular dome of Rishirifuji, a 1,721-m (4,170-ft) dormant volcano. The climb can take up to 12 hours, starting out from the Rishiri Hokuroku campsite – there are several other routes, but this one is the nearest to the port of Oshidomari. There is a small shrine at the summit, and the views are spectacular. If you cannot face such a long hike, there is a lovely three-hour trail from the lake at Himenuma to the campsite, crossing the lower slopes of two smaller peaks.

DID YOU KNOW?
Japanese boil eggs in the bubbling hot pools until they are black and eat them with evident relish.

DON'T MISS:
Taking a restorative bath in one of the hot springs.
YOU SHOULD KNOW:
Entrance fees are payable.
WHAT IS THERE TO SEE?
The Hakone Motomiya shrine, the Tokkaido Barrier and highway, and the Hakone Tozan Railway.

HAKONE

Japan

Hakone is a lovely, mountainous national park that lies south of Mount Fuji. It is dotted with lakes and hot springs, shrines and art museums, and its easy access from Tokyo makes it a perfect place to visit if you want some time out relaxing away from city life. It is possible to visit in a day, but it is much more fun to spend at least one night in a traditional, wooden Japanese *ryokan* (inn) or a smart hotel, and enjoy unwinding in one of the many hot-spring baths.

Railways, funiculars, cable-cars and buses enable you to get about the area. There are even brightly coloured 'pirate ships' on which you can travel the length of Lake Ashi, to the west of the park.

MOUNT FUJI

Japan

Japan's most recognizable landmark must surely be Mount Fuji. Situated about 100km (60 miles) west of Tokyo, this almost perfectly symmetrical volcano is venerated by the Japanese, who know it as Fuji-san, their most sacred mountain. The last eruption was in 1707, but the volcano is dormant rather than extinct. In summer people like to be at the summit to see the dawn, and at night the light from their torches can look like a thin trail of lava on the mountainside.

The small town of Fuji-Yoshido is the traditional departure point for making the ascent of Mount Fuji. Walking from here can take 11 or 12 hours before reaching the summit, and the ascent is divided into recognized sections or 'stations'.

The main climbing season is during July and August. At this time all the 17 resting huts are operational, although if you want to stay the night you will have to make an advance booking. At other times of year it is still possible to make the ascent, but there are no guarantees that any of the huts will be open, let alone the post office at the summit from which it is traditional to send a card or two. The crater itself takes about an hour to walk around, and it is often extremely cold up there – Mount Fuji is 3,776m (12,340ft) high.

DID YOU KNOW?
Over 100,000 people trek to the summit of Mount Fuji every year.

WHAT IS THERE TO SEE?
The Sengen shrine of Fuji Sengen-jinja, Fuji Five Lakes and Mount Tenjo.
DON'T MISS:
Climbing to the summit of Mount Fuji and watching the sunrise.

NIKKO

Japan

The pilgrimage town of Nikko is the site of an outstanding Shinto and Buddhist shrine complex, surrounded by wonderful mountainous landscapes, and less than two hours' journey from Tokyo.

In 1616 the powerful shogun, Tokugawa Ieyasu, left a will requesting that a shrine be built here in his honour. The site already had religious significance – the Buddhist temple of Rinnoji had been standing there since the middle of the eighth century. Ieyasu's shrine was completed within a year, but his grandson, Tokugawa Iemitsu, decided to erect a far more grandiose affair for him, the Toshogu Shrine. Iemitsu's own mausoleum is only slightly less elaborate.

WHAT IS THERE TO SEE?
The Toshogu Shrine, Rinnoji Temple, Yomeimon, Taiyuinbyo, Futarasan Shrine, Lake Chuzenji and the Kegon Falls.

FESTIVITIES
Every year, in May, a grand festival is held here to recreate Ieyasu's burial rites, featuring 1,000 or more costumed monks and warriors. The spectators are left in no doubt as to the absolute power wielded by this dynasty.

OGASAWARA ISLANDS

Japan

The Ogasawara Islands are a remote group of 30 islands in the Pacific Ocean. They were formed by an ancient submarine volcano, and are home to more than 140 species of indigenous plants as well as insects such as the Ogasawara damselfly. Of the 97 species of tree on the islands, 73 are endemic. In 1827 a British warship found and declared possession of the islands and they were not returned to Japan until 1876. During World War II the inhabitants all moved to the Japanese mainland, and by the end of the war the islands were ruled by the United States. Finally handed back in 1968 they are now part of the Tokyo prefecture, despite being about 1,000km (600 miles) away.

Only Chichijima ('father island') and Hahajima ('mother island') are inhabited, and their total population is about 2,300. Their main products are timber and fruit. Ogasawara is unspoiled and unpolluted, and the crystal-clear waters are full of coral reefs and tropical fish. This is a great place for watching whales and dolphins and there are several trips on offer. It is sometimes possible to swim with bottlenose and spinner dolphins. The small, flat island visible from Hahajima has a sweeping, white beach that is ideal for swimming, where highly endangered green turtles come to lay their eggs.

DID YOU KNOW?

The Ogasawara Islands have earned the label 'Tokyo's largest natural greenhouse'.

DON'T MISS:

Take a day trip out to the open sea for an amazing day whale and dolphin watching.

HOW DO I GET THERE?

Travel by ship from Tokyo to Chichi-jima. The ship leaves once a week and the journey takes 25 hours.

KANAZAWA

Japan

DON'T MISS:
The nearby temple at Eihei-ji, the market at Wajima
and the splendid rugged coastline of Noto-kongo.

The charming and ancient castle town of Kanazawa lies mid-way along Honshu's western coast. The name means 'marsh of gold' and comes from a story of a peasant who made his living digging potatoes, washed gold dust from the potatoes and stored it in his well. The Japanese Alps surround the city and two rivers run through it; the Saigawa, said to be a lively masculine river and the Asano, a sweet feminine river.

Kanazawa Castle seems like an enormous bird set for flight, with its white-lead roof tiles and massive American-cypress beams. It is encircled by a maze of intricately winding paths designed to protect the castle from enemies. There are still some samurai houses surrounded by mud walls, and in the Teramachi area there are 70 temples in less than 1 sq km (0.5 sq miles).

Kanazawa's crowning glory is its Gardens of Kenrokuen covering 10 hectares (25 acres) and arguably the most beautiful in Japan. They were originally designed and laid out in the 17th century. In spring, listen to the grasshoppers as you wander amongst the apricot and cherry blossoms, past cascades and over little bridges with stone lanterns. In the winter the gardens glisten with a thick carpet of snow, and ropes called *yukitsuri* support the branches of the delicate pine trees.

DID YOU KNOW?
The Isejingu shrine
is rebuilt every 20 years.

WHAT IS THERE TO SEE?
Other sights within the
national park include the
waterfalls of the Takigawa
valley, Toba – the home of
cultured pearls – and the
beautiful coastline of the
Shima Hanto Peninsula.

SHIMA HANTO

Japan

Southeast of Osaka is the Shima Hanto National Park, an area of great natural beauty and home to Japan's most sacred Shinto shrine, Isejingu (Ise Shrine), which was established during the fourth century and dedicated to Amaterasu Omikami, the sun goddess from whom, it was claimed, all of Japan's emperors were descended.

Legend has it that the shrine houses a mirror that Amaterasu gave to her grandson when he was sent to Earth to rule Japan. His great-grandson, Jimmu, became the first Emperor of Japan and the mirror has been protected here ever since, wrapped in layers of fabric. Only the Imperial family and certain priests can enter the inner sanctum, but no-one has looked into the mirror itself for more than 1,000 years.

MATSUMOTO

Japan

Matsumoto is a delightful city in the area of central Honshu known as Chubu. It is the gateway to the Japanese Alps, with all their trekking and mountaineering opportunities, but is famous in its own right for its remarkable castle.

The city is divided by the Metoba River, on the south bank of which is an area of traditional old buildings known as Nakamachi. Many of these attractive, white-walled houses have been turned into inns and shops and there is a wonderfully restored sake brewery that you can visit. To the west is the Japan Ukiyoe Museum which houses a superb collection of 100,000 woodblock prints, including works by Hiroshige Utagawa and Hokusai Katsushika.

The castle, standing in lovely grounds, is approached across a moat. Originally built in 1504, it was rebuilt almost a century later by Lord Ishikawa. He commissioned the five-tiered *donjon*, or castle keep, which is now the oldest in the country. Most Japanese castles traditionally had a hidden extra floor, and Matsumoto Castle is no exception. The view from the sixth storey over the town and mountains is superb. The castle's black, forbidding façade makes a strong impression on visitors.

DID YOU KNOW?
Most Japanese castles traditionally had a hidden extra floor.

WHAT IS IT KNOWN FOR?
Matsumoto castle, the oldest of its kind in Japan.
WHAT ELSE IS THERE TO SEE?
Mount Hotaka and Kamikochi mountain resort for access to the climbing areas and Norikura Kogen (heights).

KYOTO

Japan

TRY TO CATCH: Cherry blossom (*sakura*) season. Trees usually bloom in the last week of March and first two weeks of April in Kyoto. Sometimes almost all the trees will come into full bloom (*mankai*) at the same time and stay in full bloom for a week or even longer.

For most people who have not visited Japan, Kyoto represents the epitome of traditional Japanese culture. Images of ancient temples and imperial palaces, wooden houses, geishas elegantly performing the tea ceremony and cherry blossom drifting in the wind come to mind. In fact, although Kyoto contains all these things and more, it is also a sprawling modern city with a population of 1.5 million.

The city's golden age was during the 16th and 17th centuries when it became the centre of Japanese artistic achievement. In all, Kyoto is home to about 1,700 Buddhist temples, 300 Shinto shrines and 200 important gardens as well as imperial villas. The Higashiyama district in Kyoto is the place to aim for if you have limited time — it has an amazing concentration of sights within a reasonably compact area. The Kiyomitzudera is a temple built on a steep hill with a wooden platform overhanging the valley, giving spectacular views over the gorge. Walk through the old, cobbled lanes of Sannenzaka and Ninenzaka, with their traditional two-storey wooden townhouses known as *machiya*, and round to the temple of Kodaiji. Continue past more temples, pavilions, gardens and teahouses until you reach Ginkakuji, the Silver Pavilion. This simple, elegant two-storey pavilion is set in a spectacular garden of soft greens and a 'sea of silver sand', designed to reflect the moonlight.

DID YOU KNOW?
The Asuka-dera was the first temple built in Japan and contains the oldest Buddha image in Japan.

WHAT IS IT KNOWN FOR?
Being an ancient imperial capital and the birthplace of Japanese culture.
WHAT IS THERE TO SEE?
The region's many burial mounds and mysterious stone objects.

Right: Sakura (cherry blossom season) in Kyoto

ASUKA

Japan

Asuka is a small village in the heart of the Yamato area, the plains east of Osaka, where Japanese imperial culture first flourished. It was one of the ancient imperial capitals, and archaeological finds such as burial mounds and sophisticated artefacts dating back to 350AD have been found. Asuka was first mentioned as being the seat of Emperor Kenzo in 485AD, and during the following 250 years, 43 imperial palaces were built in this area, although, being wooden structures, virtually nothing of them remains. Most visitors go to see Asuka-dera Temple, the first true temple in Japan. Today only the main hall and a few smaller buildings are left. Around midnight on New Year's Day, the temple's bell is struck 108 times while ginger tea and *ema* (wooden tablets on which to write your wishes) are distributed to worshippers.

HIMEJI

Japan

Himeji lies northwest of Osaka, and contains the most impressive fortress in Japan. There has been a fortress here since the early 14th century, but the existing complex was built by Ikeda Terumasa in the early 17th century. It is designed to look like the shape of a bird in flight, and is often known as Shirasagijo, the white egret castle.

This fantastic place, a UNESCO World Heritage Site, is surrounded by moats and thick, defensive walls enclosing four *donjons* (castle keeps), the central one of which (Daitenshu) is five stories high. Daitenshu itself is spectacular, its five stories framed by vast wooden pillars. The view from the top is superb – all the way to the Inland Sea on a good day.

WHAT IS THERE TO SEE?
Hyogo Prefectural Museum of History, Otokoyama Senhime Shrine (Princess Sen's Shrine), the city museums of literature and art, Engyoji temple complex and the Inland Sea.

DID YOU KNOW?
Himeji featured in the James Bond film *You Only Live Twice*.

SHIMANAMI KAIDO

Japan

WHAT IS IT?
A series of bridges that connects the Inland Sea islands.
WHAT IS THERE TO DO?
Cycle along the highway and take in the breathtaking views of the islands.

The Shimani Kaido (the 'highway above the sea') is a road connecting the prefectures of Hiroshima and Ehime, from Onomichi City to Imabari City, at either end of the Inland Sea. This has been achieved by the use of a series of seven bridges linking each of the six smaller islands that lie between Honshu and Shikoku. The route was opened in 1999, and the total length of the road is about 60km (40 miles).

Each of the bridges along the route is unique. The Tatara Grand bridge is the longest cable-stayed bridge in the world, and Kurushima Bridge was the first of the three linked suspension bridges spanning the 4-km (2.5-mile) wide Kurushima Strait. Spend a few days cycling along the road and stop off at a few of the 600 Inland Sea islands to enjoy the good beaches and lovely scenery.

IZUMO TAISHA

Japan

The shrine of Izumo Taisha lies in the town of Taishamachi, at the foot of the sacred hills of Yakumo and Kamiyama. It is the oldest and most sacred Shinto shrine in Japan and is of major cultural significance. According to legend, the shrine was built by Amaterasu, the sun goddess. It is dedicated to Okuninushi-no-Mikoto, the deity of medicine, agriculture and good relationships. Once through the bronze gateway, the first building you reach is the Oracle Hall, a simple, elegant building with an enormous *shimenawa*. This ceremonial rope, made from plaited straw, is 13m (42ft) long and weighs some 1.5 tonnes. The inner shrine, designated a national treasure, is built in the unique Taisha architectural style, with an elevated floor and rafters that project from the roof.

MARRIAGE GUIDANCE
Couples come here to ask for happiness in their marriage, summoning the deity by clapping their hands four times.

WHAT IS THERE TO SEE? The Homostuden (Treasure Hall) the Shokokan exhibition hall and the Kagura Den sacred music hall.
YOU SHOULD KNOW: Entrance fees are payable.
HOW TO GET THERE: By train from Matsue.

ASO NATIONAL PARK

Japan

Almost in the centre of the island of Kyushu stands Mount Aso, not only the world's largest caldera, but possibly the most beautiful as well. The mountain is a typical active, composite volcano, the circumference of its outer caldera being 128km (79 miles). It encloses seven towns and villages and five mountains, and some 75,000 people live here, their lives completely dominated by volcanic activity.

Apart from the peaks, the scenery within the caldera is of fertile fields and gently rolling, green meadows, grazed by cows and horses. The landscape of the foothills of Eboshi is particularly lovely, with shallow crater lakes peppering the plain. High in the crater wall to the north a huge outcrop, completely covered with greenery and known locally as the 'Green Niagara', can be seen.

Most visitors to the area come to see the active volcano within the caldera, Mount Nakadake, which last erupted during the 1990s. It frequently emits such strong sulphuric and other noxious gases that it has to be closed to visitors for a day or two, and those with respiratory problems are advised not to approach the rim of the crater. The top can be reached by cable-car, by road or on foot, and looking down through the belching, turbulent, sulphur-ridden smoke to the green-blue lake beneath is an awe-inspiring experience.

DID YOU KNOW?

Yaku Island is home to some of the world's oldest trees.

WHAT IS THERE TO SEE?

Yakushima Environmental and Cultural Centre, the Sea Turtle Museum, Yakushima Fruit Garden, Shakunage Rhododendron Park and the world's oldest trees.

Right: One of Aso National Park's incredible crater lakes

YAKU ISLAND

Japan

Yaku Island is situated about 70km (45 miles) south of Kyushu's southern tip. It is a relatively small and mountainous island that boasts more than 30 peaks of over 1,000m (3,280ft). The vegetation here ranges from subtropical at sea level to subarctic on the mountain-tops, and the extraordinarily heavy rainfall ranges from 4–10m (13–32ft) per year. The combination of heavy rainfall and remote location has allowed lush, primeval forest to flourish without interference. From 800–1,600 m (2,625–5,250 ft) is a band of coniferous forest containing some of the world's oldest trees, the Yaku cedars. The most ancient of these are about 3,500 years old, and the biggest of them, known as *Jomon Sugi*, has a circumference of 16.4m (54ft), which would make it about 7,000 years old.

HATERUMA ISLAND

Japan

Hateruma (Haterumajima) is Japan's southernmost inhabited island and part of the Yaeyama island group. Its name comes from the Okinawan for coral. Out on a limb in the Pacific Ocean, Hateruma is not far from Taiwan and the Tropic of Cancer. Of the 88 constellations, 84 can be seen from here and it is a well-known observation point for the Southern Cross. Life here is simple and rustic — empty roads lead to the endless reaches of the sea and sky. There are no tour groups or large hotels, just one village in the centre of the island. The beach at Nishi, edged with pandanus trees, is thought by many to be the most beautiful beach in Japan. Diving and snorkelling here are a joy. Beneath the clear blue water is a world of coral reefs, rock arches and wonderful tropical fish.

WHAT IS THERE TO DO?
With diving, snorkelling and cycling on offer, you will be spoiled for choice.
YOU SHOULD KNOW:
There are no large hotels or tour groups on the island.

MONUMENTAL
In 1972, when Okinawa reverted to Japan, a monument was built at Takanazaki, home to Japan's southernmost police station and lighthouse. It was made of stones gathered from all across Japan.

BAND-E AMIR

Afghanistan

DID YOU KNOW?
Band-e Amir was
declared a national park,
the first in Afghanistan,
in 1973.

Visitors to Afghanistan have always marvelled at the country's raw, natural beauty. The highlights of this landscape, in the middle of the Hazarajat in the central Hindu Kush Mountains, are the legendary lakes of Band-e Amir. Here you will find six stunningly blue lakes, nestled among 3,000-m (9,850-ft) magenta-and-grey rock walls, making a stunningly beautiful and unforgettable contrast. The deep blue of the lakes is due to the combination of water purity and the high lime content.

YOU SHOULD KNOW:
Check with the Foreign
Office (www.gov.uk/
foreign-travel-advice)
or your local embassy
to ensure safe travel is
sanctioned in this often
war-torn area.

Just 75km (46 miles) from Bamiyan, the lakes of the Band-e Amir Valley are considered one of the country's natural wonders. The lakes are created by the flow of water of a succession of natural travertine terraces created through the deposition of calcium carbonate, running from the highest lake down to the ones below. The strikingly clear cobalt waters come as a shock to the senses amid this barren and rocky desert landscape. Although there is no lush foliage here, there is a variety of animal species. Wolves, foxes, hares, wild sheep and Markhor goats as well as large yellow fish, known locally as *chush,* are found in and around the lakes. Mules and donkeys, commonly used by locals for transport, can also been seen in the area.

VARANASI

India

The colourful holy city of Varanasi (Benares), a famous Hindu pilgrimage site perched on the banks of the River Ganges (Ganga), has been an important cultural, historic and religious centre of India for more than 5,000 years. Presided over by Shiva, Varanasi is to Hindus what Mecca is to Muslims or the Holy Sepulchre in Jerusalem is to Christians.

Here pilgrims come to sit on the many *ghats* (riverbank steps leading to the sacred Ganges), have a ritual bath and perform *puja* to the rising sun, in accordance with centuries of tradition. It is believed that bathing in the sacred waters results in the remission of sins and that dying here circumvents rebirth.

WHAT IS IT?
One of the ancient seats of religious learning in India, a sacred pilgrimage site for Hindus.
WHERE IS IT?
The left bank of the River Ganges in Uttar Pradesh.

LITERARY QUIP
Mark Twain said of the 5,000-year-old Varanasi, 'Benares is older than history, older than tradition, older even than legend and looks twice as old as all of them put together!'

SRINAGAR

India

DID YOU KNOW?
Srinagar is composed of two Sanskrit words: *sri*, meaning abundance and wealth; and *nagar*, meaning city.

WHAT IS THERE TO SEE?
Spectacular scenery and pretty houseboats.
WORTH A SPLURGE:
The area is known for its traditional handicrafts and dried fruits as well as its cricket bats.

Srinagar, a romantic city situated in the valley of Kashmir surrounded by glistening lakes and forested, snow-capped mountain peaks, is a lively, vibrant city with a number of stunning parks. Perched on the banks of both sides of the river Jhelum (Vyath), the city is well known for the nine ancient bridges that connect the two parts of the city as well as the houseboats floating listlessly on the city's many lakes, particularly Dal Lake.

A summer retreat for many of the great rulers of antiquity, Srinagar lays claim to one of the most pleasant climates in India and has been a tourist destination for centuries, attracting rulers from the plains of India travelling to avoid the oppressive heat of the plains. The city was popular with the Mughal emperors, who left their mark in the form of beautiful mosques and stunning gardens. The Mughal Gardens include Chasma Shahi, the royal fountains; Pari Mahal, the palace of the fairies; Nishat Bagh, the garden of spring.

Like the state of Jammu and Kashmir, Srinagar has a distinctive blend of cultural heritage and religious diversity, depicted through its holy places in and around the city.

JAISALMER

India

WHAT IS IT? A stunning city with an impressive fort and several ornate Jain temples.

Jaisalmer stands near the border with Pakistan, isolated on a ridge of yellow sandstone on the western edge of the Thar Desert and crowned by a fort containing the finely sculptured palace and several ornate Jain temples.

Founded in 1156, by the Rajput ruler Rawal Jaisal after his people fled here from their homeland, the Jaisalmer Fort is situated on Trikuta ('three-peaked') Hill. Its massive sandstone walls, with 99 sturdy turrets, loom 300m (1,000ft) above the town and are a tawny brown during the day, but turn a magical golden honey every night as the sun sets. Jaisalmer gained its prosperity through taxing merchants, but the advent of shipping routes led to its becoming a backwater once more and, fortuitously, led to the preservation of much of its architecture. The fort itself contains five interlinked palaces, including the Raj Mahal ('royal palace') and the Badal Mahal ('cloud palace'), as well as three Jain temples built from the 12th to 15th centuries, the Hindu Laxminath Temple and many exquisite *havelis* (mansions).

The landscape outside the city is desolate, but beautiful. The Desert National Park has a varied landscape and is home to wolves, desert and Indian foxes, desert cats, blackbuck and a range of birds including the highly endangered Indian Bustard.

HIMACHAL PRADESH REGION

India

WHAT IS IT?
An important pilgrimage site for Buddhists, Sikhs and Christians.
WHY IS IT IMPORTANT?
Dharamsala is home to the Dalai Lama and more than 80,000 Tibetan refugees.

Known for centuries as 'Devabhoomi', the abode of the gods, the splendid heights of the Himachal Pradesh region of the Himalayan ranges, with their great scenic beauty and aura of spiritual calm, are dotted with thousands of temples serving as pilgrimage sites for a variety of pilgrims including Christians, Sikhs and Buddhists. Full of isolated valleys and high ranges, the area is home to various styles of temple architecture such as carved stone shikharas, pagoda shrines, temples resembling Buddhist Gompas and Sikh Gurudwaras among others. The area is divided into a series of 12 districts where Hinduism, Buddhism and Sikhism are the main religions. Dharamsala, in the western area of the state, is home to the Dalai Lama and other Tibetan refugees.

TAJ MAHAL

India

....

Located outside the city of Agra in the north Indian state of Uttar Pradesh, the Taj Mahal is one of the most beautiful architectural masterpieces in the world. Shah Jahan, a Mughal ruler, ordered the construction of the Taj Mahal in honour of his wife, Arjumand Banu, to commemorate their 18 years of marriage and her death in childbirth with their 14th child. As a testament to his love for his wife he commissioned the most beautiful mausoleum on Earth.

The site, on the southwest bank of the River Yamuna outside Agra, has five main structures: the Darwaza, or main gateway; the Bageecha, or garden; the Masjid or mosque; the Naqqar Khana, or rest house and the Rauza, or mausoleum, where the tomb is located. The unique Mughal style combines elements of Persian, central Asian and Islamic architecture. Highlights include the black-and-white marble checked floor, the four 40-m (656-ft) minarets at the corners of the mausoleum's plinth and its majestic middle dome. The level of sophistication and intricacy of the monument becomes apparent when you take the time to examine the small details – for instance, in some places, one 3-cm (1.2-in) decorative element contains more than 50 inlaid gemstones. The Taj Mahal truly is a great work of art.

DID YOU KNOW?
A Mughal ruler ordered the construction of the Taj Mahal in honour of his wife.

WHAT IS IT?
One of the most beautiful architectural masterpieces in the world.
WHERE IS IT?
Outside the city of Agra, 200km (124 miles) south of Delhi.

GWALIOR

India

WHAT IS IT? An ancient site of Jain worship, notable for the architecture of its fortress, palaces and temples.
WHERE IS IT? In Madhya Pradesh, 122km (76 miles) south of Agra.

An ancient site of Jain worship, the city of Gwalior occupies a strategic location in the Gird region of north India and has served as the centre of several of northern India's historic kingdoms. Historically and architecturally fascinating, the city of Gwalior is most notable for its fortress and its palaces.

Gwalior fortress is one of the most formidable in India. On an isolated sandstone outcrop, and surrounded by high walls, it encloses a variety of buildings dating back several periods. A rampart, cut from the steep rock face, surrounds the fort, flanked by statues of the Jain Tirthankaras (people who have gained enlightenment). The Man Singh Palace stands at the northeastern corner of the enclosure, decorated with interesting tile work with symbolic images.

Within the fort are some marvels of medieval architecture including the 15th-century Gujari Mahal, a perfectly preserved monument to the love of Raja Man Singh Tomar. Converted into the Archaeological Museum, Gujari Mahal is home to the statue of Shalbhanjika from Gyraspur, the tree goddess, said to be perfection in miniature.

ORCHHA

India

Orchha is a medieval town in the Tikamgarh district of Madhya Pradesh in north-central India and is notable for its well-preserved temples and palaces on the Betwa River. Built by Bundela rulers in the 16th and 17th centuries, Orchha's stone façades continue to exude the grandeur of centuries past.

Orchha's fort complex, approached by a multi-arched bridge, has three palaces set in an open quadrangle, as well as a number of impressive temples and memorials. The most spectacular palaces are Raj Mahal, Rai Parveen Mahal and Jahangir Mahal. The soaring spires and palatial architecture of the Ram Raja Temple make it one of the most unusual in India.

WHAT IS THERE TO SEE?
Exquisite palaces dating back to the 16th century.
HOW DO I GET THERE?
By train to Jhansi from Delhi, Mumbai, Chennai or Gwalior airport, then by bus or taxi from Jhansi.

Right: The impressive fortress in Gwalior

JAIN TEMPLES

India

The Jain temples and innumerable Jain shrines dotting the Indian landscape are a testament to the Jain Tirthankars ('enlightened ones'). They spread their message of peace, non-violence, love and enlightenment as a way to salvation, freeing themselves from the continual cycle of birth and rebirth and, in the process, managing to build some of the most stunning architectural landmarks in the country. There are important cave temples, as well as carved stones and numerous illustrated manuscripts scattered across Uttar Pradesh. Some of the most notable Jain Temples include the five legendary Dilwara Temples in Rajasthan, 2.5km (1.5 miles) from Mount Abu, Rajasthan's only hill station.

Ranakpur, in Rajasthan, is one of the five most important pilgrimage sites for Jainists. Nestled in the Aravalli Hills, it is home to an extraordinarily gorgeous complex of temples, the first to have been built by the Jain community. The town of Falna donated more than 90kg (200lb) of gold for use in the decoration of the dome and internal statues. Located on the curved, boulder-strewn River Maghai, deep in the forested hills of Aravalli, the temple exploits shadow and light masterfully with its delicate lacy marble carvings and 1,500 pillars, each of which is different in design to its neighbours. Watching the sun shift through the pillars, as their colours change from gold to pale blue, is a remarkable experience.

DID YOU KNOW?
This is the only place outside China where fisherman ply the coastal waters with massive Chinese fishing nets.

WHAT IS IT?
A lovely seaside city that is the ideal starting point to tour Kerala.
WHERE IS IT?
Flanked by the Arabian Sea and the western ghats on the southwestern coast of the Indian subcontinent.

KOCHI

India

Kochi, a vibrant Indian city nestled between the western ghats in the east and the Arabian Sea in the west, is considered the gateway to breathtakingly scenic and prosperous Kerala. The history and development of this lovely seaside city has been shaped by the cultures of its various occupiers, including the Arabs, British, Chinese, Dutch and Portuguese.

Over the years, Kochi has emerged as the commercial and industrial capital of Kerala and, despite its size, it is considered the second city in western India after Mumbai. Kochi is a unique and charming amalgam of its varied cultural influences. As you stroll down Fort Kochi beach you'll see fisherman plying the coastal waters with Chinese nets against a backdrop of European-style residences.

LAKE PICHOLA

India

DID YOU KNOW?

The Lake Palace Hotel has been voted as the most romantic hotel in the world.

WORTH A SPLURGE:

Have dinner in the Lake Palace Hotel's restaurant. Sit out on the terrace for what must surely be one of the best dining views in the world.

Lake Pichola lies in the foothills of the Aravalli Hills in southern Rajasthan. It is most famous for the beautiful royal palaces that lie on its islands and around its shoreline. The chief town in the area is Udaipur, which is also known as the city of lakes, founded as a residence by Maharana Udai Singh on the advice of a hermit in 1559. After his stronghold at Chittorgarh had been sacked by Mughal invaders he moved his capital here in 1568. Among its highlights are the City Palace and Museum and the Sajjangarh Palace – which overlooks the lake from the top of a hill and was the summer palace where the royal family spent the monsoon season. There are also many smaller palaces and temples, as well as picturesque streets, fountains and gardens.

The most famous sights on the lake are the island palaces, in particular Jag Niwas, now the Lake Palace Hotel, which was built in the 1740s and is made entirely of marble. This beautiful shining white building appears to float on the lake's clear blue waters. The Jag Mandir is a red sandstone complex on the island of the same name, with cool courtyards and a small museum. It was a refuge for Shah Jahan and is said to have provided inspiration for the Taj Mahal. The massive Jagdish Temple lies within its walls.

MAKALU

Nepal

WHERE IS IT? 22km (14 miles) east of Mount Everest on the China–Nepal border in the Himalayan mountain range.
HOW DO I GET THERE? Hike from Tumlingtar airport.

Makalu is the fifth-highest mountain in the world and lies 22km (14 miles) east of Mount Everest. An isolated peak soaring 8,463m (27,766ft) into the sky, it resembles a four-sided pyramid. Chomo Lonzo, at an elevation of 7,818m (25,650ft) is a subsidiary peak separated by a narrow saddle rising just north of the higher summit.

These stunning peaks provide the backdrop for the Makalu region, an amazingly pristine area in the northwestern corner of the Sankhuwasabha district. To the west it is bordered by the Everest region, to the north by China, to the east by the Arun river and to the south by the Sabha river. Designated a national park and conservation area, the Makalu Barun Conservation Project was established to ensure the preservation of the region through its development with the least amount of impact on the natural beauty of the area, with tourism secondary on its agenda.

Makulu is one of the hardest summits to reach because of its narrow, exposed ridges and steep sides. The Makalu trek is one of the most difficult in the Himalayas – witnessing the spectacle from the Arun Valley, one can only imagine the views from the ice-capped top.

DID YOU KNOW?
This is the site where Siddharta Gautama – Buddha – was born.

LUMBINI

Nepal

Lumbini, in the Terai plains of southern Nepal, is where Siddhartha Gautama – the Lord Buddha – was born in 623 BC. The sacred place, marked by a stone pillar erected by Emperor Ashoka in 249 BC, is a UNESCO World Heritage Site.

The main attraction in Lumbini is the Sacred Garden. Spread over 8 sq km (5 sq miles), it possesses all of the significant treasures of this historic area. As part of the global initiative to promote Lumbini, many countries have built or are building temples, monastries and stupas near the Sacred Garden in the International Monastery Zone. Currently there are religious representations such as the Myanmar Temple, the International Gautami Nuns Temple, China Temple and the Nepal Buddha Temple.

WHERE IS IT?
The Rupandehi District in the Terrai plains of Nepal by the Indian border.
HISTORIC IMPORTANCE:
This is one of the four holiest places of Buddhism.

KANDY

Sri Lanka

Kandy, originally named Senkadagala after the hermit Senkada, and also known as Maha Nuwara meaning the 'Great City', is a sacred Buddhist site and the cultural centre of Sri Lanka. It was the royal capital from 1592 until 1815 when it came under British rule.

Although much of Sri Lanka's royalty suffered under the hands of the British, the city of Kandy, the last stronghold of local kings, managed to retain a rich heritage of living monuments. The best known of these is the sacred pilgrimage site of the Temple of the Tooth, which is said to house one of Buddha's teeth. Legend has it that the tooth was smuggled here in the hair of a princess after being taken from the flames of his funeral pyre. Pirated to India by an invading army, the tooth was eventually restored to its rightful place in the monument in Kandy, constructed during the 17th and 18th centuries.

DON'T MISS:
Sri Lanka's grandest celebration, the Kandy Esala Perahera (July or August). A ten-day festival ending on the night of the full moon, its highlight is a procession of drummers, dancers and elephants led by the Maligawa Tusker, a bull elephant carrying a canopy sheltering a duplicate of the Buddha's sacred tooth.

AMBALANGODA

Sri Lanka

Ambalangoda, a quiet, unspoiled beach town on Sri Lanka's southwest coast, serves as the home of devil dancing and mask- and puppet-making traditions that have been kept alive for generations. The colourful masks worn during the many festivals and ceremonies are carved from the local soft kadura wood and stained with vegetable dyes. The masks, which are associated with local legends and folklore, depict humans, demons and animals. The main types of masks included the *kolam*, *naga* and *sninii* or *sanni,* each of which is used for a different kind of ceremony, festival, opera or drama. The tradition of hanging a masked dummy on a new home to prevent evil spirits entering during building work continues in the village. Masks and other local handicrafts can be bought in the village.

DEVIL DANCING
Devil dances are performed on a variety of occasions to exorcise evil spirits and diseases, and to seek blessings from good spirits.

WHAT IS IT? A traditional beach village on the southern coast road.
WHERE IS IT? Near the resort of Bentota, 86km (53 miles) from Colombo and 24km (15 miles) from Beruwela.
WHAT SHOULD I BUY? The area is known for its masks, hand-loomed batiks and hand-woven cottons.

CAVE TEMPLES AT DAMBULLA

Sri Lanka

Dambulla is a small town known for its high concentration of cave temples, some of which have been used by local monks as meditation locations since the first century B.C. With more than 80 caves within its reach, Dambulla's major attraction is the Golden Temple of Dambulla, which is the largest and best- preserved temple in Sri Lanka. Consisting of five cave temples, each of which contains an impressive variety of Buddhist and Hindu statues and paintings that date back to between the 12th and 18th centuries. A UNESCO World Heritage Site, the Golden Temple of Dambulla has ceilings painted with intricate patterns of images depicting the life of Buddha. Statues here include Buddha, bodhisattvas (beings who help humans to achieve enlightenment), kings and gods (including two Hindu gods).

The first cave is called Temple of the King of the Gods and its well-preserved statue depicts the passing away of the Buddha. The cave also holds an additional five statues, including those of Buddha's attendant weeping at his death, Vishnu and one of the four guardian deities of the island. The second cave is the largest and most impressive at 22m (72ft) in length, with a lofty archway 6m (21ft) high guarded by stone Makara figures on either side. This cave now has 56 seated and standing statues of Buddha, as well as statues of bodhisattvas, Vishnu, Saman, King Vattagamini Abhaya (who founded the cave) and King Nissanka Malla (who paid for 50 of the Buddha statues to be gilded).

DID YOU KNOW?
Galle is the best remaining example of a European fortified city in south Asia.

WHAT IS THERE TO SEE?
The Dutch Fort and nearby Unawatuna beach.
WHERE IS IT?
The southern coast of Sri Lanka, 6km (4 miles) north-west of Unawatuna and 116km (72 miles) south of Colombo.

GALLE

Sri Lanka

Sri Lanka's fourth-biggest town, the port of Galle, was founded by the Portuguese in the 16th century. The Dutch took over in 1598, demolishing all signs of the Portuguese presence and building their own 36-hectare (90-acre) fort, which is now a UNESCO World Heritage Site. Galle is the best remaining example of a European fortified city in south Asia, and is particularly impressive for its mix of Western architecture and south-Asian traditions.

Unique to this area is stilt fishing, a traditional method in which fishermen stand in the water on tall stilts. It is an amazing feat of dexterity, and a fascinating activity to watch.

SIGIRIYA FORTRESS

Sri Lanka

WHAT IS THERE TO SEE?
A fascinating and stunning example of early architecture, engineering and hydraulics inside a massive rock fortress.
ALSO KNOWN AS:
'The eighth wonder of the ancient world'.

Sigiriya, once the capital of Sri Lanka, was built during King Kassyapa's reign (477–495AD). Lying on a steep granite peak and jutting 370m (1,214ft) into the sky, Sigiriya, a UNESCO World Heritage Site, offers the best example of an ancient Asian city centre and an excellent example of advanced Sri Lankan urban planning.

The fortress here was built in the form of a crouching lion, and entrance to the enormous rock structure was once through the lion's mouth. The gigantic paws are the only remaining feature of the lion today, but its outline still dominates the surrounding jungle-covered plains. Sigiriya is home to a magnificent complex of geometric gardens, pools, fountains and buildings. From the summit of the rock, you can see the once-magnificent royal pool, the throne and remains of the majestic palace, walkways and gardens.

ANURADHAPURA

Sri Lanka

Rediscovered in the 19th century and declared a UNESCO World Heritage Site, Anuradhapura is said to be the greatest monastic city of the ancient world. The royal capital of 113 kings and a Buddhist pilgrimage site, Anuradhapura is home to some of Sri Lanka's grandest monuments, palaces and monasteries. The city was founded by Anuradha, a king's minister, in 500BC and Sanghamitta planted Buddha's fig tree, the 'tree of enlightenment', here in the third century BC. Highlights of this city, which was hidden away in dense jungle for many years, include the Aukana Buddha and the guard stone at Thuparama (the site where Thero Mahinda, the son of the Indian Emperor Asoka introduced Buddhism to Sri Lanka which is marked by a Bo tree) and Ruwanweli Seya, which is regarded as the greatest stupa in the world. Erected in the second century BC, this

WHAT IS IT?
The greatest monastic city of the ancient world and the royal capital of 113 kings.
WHERE IS IT?
North-central Sri Lanka.

IT'S ALL IN THE DETAIL
The 13-m (43-ft) granite Aukana Buddha, which dates back to the fifth-century reign of King Dathusena, is said to be of such sculptural accuracy that droplets of rainwater falling off the tip of the nose hit the ground exactly between the toes.

POLONNARUWA

Sri Lanka

Polonnaruwa became the capital of Sri Lanka after the destruction of Anuradhapura in 993 B.C. Strategically located at the crossing of the Mahaveli River, the city, a UNESCO World Heritage Site, was used as a country residence before becoming the capital. In addition to the Brahmanic monuments built by the Cholas, Polonnaruwa is also home to the monumental ruins of the fabulous garden city created by Parakramabahu I in the 12th century.

Don't miss Gal Vihara, a Buddhist shrine, containing intricately carved and well-preserved standing and reclining statues of Buddha. Hatadage, another important shrine, was built by Parakramabahu I to house the Sacred Tooth.

WHAT IS IT?
The second capital of Sri Lanka.
WHAT IS THERE TO SEE?
Brahmanic monuments and a fabulous garden city.

MAN-MADE WONDER
The city is known for its unique irrigation system, Lake Parakrama (Parakrama Samudra), a man-made irrigation tank spread over an area of 2,400 hectares (5,940 acres).

ADAM'S PEAK

Sri Lanka

YOU SHOULD KNOW:
The steep and often difficult climb is usually made at night so that pilgrims can see the spectacular sunrise from the peak. There are various points along the way where visitors can stop, rest, cook and sleep.

Adam's Peak, surrounded by a group of mountains known as 'the Wilderness of the Peak', is best known for containing Buddha's left footprint. A pilgrimage site for the faithful since ancient times, the peak, although not the highest on the island, is the most impressive because it dominates the others around it, seemingly rising out of the ground on its own.

Soaring to 2,243m (7,360ft), the conical mountain has been compared by some to a drop of water or teardrop, its pendant shape lying on the southern forested plains of the country. According to a legend, when Buddha visited Sri Lanka he planted one foot north of the royal city and the other on Sumana-kuta, Adam's Peak, 160km (100 miles) away.

SINHARAJA FOREST RESERVE

Sri Lanka

At a mere 21km (13 miles) across, and an average of 5km (3 miles) long, Sinharaja Forest Reserve is a national treasure and a UNESCO World Heritage Site. Highlights of the park include leopards and the purple-faced langur – a species of monkey. The large bird population tends to fly in mixed feeding flocks, some of which have been known to contain up to 48 species. Rare birds seen in Sinharaja are the red-faced malkoha, the Sri Lanka blue magpie and the green-billed coucal, which is the rarest of Sri Lankan birds. The vegetation of Sinharaja is a combination of tropical lowland rainforest and tropical wet evergreen forest, with many trees averaging a height of nearly 47m (154ft). Out of the 211 woody trees and lianas so far identified within the reserve, 139 are endemic. Many of the plants at lower levels, such as epiphytes, occur only here.

PRECIOUS STATUS
Sinharaja Forest Reserve is Sri Lanka's last remaining tropical rainforest.

WHY IS IT IMPORTANT? It is home to many rare and endemic species of birds and other mammals, reptiles, amphibians and butterflies.
ALSO KNOWN AS: 'Kingdom of the Lion'.
WHEN SHOULD I VISIT? August–September and January–April.

SAMARKAND

Uzbekistan

WHAT IS IT?
One of the oldest and most important cities of Asia.
ALSO KNOWN AS:
'The Rome of the East' or 'the pearl of the Muslim world'.
WHAT IS THERE TO SEE?
Incredible architecture, an enduring history and a dazzling mixture of cultures.

A MULTICULTURAL LEGACY

Samarkand has experienced rule by the Persians, Alexander the Great, Arabs, Genghis Khan, Timur Gurkani (Tamerlane or Tamburlaine the Great), Turks and Russians, leading it to develop a culture consisting of Persian, Indian and Mongolian influences with a splash of both Western and Eastern cultures.

A UNESCO World Heritage Site, Samarkand is the third-largest city in Uzbekistan and is home to a dazzling array of architecture and culture representing its long and sometimes violent history. Majestic and beautiful, it has been called 'the Rome of the East', 'the pearl of the Muslim world' and 'the land of scientists'.

At the centre of the city lies the Registan ('sandy place'), which is surrounded on three sides by the medieval Ulugh Beg, Sherdar and Tilla-Kari *madrasahs* – universities – that sparkle with turquoise mosaic patterns. Decorated inside and out with glazed bricks, mosaics and carved marble, they are considered to be the finest representations of Islamic art and architecture in existence.

The blue, ribbed dome of the Gur Emir Mausoleum, which houses the remains of Timur and his family, dominates the skyline of central Samarkand. Inside, the broken, gigantic slab of dark-green jade commemorating this once mighty ruler is said to be the largest jade stone in the world.

Another architectural treasure, albeit much restored after earthquake damage in the 19th century, is the Bibi Khanum Mosque, named in honour of Timur's senior wife. Its dome is considered to be the largest in the Muslim world and the multicoloured decorated roof is one of the largest and most grand in Samarkand. The main gate, an impressive 35m (115ft) high, looms above a noisy, crowded market brimming with colourful fruits, vegetables and locally grown spices. The main bazaar, which lies around the mosque appears to have changed little in centuries.

Shah-i-Zinda – the tomb of the living king – houses the shrine of Prophet Muhammad's cousin, Qusam ibn Abbas, who brought Islam to this region. The beautiful shrine is one of the oldest structures in Samarkand and is a popular pilgrimage site.

ANGKOR

Cambodia

The vast, majestic temples at Angkor, the Lost City, were discovered in 1860 spread across a 64-km (40-mile) site surrounding the modern village of Siem Reap. Originally built between the eighth and 13th centuries, the temples range from a single, brick tower to vast, stone complexes such as Angkor Wat, the largest single religious monument in the world. The Khmer temples are located at two main sites. The first, at Roluos, 16km (10 miles) southeast of modern-day Siem Reap, is where a select few of the earlier temples were constructed. This was home to the first Khmer capital in the Angkor area, but in the late ninth century Yasovarman I created his new capital at Angkor itself, and it is at this much larger site that the majority of the bigger Khmer temples are located.

DON'T MISS: The Bayon, a massive complex with incredible 1,200-m (3,936-ft) bas-relief carvings including a series of mysterious Buddha faces on the third level. Ta Prohm, one of the larger complexes, enclosed by a moat, is also one of the most beautiful. It has not been restored and its location in the lush jungle gives it a romantic and mysterious aura.

CLAIM TO FAME
Angkor Wat is the largest single religious monument in the world.

MT BROMO

Indonesia

WHAT IS THERE TO SEE?
The sun rising at the crater rim of this spectacular mountain.
WHEN SHOULD I GO?
The 14th day of the month of Kasada in the Tenggerese calendar for the festival.

Mount Bromo is the most famous attraction in Eastern Java and many people from all over the world come here to make the pre-dawn trek to view the stunning sunrise over its spectacular active crater. Located in the Bromo-Tengger-Semeru National Park in the centre of East Java, the largest volcanic region in the province is the Tengger Caldera. Bromo is only one of many peaks inside the massive caldera, but it is easily recognized as the entire top has been blown off and the crater inside constantly belches white smoke. The inside of the caldera, aptly dubbed the Laut Pasir ('Sea of Sand') is an area of 10 sq km (4 sq miles) coated with fine volcanic ash. The Buddhist Tenggerese, an ethnic group inhabiting the highlands of East Java's Tengger range, live almost entirely from agriculture. On the 14th day of the month Kasada, they gather at the rim of Mount Bromo's active crater to present annual offerings of rice, fruit, vegetables, flowers, livestock and other local products and ask for a blessing from the supreme god, Hyang Widi Wasa.

YOGYAKARTA

Indonesia

The provincial capital and cultural centre of Indonesia, Yogyakarta, lies amid lush, emerald rice paddies under the shadow of Mount Merapi. Once the centre of the ancient Mataram Palace, its environs are home to many important monuments and temples, including the Gebang and Mendut temples, as well as a variety of nearby scenic beaches. The Gebang Temple to the northeast was rediscovered after a statue of Ganesha was uncovered in 1936. Built at about the same time as the nearby Borobudur temple in the eighth century, the ruins of the roof, part of the body and much of the base appeared intact upon further archaeological research. This unadorned square building measures roughly 5.25m (17ft) across and 7.75m (25.4ft) high. For a break from the sightseeing head to one of Yogyakarta's stunning beaches.

HISTORIC ARCHITECTURE
The 9th-century Pramaban Temple, which is known locally as the Temple of the Slender Virgin, is the largest in Indonesia and one of the most beautiful.

WHAT IS IT? An area of natural and historic beauty and the cultural capital of the region.
WHERE IS IT? Central Java.
ALSO KNOWN AS: Jogjakarta, Yogya, Jogia or Jogya.

BOROBUDUR TEMPLE

Indonesia

WHAT IS IT?
One of the greatest monuments in the world.
WHERE IS IT?
The Kedu plain in central Java.
WHAT IS THERE TO SEE?
An eighth-century Buddhist temple in the shape of a lotus flower.
WHY IS IT IMPORTANT?
It is an almost unique survival of a substantially intact Buddhist temple from this era.

Dating from the eighth century, Borobudur Temple in the Kedu plain of central Java is one of the greatest architectural monuments in Asia. The Buddhist temple, a UNESCO World Heritage Site, is a stepped pyramid made up of six rectangular stories, three circular terraces and a central *stupa* forming the summit. The structure forms a lotus, the sacred flower of Buddha.

The walls and balustrades are decorated with low reliefs, covering a total surface area of 2,500 sq m (8,202 sq ft). Around the circular platforms are 72 openwork *stupas*, each of which contains a statue of Buddha.

Surrounded by an idyllic landscape of emerald, rice-terraced hills and overlooked by four volcanoes, Borobudur Temple was built over a period of 80 years for the Sailendra dynasty, to resemble a microcosm of the universe, to provide a visual image of the teachings of Buddha and show, in a practical manner, the steps through life that each person must follow to achieve enlightenment.

Visitors to this pilgrimage site would first have been led around the successive levels from the base, with its friezes illustrating the consequences of living in the world of desire, then up through five levels showing how to conquer desire and attachment.

The square section of the temple then gives way to a round, unadorned summit where meditating Buddhas and saints sit in supreme peace contemplating a view of exquisite beauty. In the centre, a bell-shaped tower, or *stupa,* points to heaven, a realm beyond form and concept, known as nirvana.

SAMOSIR ISLAND

Indonesia

The island of Samosir, in the middle of Lake Toba, the original home of the fierce Toba Bataks, has many stone tombs and traditional villages. Believed to be the largest and deepest caldera lake in the world, Lake Toba spans over 1,707 sq km (436 sq miles) and reaches a depth of 529m (1,735ft). Created by an enormous volcanic eruption more than 74,000 years ago, it is a giant caldera high in the treeless mountains of northern Sumatra.

Samosir, the giant arid 'Island of the Dead' in the middle of Danau Toba, or Lake Toba, measures 45x20km (28x12 miles). The eastern coast of the island rises steeply from a small bank towards a central plateau with an altitude of 780m (2,559ft), and the land gradually descends towards the southern and western coasts of the island, which is scattered with small villages.

The island is best known for its fascinating Toba Bakat sarcophagi, which were first discovered in the 1930s. These 'adat houses', or stone graves with coffins, have been found in 26 villages. In Tomok, under the sacred Hariara tree, lies the 200-year-old stone sarcophagus of King Sidabutar's clan. Although they resemble coffins, the sarcophagi normally contain the collected skulls of an entire family or clan.

UBUD

Indonesia

WHERE IS IT?
In the centre of the island of Bali.
WHAT IS THERE TO DO?
Visit the many temples, explore the galleries and boutiques, look around the luxury resorts or just take in this paradise.

Right: Rice terraces in Ubud

Ubud, in the middle of the island of Bali, has been the island's pre-eminent centre for fine arts, crafts, dance and music for more than a century. Once a hang-out for bohemians and backpackers, Ubud has developed into a town better known for its elegant resorts, galleries and mansions for discerning art collectors and travellers.

Because of its location, it also makes a good base for visiting other Balinese attractions, but there is plenty to see and do here. Ubud is surrounded by the traditional, stunning landscape that Bali is known for, including rice paddies, scenic villages, art and craft communities, ancient temples, palaces, rivers, unique character and friendly locals.

KELIMUTU

Indonesia

Indonesia is one of the world's most geologically active countries, and among its volcanoes is Kelimutu on the island of Flores with its brightly coloured, exotic lakes. Considered a national treasure by the people of Indonesia, each of the three lakes on the eastern summit of the volcano has distinctive features and they are all worth visiting.

Many Indonesian guidebooks describe the vibrant colours of the Kelimutu lakes as resulting from the minerals in the lakes. Although partly correct, the most important determinant of colour in the lakes is oxygen. When the lake waters lack oxygen they appear green, and when they are rich in oxygen, they become a shade of deep red verging on black. The lakes are a stunning natural phenomenon not to be missed.

WHAT IS IT?
A volcano with three stunning, brightly coloured lakes.
WHERE IS IT?
On the island of Flores in Indonesia.

TAKE NOTE
These scenic lakes, considered a national treasure, were once featured on the rupiah - the national currency of Indonesia.

MANADO BAY

Indonesia

WHAT IS IT?
A series of small islands offering world-class underwater activities on some of the world's most pristine reefs.
WHERE IS IT?
The capital of north Sulawesi province.

Manado Bay, surrounded by lush, tropical peaks, serves as the gateway to north Sulawesi, particularly for those diving the volcanic islands of Bunaken, the Lembeh Strait and Bangka.

The deep waters of the Bunaken Island National Marine Park in Manado exhibit some of the highest levels of biodiversity in the world, with outstanding fish variety and world-class wall diving. The clear, warm waters contain an astonishingly high number of different species, whether corals, sponges or fish. When you are scuba diving in Bunaken you can see seven times more genera of coral than in Hawaii, 33 species of butterfly fish and more than 70 per cent of all fish species known to live in Indonesian waters. The various superb diving and snorkelling sites put the marine park in the top-ten dive sites in the world, making it a must for seasoned and beginner divers alike.

KOMODO NATIONAL PARK

Indonesia

Komodo National Park, home to the world's largest lizards, includes three major islands – Komodo, Rinca and Padar – and is located in the centre of the Indonesian archipelago. Established in 1980, the main purpose of the park was to conserve the unique Komodo dragon and its habitat. However, over the years, the goals for the park have expanded to include protecting its entire biodiversity, both terrestrial and marine. Declared a World Heritage Site and a Man and Biosphere Reserve by UNESCO, the park boasts one of the world's richest marine environments including coral reefs, mangroves, seagrass beds, seamounts and semi-enclosed bays. Dugong, sharks, manta rays, dolphins, sea turtles and at least 14 species of whale also make Komodo National Park their home.

WHERE IS IT?
In the centre of the Indonesian archipelago.
WHAT IS THERE TO DO?
Watch the impressive Komodo dragons and enjoy some of the world's best marine life.

WORLD'S LARGEST LIZARD
Komodo dragons can reach a length of 3m (10ft). Large, ferocious predators, the dragons are capable of consuming a fully grown human and can run as fast as a dog.

BUKIT LAWANG

Indonesia

The rainforests of Gunung Leuser National Park in northern Sumatra are a beautiful area for trekking and river tubing and also, most notably, home to the Bukit Lawang Orangutan Rehabilitation Centre. Located on the banks of the Bohorok River, the centre was founded in 1973 by two Swiss zoologists, Monica Borner and Regina Frey, to study and protect these fascinating creatures and to return them to their natural habitat. They gained support from the World Wildlife Fund, and made huge progress in the rehabilitation of orangutans rescued from captivity, or from the forests that are quickly being destroyed through deforestation. Other attractions in the area include a cave full of bats that fly out at dusk, watersports, the Accoustic cave and trekking in the jungle to see orangutans in the wild.

WHAT IS IT?
Home to the Bukit Lawang Orangutan Rehabilitation Centre.
WHAT IS THERE TO DO?
Tubing, trekking or watching the gorgeous orangutans.

FEEDING TIME
There are two open feedings a day, during which the orangutans may come swinging through the jungle for a free meal. The hope is that, within time, each orangutan will learn to find enough fruit in the jungle on its own, so that it no longer needs a free meal.

LUANG PRABANG

Laos

Luang Prabang must surely be one of the most beautiful cities in the world, and in 1995 it was added to UNESCO's World Heritage list, recognized as the best-preserved city in southeast Asia.

The old city is rightly famous for its historic temples and monasteries (there are more than 30 of them) and for its splendid Royal Palace, which now serves as a fascinating museum. There are lovely old French–Indochinese colonial houses, and two-storey shop houses featuring both French and Lao architectural influences. Two parallel streets run the length of the peninsula and one runs all the way around it on the river's edge. These are criss-crossed by many fascinating little lanes and back streets.

Walking in Luang Prabang is a joy — several of the streets are shaded with palms and flowering trees, sweeping, gilded temple roofs can be glimpsed every few yards, colourful prayer flags flutter in the breeze and temple gongs echo around the town. You can watch the sunset from the top of Phou Si Hill or enjoy a cool drink by the river's edge. Explore the markets or visit one of the monasteries, such as Wat Xiang Thong, and soak up the serene and spiritual atmosphere that still pervades the town despite its influx of visitors.

DID YOU KNOW?
Luang Prabang is the best-preserved city in southeast Asia.

WHAT IS THERE TO SEE?
The Royal Palace, Phou Si Hill, Wat Xiang Thong, Pak Ou Buddha caves and the Kouang Si waterfalls.
DON'T MISS:
Watching the sunset from from the top of Phou Si Hill.

VIENTIANE

Laos

DON'T MISS:
A visit to the colourful morning market (*talat sao*).

Vientiane is the capital city of the Lao People's Democratic Republic. Set on a broad curve in the Mekong river valley, it is a sleepy backwater of a city, full of charm. The city's architecture is largely low-rise, and there are old French-colonial buildings to be seen as well as two-storey Indochinese shop houses, which are often painted yellow, and lovely, ramshackle, wooden homes by the side of the river. The city centre is marked by a fountain in a square named Nam Phou Place. Almost all of Vientiane's important sights are located within walking distance from here, including a few socialist-style buildings such as the Lao Revolutionary Museum. That Luang, the old royal *stupa* is 3km (2 miles) north of the city and Wat Sisaket is the city's oldest temple. Strolling along the shady, tree-lined streets you will find it hard to believe you are in a capital city. Small groups of Buddhist monks in orange or rust-coloured robes, sporting umbrellas against the sun, invite you to visit their temples and want to practise their English on you. On the banks of the Mekong, farmers grow vegetables and water buffalo graze peacefully, barely looking up as you pass. At the morning market (*talat sao*) you can find the best of Lao weaving – glorious silks, cottons and ethnic textiles, old and new. Vientiane is changing. Where there were once hundreds of bicycles, there are now motor bikes and cars. However, the overwhelming impression you receive is of a city in a time warp, enjoying a gentle pace of life and in no particular hurry to become just like everywhere else.

TAD LO FALLS

Laos

WHAT IS THERE TO DO?
Spend a lazy day lying on a rock with the waterfall as your backdrop.
WHAT IS IT KNOWN FOR?
The elephant rides that will take you through tribal villages.
HOW DO I GET THERE?
By road from Pakxe.

The Tad Lo falls are not particularly high, in fact they are only about 10m (33ft) tall, but they are broad and long and beautifully situated in the forested hills on the northwestern edge of the Bolaven plateau in southern Laos. High above the steamy Mekong River valley, the plateau is cool and fertile, and here Laven, Alak and Katu tribal farmers grow top-quality coffee that fetches some of the highest prices in the world. Rivers plunge off the plateau in all directions, and Tad Lo is one of the most accessible and delightful. A striking feature of the lower falls are the large granite boulders that make perfect places upon which to lie and enjoy the sun, allowing you to drop down into the cool, clear water of a swimming hole, or to wade back to the shore quite safely and easily.

WAT PHOU

Laos

The temple of Wat Phou is one of the finest Khmer temple sites outside Cambodia, and is really a series of ruined temples and shrines that date from the sixth to the 13th centuries.

DID YOU KNOW?

Wat Phou means 'mountain monastery' in Lao.

Wat Phou is situated at the foot of Lingaparvata Mountain. Although it is a Theravada Buddhist site, several Hindu gods are depicted in some of the sandstone reliefs. The site itself is arranged over three main levels ascending the hill and linked by a long, stone causeway leading from a dilapidated royal residence at the bottom to stone steps that become steeper the farther up you get. On either side there are the remains of stone pillars and pedestals, and mythical creatures such as *nagas* (water serpents). There are ruined pavilions, Khmer statues lying half-buried in the grass, and fantastic carved lintels depicting Vishnu, Shiva and Kali, as well as images of Buddha.

WHAT ELSE IS THERE TO SEE?

Don Khong and Don Det islands

YOU SHOULD KNOW

There is an entrance fee.

DON'T MISS:

The annual festival of Wat Phou. It usually takes place during February.

The stairway up to the main temple sanctuary is lined with plumeria, the national tree of Laos, and the sanctuary itself is surrounded by magnificent mango trees. The view from here is extraordinary. There is an annual festival at Wat Phou that usually takes place during February, when thousands of pilgrims from Thailand and Cambodia, as well as Laos itself, converge here for almost a week.

THE PLAIN OF JARS

Laos

The Plain of Jars is a large, rolling plateau in northeast Laos, named after the mysterious groupings of stone jars to be found there in over a dozen sites. Others lie strewn across the plain and the surrounding hills. At Thong Hai Hin, or Site One, there are 250 jars that range from about 600kg (1,300lb) to one tonne, and the largest jar on the plain weighs six tonnes. Some have stone lids lying nearby.

Many different theories have been advanced regarding their purpose, but as no other material has been discovered, they remain a mystery. They may have been storage vessels, or possibly funerary urns. Even dating them reliably is difficult, although archaeologists seem to agree that they are about 2,000 years old.

The plain itself is often forgotten, as visitors concentrate on the jar sites, but it is beautiful in its own right, with its grassy meadows and rolling brown and purple hills. Villages have been rebuilt, and rice and fruit trees planted. Sadly the area is still not free of unexploded ordnance, and only the main three jar sites are considered reasonably clear, so stay on the footpaths or take a guide.

DID YOU KNOW?
In the 1950s it was chosen as the setting for the musical *South Pacific*.

WHAT IS IT?
The largest island in the Malaysian archipelago of 60 volcanic islands.
WHAT IS THERE TO DO?
Spend the day snorkelling or diving around the beautiful coral reefs, or relaxing in a hammock by the beach.

TIOMAN ISLAND

Malaysia

Tioman Island is the largest in an archipelago of about 60 volcanic islands, some inhabited, that are situated off the southern shores of the Malaysian east coast. The island boasts fabulous tropical beaches set around the mountainous interior.

Tioman Island was first recorded in the journals of Arabian merchants in the tenth century. Traders from India, Persia and China also came this way because Tioman had betelnut, sandalwood and camphor to trade and was a safe haven from monsoon storms. Many coral reefs surround the island and there are several good dive sites. It is possible to walk across the island in a couple of hours and explore the forest that is home to many species of flora and fauna.

PENANG HILL
Malaysia

WHERE IS IT?
In the centre of Penang, overlooking Georgetown.
WHAT ELSE IS THERE TO SEE?
Khoo Kongsi, Kek Lok Si Temple, Fort Cornwallis and Penang's beaches.

The island of Penang is the site of the oldest British settlement in Malaysia, founded in 1786 by Captain Francis Light. Captain Light was searching for a base where ships of the East India Company could set anchor and make repairs. He made a treaty with the Sultan of Kedah, and in exchange for military protection, received permission to colonize the jungle-covered and virtually uninhabited island. In the middle of today's busy, modern city of Georgetown rises Penang Hill (Bukit Bendera). Almost 900m (1,000ft) high, it dominates the island and from its summit there are amazing views not only of the town and the whole island but also, on a clear day, of the mountains on the mainland. The hike up Penang Hill takes about two hours, but the best way to see it is to take the funicular railway. Built by Swiss engineers, this trundles up an incredibly steep angle at a leisurely pace through the tropical forest.

TAMAN NEGARA

Malaysia

Taman Negara means 'national park', and indeed this is not only the world's oldest rainforest, but also the oldest national park in Malaysia. Almost 4,500 sq km (1,550 sq miles) are protected here. The rainforest has a wealth of biodiversity, dominated by hardwood forest in the lower areas and cloud forest at the higher elevations. There are no roads, and the only way to see it is by trekking the forest trails or by boat on the rivers. This rainforest is about 130 million years old, which means that while other parts of the planet were undergoing ice ages, this area's climate is much as it was during the age of the dinosaurs. The flora and fauna are superb – Sumatran rhinoceros, tigers, Asian elephants, sun bears, leopards and tapirs roam, and monkeys and birds chatter and call from the trees.

CLAIM TO FAME
Taman Negara is the world's oldest rainforest and the oldest national park in Malaysia.

DON'T MISS: The most amazing experience in this forest is the canopy walkway – the longest in the world at 430m (1,475ft), leading from tree to tree as high as 50m (165ft) above ground. The view of plants and wildlife living at this height is extraordinary.

SHWEDAGON PAWA

Myanmar

The Shwedagon Pawa, a great bell-shaped brick *stupa*, is the most impressive building in Yangon (Rangoon) and among the most splendid in Myanmar. The Buddhist monument is completely covered in gold, shining from the Thein Gottara hillside, the highest point in Yangon, rising 51m (168ft) above the city.

Four entrances lead onto the *stupa*, parts of which only monks and other men may visit. The contents of the base are are unknown, but according to legend, eternally flying and spinning swords protect it from intruders. It is rumoured that underground tunnels lead from here to Bagan and Thailand.

Believed to have been built single-handedly by King Okkalapa, the Shwedagon Pawa is home to many treasures including, most significantly, eight of Buddha's hairs. The Shwedagon Pawa is decorated with nearly nine tonnes of pure gold and the upper reaches are encrusted with precious stones. Last renovated during the reign of King Mindon in 1871, the temple's gold plating has, not surprisingly, been gradually deteriorating over time.

DID YOU KNOW?
Mandalay is known as 'the city of gems.'

MANDALAY

Myanmar

Mandalay is the second-largest city in Myanmar after Yangon and the former capital. It has a rich cultural tradition and a stunning landscape, dotted with the carved wooden roofs of temples and pagodas.

The city, residence to the last two kings of Myanmar – Mindon and Thibaw – is centred around the royal palace, and is known for its millionaires, its religious sites and its monks. Established by King Mindon and named Yadanabon, meaning 'where all the prosperity accumulates', Mandalay, bordered on the east by the blue-ridged Shan mountains and the lifeblood of Myanmar, the Ayeyarwady, or Irrawaddy, River on the west, continues to be the country's hub of culture, faith and communications.

WHAT SHOULD I BUY?
Head to Zegyo Market – a collection of street markets located near the city centre where you can pick up some interesting curios.

BAGAN

Myanmar

WHAT IS THERE TO SEE?
Stunning temples that
inspired the future
architecture of Myanmar.
WHAT IS THERE TO DO?
Visit the museum to see
the Myazedi Pillar – the
Burmese version of the
Rosetta Stone.

Bagan is a rich archaeological site, 145km (90 miles) southwest of Mandalay. Between the 11th and 13th centuries, the kings of the Bagan dynasty built thousands of pagodas and temples here.

Many of the most important temples are located in and around the old walled city. The Ananda temple, for example, was begun in 1091 by King Anawrahta and inspired many of the later temples. The sides of the central square block are 53m (174ft) long and 10.7m (35ft) high with a large, gabled portico on each. The six receding terraces are crowned with a pine-cone shaped *sikhara* topped by a tapering *stupa*, echoed by four smaller ones at the roof's corners. On misty mornings, the gold-clad *stupas* seem to float in the air. This is one of the richest architectural sites in the world.

PALAWAN ISLAND

Philippines

Palawan is renowned for having one of the most beautiful seascapes in the world, with thousands of square kilometres of protected coral reefs. Palawan Island has a stunning array of flora, fauna, ecology, biology and marine life, including highly endangered dugongs. Puerto Princesa Subterranean River National Park, a UNESCO World Heritage Site, with ancient cave and river networks, is an amazing place. It is thought to be the longest navigable subterranean river and its cavern contains an incredible array of stalactites and stalagmites in all shapes and sizes. Considered by many to be the Philippine's 'last frontier', the province is also home to the UNESCO World Heritage site of Tubbataha Reef National Marine Park. The Coron Reefs, in Coron Bay, Busuanga, consist of seven enchanting lakes surrounded by impressive craggy, limestone cliffs.

UNDERWATER PARADISE
Palawan is rated as one of the
top dive sites in the world and
divers come to see Japanese
shipwrecks, undisturbed reefs
and multitudes of aquatic life.

WHAT IS IT? A pristine area with gorgeous beaches, fantastic diving and tropical rainforest.
WHAT IS THERE TO SEE? The nearby Calauit Wildlife Sanctuary and the Subterranean National Park, as well as the many Japanese shipwrecks from World War II.

BANAUE RICE TERRACES

Philippines

WHAT ARE THEY?
Gigantic rice terraces carved from the mountainside.
WHERE ARE THEY?
The Luzon Province of the northern Philippines.
WHAT ELSE IS THERE TO DO?
Visit the quaint market village of Ifugao.

TRADITION
Ancestral spirits are still worshiped here and it is not unusual to see the sacrificing of three chickens or a pig to appease an angry spirit. Another tradition is that when a person dies, their body is hung from the thatched roof of their hut for three days as a sign to the villagers that the deceased has moved on to a better place. Afterwards, the bones are collected and placed inside the roof of the family's dwelling, to give comfort and protection to the living.

Considered by many to be the eighth wonder of the world, the Banaue rice terraces, a UNESCO World Heritage Site, are a feat of incredible engineering, created over the past 2,000 years by the people of Batad. This area is in the scenic Luzon Province of the Northern Philippines and contains jagged, forested mountains rising to more than 1,500m (4,292ft) above sea level. The jaw-dropping terraces, carved from the mountainside, stretch as far as the eye can see.

The terraces, a seemingly endless stairway of cultivated rice and vegetable paddies, were largely built by hand, one stone at a time, and cover an area of more than 10,500 sq km (4,000 sq miles) of mountainside. Fed by a natural irrigation system from the rainforests high in the mountains above, the local population continues to survive on the traditional farming methods employed throughout their existence.

There are no roads or electricity because the Batad prefer to live as they have for centuries, retaining a spiritual connection with the Earth and their surroundings.

Home to a number of popular hiking trails, the region has a healthy tourist population that come to gaze at these majestic creations. Four similar, albeit smaller, terraces nearby include the ampitheatre-shaped Batad terraces, the Mayoyao terraces, where organic red and white ifugao rice is grown, the stone-enclosed Hapao terraces, which date back to 650AD, and the well-known Kiangan terraces, made up of the Nagacadan and Julungan terraces.

CHATUCHAK MARKET

Thailand

Chatuchak Market, in northern Bangkok, is one of the largest and most spectacular markets in the world. Open on Saturdays and Sundays, it has about 10,000 stalls selling just about everything you can imagine to the 25,000 visitors who come here each day. You could spend every weekend here for a year and still not have seen everything. Just at the edge of Chatuchak market are two more markets, which are also open during the week. One is a food market, the other is Bangkok's largest plant and flower market.

The main market is like an Aladdin's cave, packed with treasures where you will find everything from fake designer clothes to fabulous, hand-woven tribal wear, and antiques, from opium weights to ornately carved teak screens. If you were setting up home in Bangkok you could buy everything you needed right here – furniture, bedding, kitchenware, paintings, lamps, rugs, sound systems, CDs and DVDs, musical instruments, images of Buddha and even pets.

If you are hungry, there are all sorts of food stalls selling delicious meals and if you are thirsty you can buy fresh fruit juice, delicious coffee or alcohol from one of the bars. Even if you do not buy anything, browsing is a fabulous, fascinating experience.

ANG THONG ARCHIPELAGO

Thailand

The Ang Thong archipelago is a national marine park made up of around 50 islands lying about 30km (20 miles) from Ko Samui. Most are uninhabited and were fortunately saved from the developers because the area was used by the Thai navy before it was given national park status. The islands themselves are a photographer's dream, with limestone cliffs, tropical vegetation, caves and secret lagoons, pristine white-sand beaches, coral reefs and aquamarine waters. The headquarters of the national park are situated on Ko Wua Ta Lap, where bungalow-style accommodation is available. Popular island activities include sea-kayaking tours from Ko Samui, a great way to see the islands and discover the best spots for snorkelling. It is also possible to charter boats from here, which will give you greater freedom to explore this stunning area at your own pace.

WHAT IS THERE TO SEE?
Ko Samui, Ko Pha-Ngan and Ko Tao are three of the most beautiful islands.
DON'T MISS:
The saltwater lake on Ko Mae Koh.

CHAO PHRAYA RIVER

Thailand

DID YOU KNOW?
Bangkok is known locally as Krung Thep, the 'City of Angels'.

WHAT IS THERE TO DO?
Take a river ferry to experience a more peaceful side to Bangkok.
WHAT IS THERE TO SEE?
Floating markets, temples, Bangkok's skyline, the Grand Palace, Ko Kret island.

Bangkok is a huge, sprawling city on the Chao Phraya River and is home to about six million people. It is everything and more than you would imagine a great southeast Asian city to be. One of the best ways to escape the bustle and explore the heart of the old city on the east bank, the river and the network of canals (*khlongs*) is by river ferry, tour or chartered boat. From here you can see the many beautiful temples, the Grand Palace, ramshackle old houses on stilts, 19th-century architecture, the naval dockyard and customs house and the famous floating markets.

The Royal Barge National Museum houses the kings' ceremonial barges, which were used on such state occasions as the procession at the end of the annual rainy season. Among the temples are the ancient Wat Kaeo Fa, Wat Amphawan and Wat Suwannaram. At Wat Sai floating market, tourists can buy souvenirs, while at Taling Chan a food market is held at weekends.

There are numerous boat tours during the day as well as dinner cruises in the evenings, which give visitors an opportunity to dine in luxury while watching the lit-up old buildings and beautiful skyline of the city glide past.

AYUTTHAYA

Thailand

YOU SHOULD KNOW:
Do not pose behind the Buddhas for 'comic' photos as it causes offence.

For 400 years, from 1350, Ayutthaya was the capital of Siam, and the home of 33 kings. Wealthy and powerful, merchants from all over Europe and the Far East came here. During a brief Burmese invasion in 1767, the city was all but destroyed and the new capital was established at Bangkok. Today the ancient city is a UNESCO World Heritage Site and a canal has been built to connect the three rivers that join where it stands, thus creating an island.

Ruined temples are scattered across the site, and there are others on the rivers' edges too. The main temples can be visited on foot, but if you hire a bike you will be able to see much more of this extensive site. Wat Phra Si Sanphet was the largest temple in Ayutthaya, and also served as the palace. Built in the 14th century, it has three magnificent *stupas*. The adjoining Wat Mongkhon Bophit contains one of Thailand's largest Buddha figures, which was cast in bronze in the 15th century. Some of the temples are built in the Khmer style. Many are ruined but still magnificent, and there are a great many Buddha figures, including one in Wat Phra Meru from Sri Lanka that is said to be 1,300 years old. Sadly, many figures were damaged by the Burmese invaders, and more recently art thieves have stolen some of the heads. Nevertheless, this is a sacred site for Thais, who dress many of the Buddha figures in yellow robes, scatter flower petals and burn incense sticks reverently at their feet.

DID YOU KNOW?
There are over 40,000 Buddhist temples in Thailand.

WAT THAM PHA

Thailand

Situated in the mountains above Chiang Dao stands one of the most beautiful temples in Thailand. Virtually unknown to tourists, it is sufficiently remote as to be hardly visited, and yet it is a working monastery with a serene and spiritual atmosphere. Made from stone, with a gilded *stupa*, the temple sits easily with its surroundings, and its simplicity comes as a relief after the scores of painted and glittering temples you will have already seen. To reach the temple you must climb a pathway that meanders up and through the forest. Surrounded by tall trees and with bougainvillea and frangipani tumbling down the rocky outcrops, it is some time before you catch a glimpse of the lovely mountain wat perched way above you. The view from the top is not just beautiful, it is absolutely spectacular.

WHAT ELSE IS THERE TO SEE?
The Dao Caves, the Elephant Training Centre at Taeng-Dao and Chiang Mai.
YOU SHOULD KNOW:
There is an entrance fee.

PHANG-NGA BAY

Thailand

DID YOU KNOW?

This is where the James Bond film *The Man with the Golden Gun* was made.

WHEN SHOULD I VISIT?

The winter months are best as this is when the sea is calmer.

WHAT IS THERE TO DO?

Take a kayak trip to explore the interior of Drawing Cave.

The scenery in Phang-Nga Bay is spectacular – karst (limestone) formations and islands burst from the sea. Take a tour by boat and explore the bay for the day, or, even better, go on a two- or three-day camping trip. If you take a kayak trip, you can explore the interior of some of the marvellous, semi-submerged caves – such as the Drawing Cave, full of murals – which are inaccessible to the larger boats. Another beautiful site is the Ko Panyi Muslim fishing village, built on stilts in a mangrove swamp.

Stay on an island or in Phang-Nga, a small town surrounded by forested limestone cliffs, and use this as a base from which to explore other places such as the inland cave at Wat Tham Suwankhuha, a shrine that is full of images of Buddha. In October, the annual Vegetarian Festival – a time of purification for the locals – occurs. For nine days there are processions and performances ending in a wild frenzy, with mediums in a trance walking on burning coals and piercing their cheeks and tongues with daggers and spears.

THE GRAND PALACE

Thailand

The best way to approach the Grand Palace complex is from the Chao Praya River. The palace complex and Wat Pra Kaew ('Temple of the Emerald Buddha') are set within almost 10 hectares (25 acres) of flat ground that was consecrated in the 18th century. It is surrounded by a white wall that belies the unbelievably colourful wat within. Nothing could prepare you for your first sight of Wat Pra Kaew. The colours of Theravada Buddhism are red, green, orange and yellow and along with masses of gilding and gold leaf, lotus bud patterns and columns encrusted with gleaming mosaics, these colours are everywhere – so bright they almost hurt the eye. The *stupas* are gilded and the swooping layers of the roofs are tiled in shining orange and green tiles.

WHERE IS IT?
Bangkok
HOW DO I GET THERE?
Take the Chao Praya River express, metro, skytrain or bus from Bangkok bus station.

BUDDHIST SHRINE
The Emerald Buddha is tiny in comparison to many of the famous Buddha statues in Thailand, but it is of immense significance. Its origins are surrounded in mystery, but it was first recorded in Chiang Rai, in the 15th century. It sits high up in a glass case in a huge shrine that was built specially to house it.

MEKONG DELTA

Vietnam

WHAT IS THERE TO DO?
Take a trip out to An Binh
Island and discover some
of the wildlife that inhabits
the area.
WHAT IS THERE TO SEE?
An Binh Island, Sa Dec,
Sam Mountain, Hon
Chong Peninsula.

Known to the Vietnamese as Cuu Long ('Nine Dragons') because of the nine tributaries that spread out across the floodplain, the area has been criss-crossed with canals to channel the excess flood water in the most practical fashion.

The river, with its network of tributaries and canals, is what makes the region so beautiful. It is essential for travel and transport and thousands of boats ply up and down these waterways, from tiny rowing boats to cargo boats carrying rice, fruit and sugarcane. All life is there to be seen on the water: colourful floating markets, river villages and Khmer pagodas can all be seen, and the areas not given over to farmland are rich with wildlife. Thousands of birds nest in colonies, and there are five species of dolphin to be found, including the rare Irrawaddy dolphin.

TAY NINH

Vietnam

Tay Ninh is the site of the extraordinary Cao Dai cathedral. In fact it is not just a temple, a cathedral or a pagoda it is the Cao Dai Holy See, built in 1927 by Ngo Van Chieu, who founded Cao Daism a few years earlier. The cathedral is painted in a riotous confusion of gaudy colours, and the Divine Eye, the symbol of Cao Dai, tops the balcony overlooking the central portico. The interior is where you can really see the mix of religions that are at work here. The vaulted ceiling of the nave is sky blue and decorated with stars and clouds as well as mouldings of lions and turtles. Pink pillars with green dragons twining up them mark the nave, which is dominated by a huge, blue sphere representing the heavens and dusted with stars, through which the Divine Eye takes a good look at his congregation.

A NEW RELIGION
Cao Dai is a blend of
religions: Buddhism, Taoism
and Confucianism with
additions from Christianity,
Islam and spirituality.

WHAT IS IT? The site of the Cao Dai Temple and Cao Dai Holy See, a melting pot of different religions.
WHAT ELSE IS THERE TO DO?
Visit Ho Chi Min City for an insight into the Vietnam War.

HUE

Vietnam

WHAT IS IT? The former capital of Vietnam, on the east coast.
WHAT IS THERE TO DO? A visit to Ngo Mon Gate and Thai Hoa Palace are essentials on any intinerary.

Hue is a city with a long and distinguished history and despite the bitter battles that have taken place here in recent times, during the Vietnam War, it has kept its air of romance, refinement, scholarship and spirituality. The founder of the Nguyen dynasty, Emperor Gia Long, made Hue his capital in 1802, and it soon became known for its cultural activity. On the north bank of the Perfume River, the Emperor built a huge citadel in the Chinese style, with a Forbidden City at its heart, reserved for the sovereign's use. The Imperial City which surrounds it was the hub of the administration, and the whole complex is enclosed by a wall 7m (23ft) high and 20m (66ft) thick, surrounded both inside and out by a moat and a canal.

The Imperial City was devastated first by fire in 1947, and later by some of the most terrible battles of the Vietnam War. However, some of the buildings remain and have been perfectly restored. Rebuilding has been continuous since 1975 and received a boost when Hue became a UNESCO World Heritage Site in 1993. The Ngo Mon Gate and the Thai Hoa Palace are two of the highlights, but there are ancestral altars, Chinese assembly halls, pagodas, temples, royal mausolea and fascinating museums to be explored, too. Hue is not simply a city of glorious historic relics, it is a lively, thriving place, home to five universities. In 1995 it was given independent city status by the government to mark its growing economic importance.

TUNNELS OF CU CHI

Vietnam

WHAT ELSE IS THERE TO DO?
Visit Ho Chi Minh City to gain a perspective of the importance of these tunnels.
HOW DO I GET THERE?
Take an organized bus tour.

The tunnels of Cu Chi are a relatively modern, man-made phenomenon, but their fame, deservedly, is worldwide. They are the outstanding symbol of the dogged determination of the Vietnamese desire to be free of Western colonists. The tunnels were first thought of in the late 1940s, when the Viet Minh were trying to remove the French from their country. Originally devised as hiding places for arms and ammunition, they soon became hiding places for the Viet Minh fighters. By the mid 1960s, 250km (155 miles) of tunnels threaded their way under Cu Chi and the areas around it. One even ran under the American army base situated there. These tunnels allowed the many groups of Viet Cong fighters in the area to liaise with one another at will and even to infiltrate Saigon itself.

HOI AN

Vietnam

At the heart of Hoi An, a small coastal town, is an extraordinary architectural wealth that combines Japanese, Chinese, European and Vietnamese influences that go back to its heyday in the 16th century. Many Chinese and Japanese settled here and each community had its own laws and its own governor. By the mid-18th century the Shoguns in Japan forbade foreign travel, and as the Japanese presence dwindled, the Chinese community swelled with more and more immigrants. Prosperous Chinese merchants built elegant wooden houses, interspersed with assembly halls and temples for the different ethnic Chinese communities. Today the houses are often still lived in by the descendants of those original merchants, and are furnished with astonishing antiques and memorabilia. The Assembly Halls, in contrast to the houses, are a riot of colour, with glazed roof tiles shining green, red and gold and vividly painted and decorated exteriors sporting dragons and other mythical creatures.

The Japanese covered bridge is Hoi An's emblem and best-known monument. A small Taoist temple hangs over the water and nearby is a mysterious shrine placed within the roots of an ancient banyan tree. There are also fascinating Chinese family chapels to visit, where you can learn the history of individual families from 300 years ago to the present day.

WHY IS IT IMPORTANT?
The area is steeped in history and rich with different cultures.
WHAT IS THERE TO SEE?
Cham islands and the ruins of the sanctuary at My Son.

AUSTRALASIA & OCEANIA

ULURU

Australia

Uluru (Ayers Rock) is an enormous, monolithic rock that rises majestically from the plain around it. It is part of the Uluru-Kata Tjuta National Park, which also includes the Olgas. Uluru is formed from almost vertical layers of extremely hard sandstone, the surface layer of which has become red as the result of oxidation. On the northwest and southeast sides, erosion has cut into the rock forming channels down which water pours after storms, forming spectacular but short-lived waterfalls. Most people who visit Uluru try to climb up to the summit, although the Anangu would prefer it if they did not. Every year someone dies making the attempt, and many others have to be rescued. The 9-km (6-mile) walk around the rock is probably a better option.

WHAT IS IT?
A huge rock, steeped in Aboriginal belief.
WHAT IS THERE TO SEE?
Kata Tjuta, sunset and sunrise at Uluru, helicopter tours around the rock, King's Canyon.

ABORIGINAL ROOTS
Uluru and Kata-Tjuta belong to the Anangu Aboriginal people, who manage it in tandem with Parks Australia. It is deeply significant to the Anangu, firstly as a constant source of water and food in this inhospitable desert region, and secondly as a landmark along the Songlines of Anangu culture.

KAKADU

Australia

WHAT IT IS IT?
The largest national park in Australia.
YOU SHOULD KNOW:
The park is home to two different species of crocodile, and they have been known to kill the occasional careless tourist.

Kakadu National Park is an area of 20,000 sq km (7,720 sq miles) lying about 150km (90 miles) east of Darwin, and is the largest national park in Australia. It includes the whole of the South Alligator River, which is actually home to a large crocodile population, and various other habitats including heathland, eucalyptus woods and rainforest.

The park is home to a huge range of flora and fauna — more than 10,000 species of insects, 25 per cent of Australia's freshwater fish, kangaroos, wallabies, dingoes, water buffalo and many more. There are also about 5,000 sites of Aboriginal art, from many different eras. The town of Jabiru, on the eastern side, is near the Ranger uranium mine, and has a small airport from where it is possible to arrange scenic flights across the park in helicopters or light aircraft — an incredible experience.

NOOSA

Australia

Noosa sits within a beautiful headland with the mouth of the Noosa River west of the town, a stretch of beach to the east, and the small but charming Noosa National Park covering the headland itself. It has been popular with the surfing fraternity for about 40 years, ever since the big waves that crash into the headland first came to their notice. Today all kinds of watersports are pursued upon the river and its creeks as well, such as windsurfing, kayaking and jet-skiing. It is an ideal place for boating, or you can just take it easy and go fishing at the river mouth. The headland and cliffs in the national park rise to 200m (660ft) and overlook sheltered bays and offer splendid ocean views. You may see koalas clinging to the eucalyptus but the main focus of the park's diverse habitats is the 121 different species of bird that make their homes here.

CELEB HOTSPOT
Noosa is the most exclusive part of Queensland's Sunshine Coast and is home to many celebrities.

WHAT IS THERE TO DO? Spend a day hiking in the Noosa National Park.
WHAT IS THERE TO SEE? The Glasshouse Mountains and Eumundi's Saturday market.
IF YOU DARE: Learn to kite surf or sea kayak.

THE GREAT BARRIER REEF

Australia

WHAT IS IT?
The world's most extensive coral-reef system.
DON'T MISS:
Learning to scuba dive.
WHAT IS THERE TO DO?
Visit Lady Elliot and Lady Musgrave islands; the loggerhead turtle nesting site near Bundaberg.
YOU SHOULD KNOW:
There is a reef tax payable.

The Great Barrier Reef on Australia's northeastern continental shelf is a site of exceptional natural beauty stretching for 2,000km (1,250 miles) and covering an area of about 350,000 sq km (135,100 sq miles), making it larger than the whole of Italy. It is not only the largest UNESCO World Heritage Site onEarth, but it also contains the world's most extensive coral-reef system.

The reef runs mainly north to south, passing through a number of different climates, accounting for the thousands of different species of marine life that inhabit it. It is made up of 3,400 individual reefs, including nearly 800 fringing reefs, coral islands, continental islands covered in forest, sandbars, and mangrove systems linked by huge turquoise lagoons.

The whole reef is under threat from global warming, with increasing damage to the coral itself, but it is of vital importance to the world's ecosystem, containing as it does a third of the planet's soft-coral species, the largest existing green-turtle breeding site, 30 different species of mammal, including breeding humpback whales and a large dugong population, as well as sponges, molluscs, 1,500 types of reef fish and 200 species of birds. It also contains fascinating Aboriginal archeological sites and is probably the most spectacular marine wilderness on Earth.

THE WHITSUNDAY ISLANDS

Australia

The Whitsundays are the holiday destination of your dreams. Their great and simple attraction is their generally unspoiled tropical beauty – to visit them is to be greeted by an island paradise set in crystal-clear waters and fringed by magnificent reef formations. The islands – there are 74 in all – lie just off Queensland's coast and are perfectly situated for exploring one of the truly great marvels of nature, the Great Barrier Reef. There are plenty of day cruises from different places on the islands that take you to the best places on the reef for scuba diving and snorkelling. Whitsunday Island itself is a national park. Here, you will find great, white sandy beaches, secluded bays, often spectacular marine life in the warm tropical waters, dense, green pine forests and perhaps the occasional basic camp site.

DON'T MISS:
Whitehaven Beach.
WHEN SHOULD I GO?
Arrive between June and September for humpback whale watching.

ISLAND DEVELOPMENT

A few of the islands have in recent years been quite heavily developed to cater for tourism – the expensive resort on Hayman Island is reputed to have cost A$300 million (£110 million) to build and there are tall apartment blocks and gift shops on Hamilton Island. However, most of them are still completely unspoiled.

THE GREAT OCEAN ROAD

Australia

DID YOU KNOW?

The road was built as a memorial to the Australian soldiers who died in World War I.

WHAT IS THERE TO SEE?

The Twelve Apostles, Lake Corangamite and the Princess Margaret Rose Caves.

HOW DO I GET THERE?

Drive from Torquay to Warrnambool.

The Great Ocean Road stretches for 285km (177 miles) between Warrnambool and Torquay, excavated manually along the mountainous and heavily forested coastline. The road is often very narrow, with steep cliffs to one side, and constant switchback bends to negotiate. Fortunately there are plenty of spots where you can pull over to admire the fabulous views.

The road passes through some stunning scenery, running along the shore for the whole length of the Port Campbell National Park, a stretch otherwise known as the Shipwreck Coast, the forests of the Otway National Park and along the coastal edge of Angahook-Lorne state park, which is characterized by its immense blue eucalyptus.

The Shipwreck Coast is a spectacular stretch of rugged coastline upon which at least 80 ships have come to grief. The weather is often violently stormy here and the combination of huge ocean waves and high winds have formed dramatic rock formations such as the famous Twelve Apostles. These are vast, limestone stacks that were once part of the shoreline cliffs but that, over millennia, have been eroded and now stand alone looming upwards from the wild southern-ocean floor.

YARRA VALLEY

Australia

YOU SHOULD KNOW: Tastings can be arranged at some of the wineries by prior arrangement.

The Yarra Valley, a mere half an hour's drive northeast of Melbourne, is famous for its 30 or so small wineries, which are probably the best in Victoria. With the Dandenong Range to the east, the valley rolls out ahead, towards the Great Dividing Range. This is charming countryside dotted with eucalyptus forests and tree ferns, splendid old farms, little villages and lovely gardens. It is peaceful, pretty countryside, with ranks of vines loaded with fruit on every suitable hillside.

Many visitors come here to tour the valley and visit the wineries. The area has a growing reputation for its excellent restaurants, some of which are attached to the wineries themselves. Yering Station is on the site of the first vineyard in the area, which was planted as long ago as 1838. The restaurant here has glass walls that afford lovely views of the valley beyond. All of the wineries can be visited and tastings can be arranged, whether you have come independently or as part of a tour group.

Warburton, a pretty town on the Upper Yarra River, is at the start of the 80-km (53-mile) Upper Yarra Track. This follows an old vehicle trail all the way to the Baw Baw National Park, and can be walked either in sections or continuously as a five- or six-day trek.

MORNINGTON PENINSULA

Australia

WHAT IS IT KNOWN FOR?
You can swim with seals and dolphins from many of the beaches
YOU SHOULD KNOW:
You must book in advance to visit the national park as visotor numbers are strictly limited.

Melbourne is situated on Port Phillip Bay, which is almost completely enclosed within two peninsulas. Mornington Peninsula, to the east, has three distinct shorelines – each side of the peninsula faces a different bay, and at the end, the Mornington Peninsula National Park faces the open sea.

Point Nepean, at the tip of the peninsula, is one of several parks that together are known as Mornington Peninsula National Park. The environment here is fragile and visitor numbers limited. There are beautiful walks around the park, and Cape Schanck has fantastic views. There are beaches on all sides, and one of the peninsula's most popular attractions is swimming with seals and dolphins.

BYRON BAY

Australia

WHAT IS IT?
A beautiful stretch of beach and one of the top-ten surfing beaches in the world.
WHAT IS IT KNOWN FOR?
It is a laidback place, popular with those seeking an alternative lifestyle.

Byron Bay is a gorgeous 30-km (18.5-mile) stretch of sandy beaches with a small town of the same name at one end. Originally the town was best known for its abbatoir, and was, until the late 1960s, an ordinary working-class town. Then the area became popular with surfers because Lennox Head, which is just a short distance away, is one of the top-ten surfing beaches in the world. From May to July hundreds of professional surfers gather here to ride the big waves.

By the 1970s the hippies had arrived, and as time went on, their community grew and prospered. It is a perfect spot in which to live an alternative lifestyle, although these days Byron Bay has become very popular with both backpackers and more wealthy holiday-makers. The wide choice of accommodation reflects this, varying from campsites and hostels to the most luxurious upmarket resorts favoured by the rich and famous.

ROTTNEST ISLAND

Australia

Rottnest Island is situated in the Indian Ocean, 19km (12 miles) west of Fremantle, on the south-west coast of Australia, close to Perth. It is renowned for its superb diving and snorkelling, and is a perfect spot for a relaxing break. It is 11km (7 miles) long and 4.5km (2.8 miles) across at its widest, with one settlement at Thompson's Bay on the east side. During the 19th century the island became a barbarous penal colony for native Australians, but today its old colonial architecture, fabulous beaches and Mediterranean climate have made it a popular destination for western Australians. There are beautiful coves with small, sandy beaches and pristine, sparkling water with offshore reefs altogether superior to anything found on the nearby mainland coast.

MISTAKEN IDENTITY
The island was named by its discoverer, Willem de Vlamingh, who saw a quokka and believed it to be a rat.

YOU SHOULD KNOW: Private cars are not allowed on Rottnest, and the best way of exploring the island is by bicycle – you can ride right round it in less than three hours.

SYDNEY HARBOUR

Australia

Sydney Harbour is probably best seen first from the water. When those who have never visited Australia think of that country, the picture in their mind's eye is, more often than not, that iconic image of Sydney Harbour. Sydney is a beautiful city anyway, but its fabulous location lifts it to a position where it is a genuine contender for the title of the world's most beautiful city. Sydney is divided by Port Jackson, with the south and north shores linked by both the bridge and a tunnel. The busy waterfront of Circular Quay is packed with boats: harbour and river ferries, water taxis and cruisers all ply their trade from here, and many of Sydney's classic views can be seen from this spot. Pedestrians can walk the length of Harbour Bridge to enjoy marvellous views across the sparkling waters of the harbour itself.

WHAT IS THERE TO DO?
See the harbour from the water with a boat tour.
WHAT IS THERE TO SEE?
Darling Harbour, the Royal Botanic Gardens, the Museum of Contemporary Art, Manly.

THE OPERA HOUSE
Sydney Opera House took 16 years to complete and came in at ten times its original estimated cost, but it is now one of the world's most famous landmarks.

THE BLUE MOUNTAINS

Australia

DID YOU KNOW?
The Blue Mountains are so named because of the blue vapour that rises from the millions of eucalyptus trees growing there.

DON'T MISS:
Make sure you go up to Sublime Point Lookout for spectacular, panoramic views.
IF YOU DARE:
Abseil down the cliff faces in the Blue Mountain National Park.

The Great Dividing Range stretches right up the east of Australia, from Melbourne in the south to Cairns in the north. The area nearest to Sydney is known as the Blue Mountains. When Sydney was first colonized, it was thought that the Blue Mountains were impassable after several unsuccessful expeditions. In 1813 William Wentworth, Gregory Blaxland and William Lawson, who followed the ridges rather than the valleys, found their way across, thus enabling the western plains to be opened for settlement.

At the top of the range, at an altitude of over 1,000m (3,300ft), is an extraordinary plateau into which over the millennia rivers have carved deep valleys. The scenery is spectacular, cut by ravines and walled canyons, and by the early 20th century three mountain resorts had been established here. Today the villages and towns lie on a mountain ridge surrounded by the Blue Mountain National Park, a wonderful place for walking, climbing and abseiling. In 1994 a group of canyoners discovered a stand of 30-m (100-ft) high Wollemi pines, previously only known from fossil material. Designated a World Heritage site in 2000, the Blue Mountains are now protected, and abseiling on the Three Sisters — the mountains' most famous peaks, which had suffered marked erosion — has been banned.

WINEGLASS BAY

Australia

Wineglass Bay is situated on the rugged Freycinet Peninsula, part of the Freycinet National Park, on the east coast of Tasmania. The peninsula is made up of granite mountains that sweep down to sparkling, vivid-blue coves, the most beautiful of which is Wineglass Bay, so called because of its perfect shape. A stunning, white sandy beach fringes the bay, set off by strange rocks that appear orange thanks to the lichen that has colonized them.

The peninsula enjoys some of the most beautiful coastline in Tasmania and a pleasantly mild climate. Coles Bay, at the north of the park, is a deep inlet with an imposing backdrop of three pink-granite rocks, known as The Hazards, that rise straight from the sea to 300m (1,000ft) high. Coles Bay makes a good base for visiting the national park, although it is possible to stay within the park itself.

There are many walking trails to be explored but very little water, so you will need to carry plenty with you, and take advice as to the safety of drinking the water from streams. Walks start from the car park, and from there up to the lookout point over Wineglass Bay and down to the beach and back could take as long as five hours. Another, lovely, way of seeing the bay is to take an organized cruise or hire a boat from Coles Bay, and approach it from the sea.

DID YOU KNOW?
Walkers from all over the world come to hike the Overland Track.

WHAT IS IT?
Lake St Clare, situated at the foot of Cradle Mountain, is Australia's deepest freshwater lake.
WHAT IS THERE TO DO?
Spend a day rafting on the Franklin River.

CRADLE MOUNTAIN

Australia

Cradle Mountain stands brooding over the northern end of the Cradle Mountain-Lake St Clare National Park, which itself is part of the enormous wilderness that forms Tasmania's World Heritage Area. It is a craggy peak that was formed by glaciers and forms a stunning backdrop to the lovely Dove Lake that lies below it. There are many great walking opportunites in this area, ranging from easy, ten-minute strolls through rainforest or a three-hour walk around the shores of Lake Dove, to a hard, full-day's hike to the summit of the mountain. The most famous hike, the Overland Track, runs from Cradle Mountain to Lake St Clare, Australia's deepest freshwater lake, which lies at the southern end of the park. This is one of Australia's best-known bush trails, and it draws walkers from around the world.

BAY OF FIRES

Australia

Mount William National Park is in the northeast corner of Tasmania, and the Bay of Fires is the local name for the unparalleled coastline that is found here.

DID YOU KNOW?
The bay owes its striking appearance to granite boulders covered in bright orange lichen.

WHAT IS THERE TO DO?
If you are a keen fisherman, spend a day fishing for the Australian bass.
DON'T MISS:
Take a guided walking tour around the coastline

Mount William National Park was set aside as a wildlife refuge in order to protect the bountiful wildlife within – the birdlife is particularly rich, with raptors such as sea eagles, wedge-tailed eagles and peregrine falcons, all of which are able to find plentiful food in the area. Wallabies, wombats, echidnas, brush-tailed possums and Tasmanian devils are also to be seen, and this is the only area of Tasmania where forester kangaroos maintain a strong community. In spring the park is a mass of wildflowers that attract butterflies and other insects as well as numerous smaller birds – more than 100 different species of which occur in the park.

The shoreline is empty and beautiful. Secluded, white sandy beaches are tucked between sand dunes and granite outcrops, and from the ridgeline magnificent views of heathland, woods and coastline stretch out around you. Anson's Bay is one of the few places in Tasmania where the Australian bass may be caught, and there are also great opportunities for snorkelling and scuba diving.

SPIRITS BAY

New Zealand

Cape Reinga is at the northern tip of New Zealand's North Island, on the Aupuri Peninsula. A mere 500m (5,640ft) offshore, the seas are wild and dangerous where the warm South Pacific meets the Tasman Sea. A lighthouse stands at the point; painted white it flashes its warning light every 26 seconds. Staff at the small post office will stamp your cards with its own unique postmark, but other than that you are alone with Mother Nature. Spirits Bay, east of the Cape, is windswept and remote, with amazing pale-pink sand. In the Maori language *reinga* means 'place of leaping' and Maoris believe that at the moment of death, the soul journeys to Cape Reinga, where it climbs down the roots of an ancient Pohutakawa tree to plunge into Spirits Bay, the final leg of its journey to the spirit world. This is a sacred place and visitors are politely requested not to eat and to behave with respect during their visit to the site.

The best way of travelling to Cape Reinga is by specially designed bus. You can drive yourself in a 4x4 or even on a quad bike, but it is a really tricky journey. The problem is Ninety Mile Beach, south of the Cape. Although it is in fact only 88km (55 miles) long, you do actually drive along the beach, with the surf on one side and vast sand dunes on the other, negotiating the occasional patch of quicksand along the way. If you go by bus, you will probably get the opportunity to surf a sand dune as part of your excursion.

DID YOU KNOW?
The area is home to about a third of New Zealand's Maoris.

WHAT IS THERE TO SEE?
The Polynesian Pools, the Hakereteke Stream, Ohinemutu and Lake Okataina.
WHAT IS THERE TO DO?
Visit a restored Maori village dating back to the early twentieth century.

ROTORUA

New Zealand

Rotorua is at the southwest end of Lake Rotorua, on a volcanic plateau. The extraordinary amount of thermal activity in the area, with more than 1,200 geothermal features, has made it North Island's top tourist attraction, and the countryside around it is a mass of lakes, volcanos, dense pine and redwood forests, hot springs and geysers.

The most dramatic thermal scenery is found at the Whakarewarewa Thermal Reserve, a weird and wonderful nature park that looks as though it belongs on another planet altogether. Huge pools of mud bubble and gurgle, steam rises from cracks in the rocks and geysers erupt without warning. The most spectacular of these is the Pohutu geyser, which can blow as high as 30m (100ft).

BAY OF ISLANDS

New Zealand

TRAVELLERS' TIP:
Take the Cream Trip cruise, which delivers post and supplies to farmers in remote locations, taking you up and down little inlets and hidden bays for five hours of peaceful relaxation and gorgeous views in every direction.

The Bay of Islands is a maritime park that lies off the northeast coast of New Zealand's North Island, in a region known as Northland. Altogether there are some 150 islands of varying size dotted about the clear blue waters of the bay. The bay is one of the world's most popular areas for big-game fishing, and from December until June fishermen do their best to catch striped and blue marlin, yellowfin tuna, broadbill and sharks.

For those who prefer to look at wildlife but not hunt it, there are wonderful opportunities to go dolphin- and whale-watching. One of the best-known companies offering trips is so confident that it volunteers an extra trip for free if you have the bad luck not to see a dolphin or whale the first time round. You can even swim with the dolphins, which is the experience of a lifetime.

BLENHEIM

New Zealand

Nelson and Blenheim are towns in the north of the South Island of New Zealand, in what is known as the Marlborough area. Nelson lies in a fertile area, on the coast of the Tasman Bay, and it is a really attractive town with old-fashioned, colonial-style wooden buildings and a laid-back, arty atmosphere. Blenheim is the largest town in the region, and is almost entirely devoted to the wine industry.

The climate in this region is almost Mediterranean in summer, and not only does Nelson have great beaches nearby, but it is surrounded by orchard-filled valleys and vineyards. Altogether there are more than 4,000 hectares (10,000 acres) given over to vines, and over 40 wineries, many of which welcome visitors.

BEST WEATHER

This part of the island is the sunniest place in New Zealand.

TRAVELLERS' TIP: Merlot, Cabernet Sauvignon, Chardonnay, Pinot Noir and Riesling are among the grape varieties that thrive here, and the best way to try them out is to organize your own wine tour if you can. Organized tours are easy to find, but tend to take you to too many places to really be able to enjoy any of them.

MILFORD SOUND

New Zealand

WHERE IS IT?
In Fiordland on the isolated west coast of lower South Island.
WHAT IS IT KNOWN FOR?
The Milford Track is known as one of the most beautiful walks in the world.
WHAT IS THERE TO SEE?
Bowen and Sutherland falls, Cleddau Canyon, Milford Sound Underwater Observatory, Te Anau Wildlife Park.

WHAT'S IN A NAME
The sound got its name from John Grono, a sealing captain who discovered it in 1822 and named it after his birthplace, Milford Haven in Wales.

Milford Sound is in Fiordland, on the isolated west coast of lower South Island. It is the best known of the fiords and sounds that were gouged out of the coast by glaciers some 15,000–20,000 years ago, and it is the only one that is accessible by road. This vast and glorious wilderness of forests and mountains, lakes and waterfalls contains some of the best of New Zealand's hiking trails.

The far end of the sound is dominated by the 1,412-m (4,633-ft) Mitre Peak, but it is the combination of the constantly changing light, clouds, sunshine, pouring rain and rainbows that make it such a dramatically beautiful place. Captain Cook famously passed the entrance to Milford Sound twice, in 1770 and 1773, without discovering the entrance, which was hidden in mist on both occasions.

The Milford Track is a four-day hike from Lake Te Anau across the Mackinnon Pass to Milford Sound. It is renowned amongst hikers as one of the most beautiful walks in the world, taking in rapids, mountain passes, alpine fields, rainforest and the Sutherland Falls, one of the world's highest. Fiordland has a huge amount of rain – 7,600mm (300in) per year and the forest reflects this – giant trees wreathed in moss and vines, lichen and ferns, and all dripping with water. If walking doesn't appeal, take a cruise to the mouth of the sound – you will see Sinbad Gully, a classic glacial valley that is the last refuge of the endangered kakapo, as well as seals and dolphins and even penguins if you are there in the autumn.

QUEENSTOWN

New Zealand

WORTH A SPLURGE:
Take a guided helicopter tour for superb views of the mountains.

Queenstown is a beautifully situated resort town on the shores of Lake Wakatipu. A backdrop of mountains, the Southern Alps and the Remarkables, stretch away into the distance, with their snow-covered peaks reflected in the calm, blue waters of the lake. The town is perfectly positioned for all sorts of outdoor activities, at all times of year. In winter, many people come to ski here – there are slopes within half an hour's drive for skiers of every level of ability, as well as cross-country skiing and, in good weather, guided tours by helicopter or ski plane can be arranged to take you to remote peaks that are otherwise inaccessible.

In summer you can try white-water rafting, trekking or horse-riding, fishing, scenic helicopter rides, and cruises around the lake. Jet-boat riding is a New Zealand invention, and is not for the fainthearted. The specially-built boats are powered by gas turbine – water is pumped out through a nozzle at high speed and the boat, which can reach 70kph (44mph), skims over the surface of the water as it whizzes through mountain canyons, spinning round in a terrifying fashion. Queenstown is also the home of bungee jumping. The first commercial bungee operation was set up here by A.J. Hackett in 1988. Kawarau Suspension Bridge was the original site, but today there are four others to choose from.

DID YOU KNOW?
This group of 15 islands are named after Captain Cook who landed there in the 1770s.

AITUTAKI

Cook Islands

DON'T MISS:
A lagoon cruise to the islets of Akaiami and Tapuatae, *ika mata* – marinated raw fish with coconut sauce. Aitutaki's dancers, who are famous throughout the Cook Islands.

The 15 Cook Islands are scattered over 1,830,000 sq km (706,380 sq miles) of the South Pacific, yet have a total land area of only 240 sq km (93 sq miles). Aitutaki is a coral atoll with low-rolling hills, banana plantations and coconut groves. Along with the small, uninhabited islets to the south and east, Aitutaki is surrounded by a barrier reef, thus creating the spectacular turquoise lagoon that makes it such a perfect place for swimming, snorkelling and scuba diving. Although it is the second-most visited of the Cook Islands and tourism has now become the main source of income, Aitutaki is still very unspoiled. The palm-fringed, white sandy beaches and the magnificent clear sea, coupled with the wonderfully relaxed pace of life on Aitutaki, contribute to making this remote island the stuff of which dreams are made.

THE MARQUESA ISLANDS

French Polynesia

DID YOU KNOW?

Paul Gauguin, the French impressionist painter came to live here in 1901 and his final resting place is on Hiva Oa.

HOW DO I GET THERE?

Either fly from Papeete or Rangiroa to Nuku Hiva, the largest island, or take one of the cruise ships or freighters that sail monthly from Papeete, calling at all six of the inhabited Marquesas.

The 7,500 inhabitants of the Marquesa Islands could reasonably lay claim to living in the remotest place in the world. Farther from a continental landfall than any other group of islands on Earth, the Marquesas poke out of the open Pacific just south of the equator and about 1,400km (870 miles) northeast of Tahiti. Unlike many of the islands in the South Pacific, the Marquesas are, because of their remoteness, almost entirely unspoiled. They are wild and rugged islands with steep cliffs and valleys leading up to high central ridges. Brooding volcanic pinnacles pierce the landscape, while the lush vegetation is overflowing with bougainvillea, orchids, spider lilies, ginger and jasmine, as well as all manner of fruit from grapefruits and bananas to mangos and papayas.

Of the 12 Marquesa Islands, known in the local Polynesian language as 'Land of the Men', only six are inhabited, with most of the population living in the narrow fertile valleys, leaving the interiors to the hundreds of wild horses, cattle and goats. The birdlife is extraordinarily rich and varied and the waters around the islands are teeming with fish and lobsters. The size and quality of the ocean waves as they reach many of the beaches of the Marquesas make the islands a hotspot for surfers.

RANGIROA

French Polynesia

WHAT IS THERE TO DO?
Explore some of the world's
best diving sites.
WHAT IS THERE TO SEE?
The bird sanctuary on Motu
Paio or one of the many
working pearl farms.
DON'T MISS:
Take a lagoon cruise in a
glass-bottomed boat.
HOW DO I GET THERE?
Fly from Tahiti or Bora Bora.

About 200km (120 miles) north of Tahiti, Rangiroa is the most populous of the Tuamotu Islands, an archipelago of 78 low islands or coral atolls spread over several hundred kilometres of the eastern Pacific. It is the largest atoll in Polynesia and the second largest in the world. With some 220 *motus*, or islets, none more than a metre in elevation, separated by over 100 small channels, Rangiroa's lagoon is about 80x25km (50x16 miles), giving an area of more than 1,000 sq km (nearly 400 sq miles) of magnificently clear water. The incomparable brilliance and colours of the lagoon, from jade-green to purple, completely overwhelm the first-time visitor to Rangi, as everyone calls it.

The marine life in the lagoon is truly astonishing – there are thousands of colourful fish of all shapes and sizes, together with several varieties of mostly harmless reef sharks. Rangiroa lagoon is world famous for its unsurpassed snorkelling and scuba diving. Outside the reefs is a breathtaking array of large species along the walls of the drop-offs, including squadrons of eagle rays and schools of sharks, barracuda and tuna.

Surrounded by two legendary bodies of water, Moana-tea ('Peaceful Ocean') and Moana-uri ('Wild Ocean'), the main villages of Avatoru and Tiputa offer the visitor a unique look at the South-Pacific lifestyle of the residents. Along the few roads, coral churches, craft centres, local restaurants and tiny shops provide enjoyable, land-based experiences to complement the many activities awaiting the visitor in the lagoon. Rangiroa offers the visitor sunshine, white coral beaches and an immense playground for watersports and activities.

EUROPE & THE MIDDLE EAST

THE SPANISH RIDING SCHOOL

Austria

The Spanish Riding School (the *Spanische Hofreitschule*), is a unique institution in central Vienna. It is the oldest riding school in the world and the last to train the horses and their riders in classic dressage routines.

YOU SHOULD KNOW:
You need to book
well in advance to see
performances.

Originally the school was based at the Imperial Palace, but Emperor Charles VI commissioned a Baroque Riding Hall to teach aristocratic youths riding skills. Completed in 1735, the hall looks more like a ballroom, complete with balconies and chandeliers. Performances here are booked out well in advance, but if you can't get tickets, you could instead see the morning training session, also set to music, or take a tour of the stables.

The riders all wear the traditional two-cornered hats and brown frock coats, and the horses all have gold-and-red saddlecloths. The performances include individual and two-horse displays, as well as the Grand Quadrille which consists of 16 horses in formation, performing something approaching a ballet, set to classical music.

WHAT IS IT KNOWN FOR?
Salzburg is the birthplace of Mozart.
WHAT IS THERE TO DO?
Take a horse-drawn carriage around the city and enjoy the sites.
WHAT IS THERE TO SEE?
The Mozart museums; the Residenz; Schloss Hellbrunn; St Peter's Abbey Church (Stiftkirche St Peter).

SALZBURG

Austria

The old city of Salzburg is in a beautiful location between the Salzach River and the Mönchsberg, overlooked by the Hohensalzburg Fortress.

Salzburg is famous as the birthplace of Mozart and although the city was not generous towards him during his lifetime, it does its level best to make the most of him now. Everywhere you go Mozart's music is being played, and there are two Mozart museums and even chocolate balls called *Mozart Kugeln*.

The Hohensalzburg Fortress was built for the prince-archbishops and although it is interesting to see the lavish lifestyle that they led, one of the main reasons to come here is for truly astonishing views over the Alps and the city.

Right: The cityscape of Salzburg

GRAZ

Austria

Graz is a delightfully relaxed city situated in southeastern Austria. It is set around the banks of the Mur River, and the old town centre with its red roofs is dominated by the Schlossberg, the hill that rises above it. This UNESCO World Heritage Site is a picturesque place, full of cultural interest and wonderful architecture from Baroque palaces to innovative modern constructions.

WHAT IS THERE TO SEE?
The Carillon (Glockenspiel);
the Clock tower (Uhrturm);
the Stadtpfarrkirche, a
Baroque parish church.
WHAT IS THERE TO DO?
A trip to the Murinsel
(Mur Island).

The Landesmuseum Joanneum is a vast natural history museum, but perhaps a more obviously Austrian museum is the Landeszeughaus with its amazing collection of more than 30,000 items of armour and weapons largely from the 17th century. Graz is full of museums but it is far from being a museum piece of a city – it has three universities, and a vibrant atmosphere.

The architecture is the main attraction for visitors. Among the highlights is the Landhaus's fabulous Italian Renaissance courtyard, with triple-tiered arcades. The Schloss Eggenberg, a Baroque palace built in the 17th century, has an extraordinary interior dedicated to astronomical and mythological themes, as in the memorable Planet Hall. There is also a fine cathedral, the Domkirche.

WHAT IS IT KNOWN FOR?
Being a nurturing place for
classical music in the
18th century.
WHAT IS IT?
One of the most culturally
important cities in Europe.
WHAT IS THERE TO SEE?
Kunsthistorisches Museum,
Schloss Belvedere, Palais
Liechtenstein, Karlskirche...
You would need days to
really see all the marvels this
great city has to offer.

VIENNA

Austria

The magical city of Vienna stands on the Danube River, with wooded hills to the north and west. The Danube runs through two man-made channels, built to prevent flooding, which have created a narrow island in the middle. The city is elegant and cultured, and is famous for its art and music. The old city centre is a UNESCO World Heritage Site.

The most recognizable landmark in Vienna is the slim, graceful spire of St Stephen's Cathedral (Stephansdom). Built on the site of an earlier church, some of which is incorporated into the present one, it is a 14th-century Gothic masterpiece with a gleaming tiled roof sporting the symbolic Austrian eagle. Inside and out are wonderful sculptures, and the pulpit and the altar are particularly fine.

Right: Karlskirche, Vienna

ALPBACH

Austria

Alpbach is a perfect example of a gorgeous Tyrolean village. In the summer it is a splendid place for hiking and in winter, for skiing and snowboarding.

The village is small enough to have a relaxed, intimate atmosphere, and although the pubs and bars stay open late, it all feels very laid back.
Now just 45 minutes from Innsbruck, Alpbach is popular with visitors both for its scenery and the first-class recreation it affords. It offers skiing for people at every level, from complete beginners to the black runs on the Wiedersbergerhorn.
The nearby Vorder-Unterberg Farm, which was built in the 17th century and lived in until 1952, is now a museum giving a fascinating glimpse into the traditional way of life of the region's mountain farmers.

DON'T MISS:
Hiking around the Galtenberg mountain and in the area of Inneralpbach; climbing the Gratlspitz ridge; the Golden Roof in the Old Town in Innsbruck.

TRADITIONAL ARCHITECTURE
High up in a valley, the village was isolated and little visited until the road was built in 1926. Because of this relative lack of contact with the outside world, the locals retained their traditional, distinctive style of building wooden chalets with sloping roofs and balconies.

BRUGES

Belgium

DID YOU KNOW?
Bruges is known as 'The Venice of the North'.

DON'T MISS:
The Groeninge museum, the Memling Museum, the Church of Our Lady, the Beguinage (the Market Place).

WHAT IS IT KNOWN FOR?
Moules and chocolate are specialities of the area.

Bruges is one of the most beautiful medieval cities in Europe. Often referred to as the 'Venice of the North', it is criss-crossed by canals, the main ring of which encloses the historic centre. It is a wonderful city with cobbled streets and lovely gabled houses that cast their reflections onto the water.

There is much fine art and architecture to see in Bruges. The Church of Our Lady (Onze Lieve Vrouwekerk) boasts the highest brick spire in Europe and contains a sculpture of the Madonna by Michelangelo. The Basilica of the Holy Blood (Heilig Bloed Basiliek) is another famous church that displays a phial said to contain the blood of Christ. The Groeninge Museum contains paintings from six centuries, including works by Hans Memling and Jan Van Eyck, who lived and worked here.

If you tire of cultural sightseeing, take a trip on a canal or just sit in a pretty, peaceful spot and try one of the 350 or more beers.

KAREN BLIXEN MUSEUM

Denmark

Karen Blixen was a Danish writer who became known throughout the world as Isak Dinesen, the author of the bestselling novel *Out of Africa*. Her family home, situated less than half an hour's drive north of Copenhagen, became a museum after her death here in 1962. She is buried in the grounds

WHAT IS IT?
The musuem and former home of Denmark's first lady of literature.

The living rooms are almost exactly as they were while the author was still alive. Some of the furniture was brought back from Kenya, including the favourite chair of her lover, Dennis Finch Hatton. One room is now a gallery displaying some of her art (she studied at Copenhagen's Academy of Art in her youth), including portraits that she painted while in Africa. Two others are devoted to Blixen's personal library. Poems, drawings, letters and manuscripts are also on display.

In 2004, two more rooms were opened, one of which is dedicated to the birds she loved so much. Behind the house are 5.7 hectares (14 acres) of garden, meadow and a grove of beech trees, which she made a bird sanctuary in the 1950s. Some 40 different species of bird breed here, in an area supervised by the Danish Ornithological Society.

YOU SHOULD KNOW:
There is an open-air stage with daily shows and an internationally renowned concert hall. At night, the park is lit with thousands of coloured lights that reflect off every surface. The lake in particular looks wonderful, especially when there are firework displays. These take place every weekend in summer. The gardens are very popular with children, for whom there are all sorts of traditional fairground amusements.

TIVOLI GARDENS

Denmark

The Tivoli Gardens, in Copenhagen, are one of the city's best known and loved attractions. It is situated on what was once part of the fortifications that surrounded Copenhagen. In 1841 King Christian VIII was persuaded to allow the establishment of an amusement park here in order to 'provide the masses with suitable entertainment and fun', and Tivoli has been doing just that ever since. The gardens receive some five million visitors a year, more than any other tourist attraction in the country. They are popular with young and old alike and open until midnight all week and 1am at weekends. The gardens are planted with thousands of brightly flowering summer bedding plants, and people stroll along paths beneath old, shady trees, before heading to one of the many cafés or restaurants in the park, some of which are among the most stylish in the city.

TALLINN
Estonia

DON'T MISS:
The Town Hall, St Olaf's Church (Oleviste kirik), Kiek in de Kok tower, Kadriorg and the National Art Museum (Kunstimuuseum, known as KUMU), the Estonian islands of Saaremaa, Muhu and Hiiuma.

Estonia has been invaded time and again in its long history, most recently by Soviet Russia, but fortunately the medieval centre retains its charm. Declared a UNESCO World Heritage Site in 1997, today the historic centre of Tallinn is a popular tourist destination.

The best way to enter Toompea (the Old Town) is through the Pikk Jalg gate tower, built in 1380. You will soon reach Castle Square (Lossi plats), which is dominated by Alexander Nevsky Cathedral, its distinctive onion domes denoting its Russian Orthodoxy. The lower town is a mass of winding, cobbled streets and arches, and story-book, pastel-coloured houses. Town Hall Square (Raekoja plats) contains merchants' houses dating from the 15th century, and some splendid guildhalls such as the Great Guild, now housing part of the State History Museum (Eesti Ajaloomuuseum).

THE FINNISH ARCHIPELAGO
Finland

The greatest treasure of the Finnish landscape is its archipelagos, particularly the southwestern archipelago with more than 20,000 islands and skerries. It is a unique maritime landscape that captures the imagination of everyone who sees it. Turku is Finland's oldest city, largest port, and its former capital. This is a good base for visiting the islands, particularly by bicycle, as there is a fantastic system of free ferry services that cross back and forth all the time between islands. The biodiversity here is exceptional, and you can see wonderful seabirds, elks and seals as you soak up the tranquil, rural charm of the inner islands, the huge lighthouses of Bengtskar, Isokari and Uto and the astounding beauty of the seascapes.

DID YOU KNOW?
The area is a UNESCO Sea Biosphere Reserve.

WHAT IS IT? A collection of over 20,000 islands and skerries.
DON'T MISS: The Blue Mussel Visitor Centre at Kasnas, the harbour village of Naantali and the town of Kotka, Helsinki.
WHEN SHOULD I GO? The best time is from May to September.

MONT-ST-MICHEL

France

The view of Mont-St-Michel rising from the rippling sands that surround it is one of the iconic images of France, but no matter how often you have seen pictures of it, your first sight of the real thing is quite spectacular. The 80-m (260-ft) high granite rock rising from the bay has a long religious history. Legend has it that the Archangel Michael appeared to the Bishop of Avranches (later St Aubert) and told him to build a chapel here. A settlement grew up around the base of the mount and it became a place of pilgrimage. In 966 the Duke of Normandy replaced the chapel with a Benedictine Abbey but in 1203 it was burned down by Philippe-Auguste's troops. He made reparation for this by building the great Gothic abbey that we see today, although the fortifications were added by Charles VI. After a period of decline, Napoleon made the abbey a prison. In 1874, it was declared a national monument and restoration work began.

Mont-St-Michel is separated from the mainland by 1km (0.6 miles) of water that becomes a floor of shifting sand and mud at low tide. The causeway was built in 1879 – before that pilgrims had to brave the tides that could sweep in and drown them.

WHAT IS IT?
A chapel built on an 80-m (260-ft) high granite rock, cut off from the mainland by 1km (0.6 miles).
WHAT IS THERE TO SEE?
La Merveille; walk around the base of the mount.

ÉTRETAT

France

WHAT IS THERE TO DO?
Climb to the top of the Falaise d'Aval for a view of the rock formations.
DON'T MISS:
Palais Benedictine in Fécamp; Honfleur; Trouville-sur-Mer and Deauville.

Étretat is a large village situated on what is known as the 'Alabaster Coast', west of Dieppe and north of Le Havre, in Normandy. Its high, white cliffs, the Falaises d'Étretat, are as well known to the French as the White Cliffs of Dover are to the British.

Étretat has been a draw for artists and writers since the 19th century. Victor Hugo loved it here and Guy de Maupassant lived here. Courbet, Degas and Matisse all came here to paint, but it was Alphonse Carr, the editor of Le Figaro, who made it fashionable with Parisians. Today, it is still a popular little resort in summer, but in winter it reverts to being the quiet and beautiful place it has always been, with the sweeping promenade and shingle beach empty but for the odd solitary walker.

WHEN SHOULD I GO?
May and June are the months when the wisteria is in flower above the Japanese bridge, but the garden is magical whenever you go. The lily pond looks its best in late July and early August when the lilies are in bloom.

MONET'S GARDEN

France

The Impressionist painter, Claude Monet, lived at Giverny for 43 years, from 1883. He first saw it from the window of a train, and fell in love. Though the world may consider Monet to be the grand master of Impressionism, he thought these beautifully crafted gardens that run down to the Epte River were his true masterpiece.

Gravel paths lead from one part of the garden to the next. At every turn a slightly different view is offered, and the light changes, too, not only because of the weather and the passage of the sun but also according to the position of the weeping willows and rhododendrons. This changing light was what entranced Monet, who painted his gardens over and over again. The gardens now contain more than 100,000 perennials and almost as many annuals are planted every year, providing a profusion of flowers, scents and butterflies.

CHARTRES CATHEDRAL

France

The market town of Chartres lies about 96km (60 miles) south-west of Paris and it has been famous throughout the Christian world for centuries, thanks to its magnificent cathedral.

In 875, Charles II presented the *Sancta Camisia* to Chartres. This was the garment supposedly worn by the Virgin Mary when she gave birth to Christ, and its presence led to an immediate influx of pilgrims. In 1194 the existing church burnt down, but the relic, seemingly miraculously, was untouched. Funds flooded in to enable a new church to be built, and by 1260, the new, glorious Chartres Cathedral (Cathédrale Notre-Dame de Chartres) had risen from the ashes. It was recognized as a UNESCO World Heritage Site in 1979.

HIDDEN GEMS
During both world wars, the thousands of panes from the 172 stunning stained-glass windows were carefully taken apart and hidden in the Dordogne for safekeeping.

WHAT IS IT KNOWN FOR? The exquisite stained glass has made the cathedral famous.
DON'T MISS: The view from the tower; Jehan-de-Beauce; the Musée des Beaux-Arts.
YOU SHOULD KNOW: There are entrance fees payable for the crypt and treasury, and climbing the tower.

PLACE DES VOSGES

France

The Place des Vosges is a beautifully proportioned, elegant square, situated in the Marais area of Paris. It is the oldest square in Paris, and the first example of planned development in the city. In 1559 Henri II was killed during a jousting tournament near the Hotel des Tournelles, which stood on what is now the north side of the square. His widow, Catherine de Medici, had the palace demolished, and the huge space became a horse market. In 1605, Henri IV commissioned the square to be built in honour of Louis XIII's marriage and 36 rose-pink brick-and-stone arcaded mansions were built, all surrounding a central square. The houses were built to a specific design – the height and width of the façades are the same, and the roofs are half the height of the façades. Henri IV named it the Place Royal, and it soon became the home of many aristocratic families. In 1800 it was renamed the Place des Vosges, when the administrative department of the same name became the first in the country to pay its taxes to Napoleon. The Marais went into decline for a long period during the 19th and early 20th centuries, but today it is as fashionable as ever, and the Place des Vosges is full of chic shops and interesting restaurants. Many famous people have lived here: Cardinal Richelieu, Blaise Pascal and Madame de Sevigné to name but a few. One of its best-known inhabitants, however, was Victor Hugo, who lived on the second floor of number six, and wrote much of *Les Misérables* there. His home is now a museum, and is the only one of these lovely houses that is open to the public.

WHAT IS IT?
The Louvre is the world's largest museum and was, at one time, the world's largest palace.
WHAT IS IT KNOWN FOR?
The Louvre is home to the *Mona Lisa*.

THE LOUVRE

France

The Louvre is the world's largest museum, a classically grand building that stretches for about 1km (0.6 miles) between the Seine and the rue de Rivoli in Paris. At one time, it was the world's largest palace. Its life as a museum began less than a month after the execution of Marie Antoinette, when the leaders of the Revolution decided that the public should be able to enjoy the royal art collection.

The museum houses some 400,000 items, of which 35,000 are on display. The collections are divided into eight sections: Oriental antiquities, Egyptian antiquities, Greek, Etruscan and Roman antiquities, Islamic art, sculpture, paintings, *objets d'art* and graphic arts. The Denon wing is the most visited area of the museum, housing a wonderful collection of Italian masterpieces and the *Mona Lisa*.

NOTRE-DAME
France

Notre-Dame is a Gothic masterpiece on the Île de la Cité in the Seine, Paris. The site on which it stands has been a place of worship since Roman times, when a temple to Jupiter was built here. The glory of the cathedral is its façade, with its lovely rose window and gallery above, and the flying buttresses to the side, holding up the choir. There are three magnificent entrances: to the left is the Portal of the Virgin, with signs of the zodiac and the coronation of the Virgin Mary; to the right is the Portal of St Anne, which features the Virgin and Child – possibly the cathedral's finest piece of sculpture; and the central Portal depicts the Last Judgement.

In the 1820s the cathedral went through some major restoration, partly through the popularity of Victor Hugo's *The Hunchback of Notre-Dame* and partly through a 19th-century revival of interest in Gothic architecture. The architect, Viollet-le-Duc, added the steeple and the gargoyles, which you can get a good look at if you can face walking up the 387 steps of the tower.

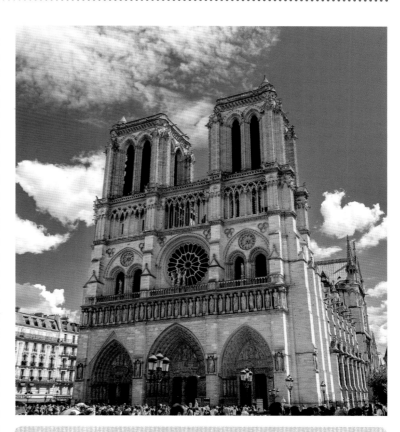

WHERE IS IT?
On the Île de la Cité in Paris.
WHAT IS IT KNOWN FOR?
Victor Hugo's *The Hunchback of Notre-Dame* made this one of the most famous cathedrals in the world.
WHAT IS THERE TO SEE?
Crypte Archaeologique; Kilometre zero.

SAINTE-CHAPELLE

France

The Sainte-Chapelle is a tiny, exquisite chapel situated on the Île de la Cité, east of the Pont Neuf in Paris. Originally it was part of the old royal palace, which was used by French kings until 1358, when they moved into the Louvre for safety. It is the only part of the palace that remains, but its graceful 74-m (243-ft) spire soars above the massive façade of the neighbouring Palais de Justice, which might otherwise render it almost invisible.

The chapel is built on two levels. The lower level was for the palace servants, whilst the courtiers and royalty used the upper level, which is reached by a spiral staircase. This upper chapel is one of the finest examples of High Gothic architecture in existence, and it is renowned for the dazzling stained-glass windows that make up virtually all of the walls. The windows tell the story of the Bible from Genesis to the Apocalypse. They are supported by clusters of delicate columns, whose fragile appearance belies their great strength. When the sun streams through the gorgeous red-and-blue glass you see precisely why the Sainte-Chapelle is described as a 'jewel box'.

WHAT IS IT?
A fine example of High Gothic architecture.
WHEN SHOULD I GO?
Arrive in summertime and enjoy the concerts in the chapel.

FONTAINEBLEAU

France

The Château de Fontainebleau stands in the midst of a forest, about 55km (35 miles) south of Paris. It began life as a hunting lodge during the 12th century, but it was not until the 16th century that Francois I was inspired to turn it into a palace, and commissioned several well-known Italian artists, including Francesco Primaticcio, Benvenuto Cellini and Rosso Fiorentino, to adorn the interior. Fontainebleau remained a popular getaway for royal hunting trips until Louis IV became obsessed with the palace at Versailles, and it was in fact Napoleon Bonaparte who brought it back to its former glory. Both his *Petits Appartements* and the Musée Napoleon provide a fascinating glimpse of his life here. It was here, too, on the 17th-century exterior, horseshoe-shaped staircase that Napoleon, having abdicated, said farewell to his army and was then removed to Elba.

WHAT IS THERE TO SEE?
The Louis XV staircase; the Cour Oval.
YOU SHOULD KNOW:
The palace is closed Tuesdays.
HOW DO I GET THERE?
Travel by car, train or bus from the Gare de Lyon.

THE LOIRE AND ITS CHÂTEAUX

France

There is a wealth of history, art and architecture to be found in the Loire and it is also famous for its food and wines – Sancerre and Muscadet, Chinon and Bourgeuil to mention but a few. This is a wonderful place to explore and enjoy.

It is an immensely fertile area, which – along with the easy transport provided by the river – made it highly desirable to wealthy lords and royalty, so the string of fabulous châteaux that can be seen today were built. There are so many of these gems that you could spend weeks trying to visit them all. This is no doubt why UNESCO designated the whole area a World Heritage Site instead of attempting to pick out individual châteaux for that distinction.

Chenonceaux, built in 1520 by a tax collector for his wife, is often thought to be the most romantic of castles. Its design was always controlled by the women who lived here, including Diane de Poitiers and Catherine de Medici. Azay-le-Rideau is a classic fairy-tale palace with its white walls and early-Renaissance style. It stands in lovely gardens on its own little island in the Indre River. The château at Villandry is renowned for its ornamental 'garden of love' and its wonderful kitchen garden. Fontevraud Abbey, which contains the tombs of the Plantagenets, is a superb complex of Romanesque buildings and the largest abbey in France.

DID YOU KNOW?
The Loire Valley is often referred to as 'the Garden of France'.

WHAT IS IT KNOWN FOR?
Vineyards producing famous wines such as Sancerre and Muscadet.
DON'T MISS:
The Angers Tapestry, the Châteaux de Chambord, Chinon and Blois.

BELLE-ILE-EN-MER

France

Belle-Ile-en-Mer lies in the Atlantic Ocean, off the tip of the narrow Quiberon peninsula in southwestern Brittany. It is the largest of Brittany's islands at 18km (11 miles) long, and true to its name, it is indeed beautiful. The sheltered, eastern coast of the island is carved with deep estuaries, and there are a number of small fishing villages surrounded by fertile, cultivated land. The island is hilly, and the northwestern coast, the Côte Sauvage, is a place of high cliffs, lashed by fierce seas.

WHAT IS IT?
The largest of
Brittany's islands.
HOW DO I GET THERE?
Travel by ferry from Quiberon.

The island is a lovely, peaceful place on which to spend a holiday. There are 90 beaches to explore – Donnant beach on the western shore is probably the most popular, and south east of Le Palais you will find the white sands of Grands Sables, which is the longest on the island. Sauzon is a picturesque fishing village running down one side of an estuary to the west of Le Palais, with picture-postcard houses looking at the rocky cliffs opposite. There are several major rock formations in the north of the island – Monet even painted one.

THE MARAIS POITEVIN

France

YOU SHOULD KNOW:
Niort is a small city about 50km (30 miles) south-west of Poitiers and is a good base from which to explore the Marais Poitevin. It has several medieval buildings including the old town hall, a castle keep built by Henry II of England, and a fine 15th-century church, the Église Notre-Dame.

Between La Rochelle and Poitiers, in the Poitou-Charentes region, is an area known as the Marais Poitevin. This is a strange and beautiful region of natural marshland, criss-crossed by lazy rivers, streams, canals and dykes. Designated a regional park, it is often called *La Venise Verte* – the Green Venice. This is an apt name as many of the farmers here have to travel by boat, as they have no access to their fields by road. This is a lovely, timeless and tranquil place to visit. You can walk along the footpaths or take bikes, but probably the best way to see it is by boat. Weeping willows overhang the water forming green tunnels over the canals, which are themselves at times so covered in weed that they look like solid paths. Water-loving plants – irises, marsh marigolds and rushes – abound and everywhere you hear the sound of birdsong and very little else to disturb the peace.

GORGES DU TARN

France

WHAT IS IT?
One of France's most beautiful gorges.
WHAT IS THERE TO DO?
Take a trip in a glass-bottomed boat from La Malène.

The River Tarn is 375km (233 miles) long and flows from Mount Lozère to Moissac, where it enters the Garonne at the southern end of the Massif Central. The precipitous gorge, carved out of the limestone rocks of the Grands Causses, is one of the most beautiful in France. Its steep sides are swathed in pine forest, and extraordinary karst formations can be found here.

At Le Rozier, a pretty little village, the Tarn is joined by another river, the Jonte, and this is the beginning of probably the most appealing section of the gorge, a 60-km (37-mile) stretch that ends at Florac. Follow the road from here to the cliff-top at Point Sublime for some of the best views of stark rock faces and dramatic cliffs. The imposing 15th-century Château de la Caze stands close to the Cirque du Pougnadoires, a large, natural amphitheatre that, during the summer months, is the site of a fabulous *son-et-lumière* spectacle.

THE AVEN-ARMAND CAVE

France

The entrance to the amazing cavern of Aven-Armand was discovered by Louis Armand in December 1897. Situated on the Causse Méjean, a limestone plateau close to the small village of Lozère, it is possibly the most beautiful cave in the country. The cave is vast, 110m (360 ft) long by 60m (200 ft) wide and 45m (150 ft) high – large enough to house Paris's Notre-Dame comfortably. The Virgin Forest, as it is known, is a forest of stalagmites, more than 400 of which are more than 1m (39in) high. Many reach 15 to 20m (66ft), and the most famous of them all, the world's tallest stalagmite, tops 30m (100ft) in height. Walking through the Aven-Armand makes you feel you have been transported to some Tolkienesque wonderland.

DARING DESCENT
After its discovery in 1897, for 30 years the only way to see the cave was by climbing down a rope ladder or by being winched down in a bucket.

WHAT IS IT? A vast cavern that houses the world's tallest stalagmite.
WHAT ELSE IS THERE TO SEE? The Dargilan grotto; Montpellier-le-Vieux.
YOU SHOULD KNOW: The cave is closed in December.

LES GORGES DU VERDON

France

Les Gorges du Verdon is found high up in the Haut-Var region of Provence. This natural wonder is a vast chasm cut by the Verdon River over the course of time. Roads run around both sides of the gorge, which is up to 800m (2,625ft) deep at some points. The entire circuit is 130km (80 miles) long, and the narrow ribbon of the river far below winds its way through the full 21km (13 miles) of the gorge into the man-made Lac de Sainte-Croix. This is the largest gorge in Europe and is sometimes referred to as Europe's 'Grand Canyon'. It has been formed by water eroding the soft limestone rock over some 25 million years. The water gradually worked its way through the limestone plateau, gouging out caves and tunnels as it flowed. These caverns grew larger until finally the roof of the plateau caved in, forming this dramatic V-shaped gorge. In some places at the top, the walls of the gorge are as much as 1,500m (4,920ft apart), but at the valley floor the gorge can be as little as 6m (20ft) across. In 1997, the Parc Natural Régional du Verdon was set up to protect this unique, beautiful landscape.

BEST VIEW:
Drivers can stop at the lookout point of the Balcons de la Mescla, which affords an amazing view right down to the valley floor. West of this point the road has been designed to give the best possible views, but drivers need to keep their eyes on the road!

MERCANTOUR NATIONAL PARK

France

WHAT IS IT KNOWN FOR?
Containing the largest high-altitude lake in Europe.
WHEN SHOULD I GO?
The best time is from June to October.

This national park stretches for about 75km (47 miles) in a narrow, mountainous ribbon between Barcelonette in the Alpes Maritimes to Sospel, about 20km (12.5 miles) north of Monte Carlo. Although it is almost completely uninhabited it is criss-crossed with trails and refuge huts for hikers.

The park contains several peaks, the highest being La Cime du Gélas at 3,143m (10,312ft), as well as the largest high-altitude lake in Europe, the Lac d'Allos. It is a beautiful, completely unspoiled area, with stunning waterfalls and gorges, but it is best known for its flora and fauna. Inland there are unusual alpine plants such as the multi-flowering saxifrage as well as unique types of orchid and lily. Closer to the coast more typical maquis plant life can be found, the tough, aromatic species for which the Provencal hinterland is famous.

TOULOUSE-LAUTREC MUSEUM

France

Albi is situated on the banks of the River Tarn about 75km (50 miles) north-east of Toulouse. The painter Henri de Toulouse-Lautrec is Albi's most famous son and one of France's most famous artists.

The Toulouse-Lautrec Museum is housed in the Palais de la Berbie, a red-brick fortress of which the oldest sections date back to the 13th century. Originally the home of the bishops of the Midi region, the gardens were designed in the reign of Louis XIV in the French style, with terraces and knot gardens that offer great views of the Tarn. The museum's collection is extensive and holds more than 1,000 works, including all the posters he made for the nightclubs in Montmartre, including the Moulin Rouge.

CITY SIGHTS
Albi is also home to the wonderful Gothic cathedral of Ste-Cécile, which is visible for miles around.

YOU SHOULD KNOW: As soon as he was 18, Toulouse-Lautrec made his way to Paris, where he quickly became both fascinated by and obsessed with the seedy and Bohemian lifestyle that he found in the areas of Montmartre and Pigalle. He sketched and painted prolifically, perfectly capturing the atmosphere of the bars, music halls and brothels he frequented.

ORANGE

France

Orange is situated in northwest Provence, in a fertile region that is famous for its wines – in fact it is only 10km (6 miles) north of Châteauneuf-du-Pape. Its name is thought to derive from its original Roman name of Arausio, and it was the home of the counts of Orange, a title created by Charlemagne in the eighth century.

WHAT IS IT KNOWN FOR?
Its superbly preserved Roman theatre.
WHAT IS THERE TO DO?
Attend one of the performances in the Théâtre Antique.
WORTH A DIVERSION:
The village of Châteauneuf-du-Pape.

Orange is best known for its superb Roman theatre. Built in the first century AD, the Théâtre Antique is built at the base of the hill at the south end of the old town, and it is the best-preserved Roman theatre in Europe. Its vast, stone stage wall is one of only three left in the world, and it rises to 36m (118ft), so sounds bounce back off it towards the seating that is built into the hill itself. In an alcove in the centre of the wall stands a large statue of Augustus Caesar, the man responsible for its foundation. The acoustics here are virtually perfect and today the theatre is still used for theatrical and operatic productions, for which it still draws large audiences. You can follow a footpath up the hill behind the theatre to the scattered ruins of the 17th-century castle of the Princes of Orange where Queen Juliana of Holland planted an oak tree in tribute to her ancestors. This gives you the best view of the theatre and the city.

ALSO KNOWN AS:
The City of the Popes.
WHAT IS THERE TO SEE?
Palais du Roure Museum, Rocher des Doms, Musée Calvet.
DON'T MISS:
Visit the Petit Palais to see Botticelli's *Virgin and Child*.

AVIGNON

France

Avignon stands on a bend in the Rhône River, some 95km (60 miles) northwest of Marseille. Despite its superb medieval monuments and its bridge made famous by the nursery rhyme, it is a thriving, energetic city rather than a museum piece.

Known as 'the city of the Popes', the third pope of Avignon, Benedict XII, began building the vast, fortified Palais des Papes in 1335 and it was finished by his successor, Clement VI a couple of decades later. It is divided by the Great Court – to one side of this the building is austere while to the other it retains visible evidence of the lavish, secular lifestyle of Clement VI. The palace was desecrated during the French Revolution and its treasures looted, but the scale of the rooms with their frescoes and tiles shows how luxurious life was here.

LES CALANQUES
France

WHAT ELSE IS THERE TO SEE?
Cap Canaille, Marseilles and the Château d'If.
WHAT IS THERE TO DO?
Hike up to Calanque en Vau for the best view over the cliffs.

Les Calanques are a series of long, narrow inlets, like mini fjords, cut into the limestone cliffs around Cassis on the Mediterranean coast. Cassis is a pretty coastal town tucked in between tall, white cliffs and the sea. Its picturesque fishing port is overlooked by the Château de Cassis, a medieval castle now owned by the Michelin family.

It is easy enough to hike up the well-signed footpath that runs along the cliffs to the Calanque de Port Pin, but it is worth making the extra effort to reach Calanque en Vau, the most beautiful of the lot. From the top of the cliff here you can look over the white rocks to the sparkling turquoise sea and the tiny, but perfectly formed, beach. An easier way to get here is by boat from Cassis — tours leave from the harbour at regular intervals — or you could rent a kayak and make your own way. The swimming and diving here are fabulous.

ARLES
France

Arles is situated on the banks of the Rhône River, just north of the Camargue and the Mediterranean. Its medieval buildings, Roman arena and treasure trove of other antiquities have drawn visitors here for centuries. The ancient theatre was once able to hold 20,000 spectators, and nowadays is used as a concert venue. The *Venus of Arles*, now housed in the Louvre, was found here. The real splendour is the Roman arena, Les Arènes, which can still hold about 12,000 people, and dates from the end of the first century. In the eighth century it was turned into a fortified village, but its towers are virtually all that remain from that period. Today it is used for the bullfights and races that are put on in summer.

HISTORY
In the first century BC, Julius Caesar conquered Marseille and designated Arles a Roman colony. It quickly became a wealthy commercial centre and one of the main cities in the region.

DON'T MISS: Musée de l'Arles Antique, Cryptoportiques du Forum, Les Alyscamps and the International Photography exhibition.
WHEN SHOULD I GO? Arrive in the summer and see the races and bull fights put on in Les Arènes, the Roman arena.

THE CAMARGUE

France

The Camargue is a vast area of marshlands formed by the delta of the Grand Rhône and the Petit Rhône rivers as they near the Mediterranean Sea. It is a protected area, full of wildlife and rich with beauty. The grasslands and lagoons (*étangs*) are the home of the famous black bulls, which roam at will and are tended by *gardians*, the French equivalent of cowboys, who ride the unique Camargue horses, thought to be the descendants of an ancient breed. These are brown or black at birth but become white in their fourth year and, like the bulls, they also run free. The whole area is rich in wildlife, with beavers, badgers, wild boar and, above all, birds. In all, 337 bird species can be found here, and the best known are the flamingoes, the symbol of the region. The Étang Fangassier is the only area in Europe where flamingos breed in any number.

WHAT IS THERE TO SEE?
Les Stes-Maries-de-la-Mer; the Romany festival in May; the Parc Ornithologique.
WHAT IS IT KNOWN FOR?
The area is famous for its wild horses and the flamingos.

FOOD SUPPLIES
The northern marshes were drained some 60 years ago, and re-filled with fresh water in order to grow rice. By the 1960s the Camargue produced 75 per cent of all the rice eaten in France.

OLD MARSEILLE
France

WORTH A TASTE:
The famous bouillabaisse.
DON'T MISS:
The beautifully restored
Hospice de la Vieille Charité,
a 17th-century workhouse
with a stunning Baroque
chapel and pink stone
arcades.

The area around the old port of Marseille is the true heart of the place, and Le Panier, the old town, lies to its north. The boulevard La Canebière runs northeast from the port and around it is the colourful Maghrebi quarter, full of markets selling exotic vegetables, colourful African fabrics and pungent eastern spices.

Two fortresses stand guard over the harbour entrance, but the basilica of Notre-Dame de la Garde, standing high above the city to the south of the port, is probably its best known landmark. The vast statue of the Madonna and Child covered with gold leaf, that stands on top of the basilica tower, can be seen far out to sea. Le Panier is the oldest part of town, a rabbit warren of narrow streets and stone stairways, but it suffered some serious damage during World War II when the Nazis used dynamite to clear the area of undesirables such as Jews and resistance fighters.

ST-TROPEZ
France

No visit to the Côte d'Azur would be complete without at least popping into St-Tropez for an hour or so, even at the height of summer when the traffic is dreadful, the port thronged with expensive-looking, sun-bronzed people and the harbour is chock-a-block with floating palaces. St-Tropez is lucky enough to be near a good many sandy beaches, unlike much of the rest of the Côte d'Azur, and it also has lovely, pastel-coloured houses and winding streets, squares surrounded by plane trees and old men playing *pétanque* in the shade. There are, of course, endless chic boutiques, restaurants and ice-cream parlours too, and you could do worse than people-watch from a harbour-side café. If you want to see the town when it is less crowded, come out of season, buy a picnic and a bottle of wine and enjoy it on the beach.

CITY CHIC
1956, when Brigitte Bardot arrived to make a film and decided to stay, marked the beginning of St-Tropez's current fashionable status.

WHAT IS IT KNOWN FOR? Being the beach-holiday destination of the rich and famous.
WHAT IS THERE TO SEE? Musée de l'Annonciade, the baie de Pampelonne and Ste-Maxime.
YOU SHOULD KNOW: The museum and some of the beaches charge entrance fees.

LÜBECK

Germany

Lübeck, the second-largest city in Schleswig-Holstein, in northern Germany, served as the capital of the Hanseatic League. Sited on the Trave River, it is the largest German port city on the Baltic Sea. Its old town is a well-preserved ensemble of churches, merchants' homes, narrow alleyways and warehouses that have been recognized by UNESCO as a World Heritage Site.

DON'T MISS:
Boat trips round the beautiful harbour – the origin of the city's wealth and power – leave from the Holsten bridge (Holstenbrücke), opposite the old Salzspeicher (salt warehouses).

The old town of Lübeck, the heart of the city, is dominated by church steeples, showing how wealthy it once was and includes the Cathedral (Dom), St Mary's (Marienkirche); St Peter's (Petrikirche); St Aegidien's (Aegidienkirche) in the craftsmen's district and St Jacob's (Jakobikirche), the seafarers' church. The oldest, the Dom and the Marienkirche, date back to the 13th and 14th centuries. The old town's many narrow lanes and alleys are lined by Gothic, Renaissance, Baroque and Classical town houses with red-brick, gabled façades. The impressive Town Hall (Rathaus), still in use, and the Art Nouveau Stadttheater, the Heiligen-Geist-Hospital and the Schiffergesellschaft can also be found here. The sounds of Brahms and Mozart sometimes float through the windows of the Hochschule für Musik (college of music), lending another layer to the city's already heady European charms.

BREMEN MARKET PLACE

Germany

WHAT IS IT?
A port town once considered the 'Rome of the North' for its architectural treasures.

DON'T MISS:
The Böttcherstrasse, running from Marktplatz to the Weser River, is a brick reproduction of a medieval alley, which has boutiques, cafés, a museum and art galleries.

Bremen, Germany's oldest coastal city, once a small fishing settlement, is now second only to Hamburg among the country's ports. Recognized as a UNESCO World Heritage Site, its Marktplatz (market place) is home to significant buildings dating back to the 13th century. The Rathaus (town hall) looming above the market place, was developed by the Holy Roman Empire in the early 15th century. Built in the Gothic style, the building was renovated in the local 'Weser Renaissance' style in the early 17th century. Across the square from the Rathaus stands the Schötting, a 16th-century guildhall, a mixture of Gothic and Renaissance architectural styles. In contrast to, but also complementing, this ancient masterpiece is the home to Bremen's parliament, the Haus der Bürgerschaft, a 1966 modern structure of glass, concrete and steel.

BERLIN
Germany

Since the reuinification of Germany in 1990, Berlin has emerged from its sometimes dark past and reinvented itself as a vibrant, forward-looking, modern centre of culture and Europe's capital of cool. The city has more than 170 museums and galleries that cover subjects as diverse as old-master paintings, 20th-century and contemporary art, ancient Egypt, the city's past, Bauhaus design and architecture, its Jewish residents, erotica, the ancient Greek architecture in the Pergamon Museum, technology, natural history, ethnology, Indian art and European culture, as well as its more recent history in the Haus am Checkpoint Charlie and the Berlin Wall Memorial.

Berlin is also a magnet for the young, and its vibrant nightlife and club scene are second to none. Among its many annual festivals are PopKomm, Myfest and Christopher Street Day, the last of which is among Europe's largest gay pride festivals.

Berlin, both old and new, historical and modern, is a fascinating city well worth the trip.

WHAT IS IT?
The historic capital of Germany.
DON'T MISS:
The Berlin Wall memorial, the Brandenburg Gate, more than 150 museums, including those on the UNESCO World Heritage Site of Museum Island and beautiful modern architecture.
WHAT IS THERE TO DO?
Enjoy the vibrant nightlife, stroll along Unter den Linden or visit one of the operas.

COLOGNE CATHEDRAL

Germany

Cologne Cathedral (Hohe Domkirche St Peter und Maria) is one of Germany's most famous landmarks; its towers have been a friendly outline on the city's skyline since 1880. It is the third church on the site. The first was commissioned in the fourth century by Maternus, the first Christian bishop of Cologne, and a second cathedral was completed in 818, but burned down in 1248.

TRAVELLERS' TIP:
Pre-booking a ticket for the guided tours is necessary – few are available on the day, especially for tours of the tower, roof or crypt.

In 1164, the Holy Roman Emperor, Frederick Barbarossa, had presented the relics of the Magi to the Archbishop of Cologne, Rainald von Dassel, and it was decided that these should become the focal point of the new building because of their importance to pilgrims. The foundation of the new building was laid by Archbishop Konrad von Hochstaden on 15 August 1248 and work continued on and off for another 632 years. Unusually, subsequent builders kept more or less to the original design style.

The cathedral is 144m (472ft) long, 86m (282ft) wide and the twin towers at the west end of the building reach a height of 157m (515ft), making it the largest church in Germany.

WHAT IS IT?
A collection of important modern buildings, furniture and art.
WHERE IS IT?
The most important surviving Bauhaus buildings are in Dessau and Berlin. Together these sites have been listed as a UNESCO World Heritage Site.
WHY IS IT IMPORTANT?
These buildings are examples of the school of thought that revolutionized 20th-century architecture and design.

BAUHAUS

Germany

In the social and political turmoil after the end of World War I, Walter Gropius and a group of like-minded designers and artists merged Weimar's art school with Henry van der Velde's College of Arts and Crafts to create a new design school, the Staatliche Bauhaus. The aim was to start a new style of design and architecture to suit the needs of what he saw as a new age, in which aesthetics, function and technology worked together to produce objects that were at once aesthetically pleasing, efficient and capable of being mass-produced cheaply. Products from the school included pottery, furniture and wallpaper.

The most important surviving Bauhaus buildings are in Dessau, where the school moved in 1925, and includes the Bauhaus school complex itself which is once again functioning as a design school.

THE BLACK FOREST

Germany

The Black Forest, synonymous with cuckoo clocks, folklore and primeval woodland punctuated by charming, gabled fairy-tale cottages, is one of the most popular tourist centres of the German countryside.

The northern region is crossed by broad, densely wooded ridges, thickly forested slopes and small picturesque lakes, such as the Mummelsee and the Wildsee. It includes the 270-km (167-mile) Black Forest Spa Route, linking many of the spas in the region, from Baden-Baden to Bad Wildbad. A trip to the area would not be complete without a soak in their warm waters.

In the south you will find the most spectacular and dramatic mountain scenery in the area, culminating in the Feldberg, at 1,493m (4,899ft) the highest mountain in the Black Forest. The region also has two large glacial lakes, the Titisee and the Schluchsee. Freiburg, a romantic university city with vineyards producing dry Baden wines and a superb Gothic cathedral with perfect spires, is also located here.

WHAT IS IT?
A magical, fairy-tale resort area amidst dense forests in Baden-Württemberg, southwest Germany.
WHAT IS THERE TO SEE?
Charming architecture in a dreamlike alpine setting.
WHAT IS THERE TO DO?
Drink wine, hike, paddle in the rivers, visit a spa.
WHAT SHOULD I BUY?
A cuckoo clock.

BERCHTESGADEN

Germany

Berchtesgaden National Park, the only alpine national park in Germany, is located in southeast Germany in Bavaria, bordering on the Austrian state of Salzburg. Its high-mountain landscapes are characterized by dense forests, steep rock faces, rugged cliffs, deep gorges and glaciers, complemented by idyllic pasture and gentle valleys. The Park covers an area of 210 sq km (81 sq miles), including the Watzmann massif, which rises to an impressive 2,713m (8,901ft), and the Königssee, a gorgeous 5.2-sq-km (2-sq-mile) glacial lake surrounded by majestic mountains and favoured by the Bavarian royal family.

The town of Berchtesgaden lies just north of the national park. Famed for its rich salt deposits, the town dates back to 1102 and its salt mine attracts up to 40,000 visitors a year.

WHAT IS IT?
An area of stunning natural beauty from its craggy peaks to its luscious valleys.
WHAT IS THERE TO DO?
Hike, swim, wander and enjoy the natural spoils around you.

WILDLIFE
The national park, which was declared a UNESCO biosphere reserve in 1990, has populations of chamois, roe deer, red foxes and griffon vultures. Bearded vultures, golden eagles and snow finches are more rarely spotted.

AACHEN CATHEDRAL

Germany

WHAT IS THERE TO SEE?
Its treasury has some of the most important ecclesiastical jewels in northern Europe including the Cross of Lothair the Bust of Charlemagne and the Persephone sarcophagus.

The first part of Aachen Cathedral, frequently referred to as the 'Imperial Cathedral,' is the diminutive Palatine Chapel, which was begun in 786 by Charlemagne, then King of the Franks and later the first Western Roman Emperor for some 400 years. It is in the form of an octagon with a cupola, surrounded by a 16-sided ambulatory, and is based on the design of the Byzantine church of San Vitale in Ravenna, in Italy and includes some material looted from other buildings there. The oldest cathedral in northern Europe, it is recognized as a UNESCO World Heritage Site and combines architectural elements from Classical, Byzantine and Germanic-Franconian styles. When he died in 814, Charlemagne was buried here in a shrine. The popularity of the shrine as a site of pilgrimage made it imperative for the building to be extended, and it is the Gothic 'glass chapel' or choir hall for which the cathedral is best known today

REICHENAU

Germany

For more than 1,000 years, the Benedictine complex on Reichenau Island in Lake Constance (the Bodensee) in southern Germany was an important religious site on the main trade route between Italy and Germany. It has been listed by UNESCO as a World Heritage Site because of its importance both as the best-preserved ancient monastery north of the Alps and for its role in the development of Christian art. The island's museum is housed in a 12th–15th-century building, which is one of the oldest half-timbered buildings in southern Germany. In the past it has served as the monastery bailiff's court and the town hall. As well as telling the story of the monastery, it has exhibits about life on this tranquil island and the surrounding area.

HISTORY
The monastery was founded by St Pirmin in 724 and the oldest remaining part of the church was consecrated in 816. In the tenth and 11th centuries, it was home to an extensive library.

WHAT IS IT? A UNESCO-listed abbey of historical and archaeological importance.
WHERE IS IT? Lake Constance in Baden-Württemberg in southern Germany, between the Gnadensee and the Untersee, west of the city of Konstanz.

NEUSCHWANSTEIN

Germany

WHAT IS IT?
A 19th-century castle in the Bavarian Alps and one of Germany's most popular tourist destinations.
WHERE IS IT?
Southwest Bavaria near the Austrian border.
WHAT IS THERE TO SEE?
The whimsical castle that inspired the Disney castle.
FILM CONNECTION:
The 1968 film *Chitty Chitty Bang Bang* was partly filmed here.

Built on a 92-m (300-ft) hill, Neuschwanstein, the royal palace in the Bavarian Alps of Germany, is the most famous of the three royal palaces built for Louis II of Bavaria, sometimes referred to as 'Mad King Ludwig'.

Named after the Swan Knight of Wagner's opera *Lohengrin*, the castle was exquisitely designed by Christian Jank. Located near the Hohenschwangau, where Ludwig was brought up in southwestern Bavaria near the Austrian border, the enormous and whimsical castle is so spectacular that it inspired Walt Disney to use it as a model for Cinderella's castle, used on the Disney logo.

Ludwig was removed from power before the completion of the castle, which was opened to the public after his mysterious death in 1886. An embodiment of 19th-century Romanticism, the castle is reached by a meandering road that leads from the valley to the front gate. The castle is a mixture of medieval detail, such as narrow spiral staircases and a plethora of turrets and towers, and advanced engineering features such as forced-air heating, running water on all floors and toilets with an automatic flush. After 17 years' work, only 14 of the 360 rooms were finished before Ludwig's death, but these alone are worth the trip. The Throne Room was designed in elaborate Byzantine style as the Grail-Hall of Parsifal. Inspired by the Aya Sophia in Istanbul, the two-storey throne room has a series of pillars made of imitation porphyry and lapis lazuli. Ludwig's obsession with the legends on which Wagner based his operas continues in the other rooms on this floor: *Tannhauser* in the study, grotto and conservatory, *Lohengrin* in the salon and study, the *Nibelungenlied* in the dining room and lower hall and the *Meistersinger von Nürnberg* in the dressing room. The bedroom, which is neo-Gothic in style, features paintings of scenes from *Tristan and Isolde*.

But Neuschwanstein is about more than one man's obsession with his medieval ancestors; it is a beautiful, visionary place, which sits perfectly within the stunning landscape of the Bavarian Alps.

THE RHINE VALLEY

Germany

A UNESCO World Heritage Site since 2002, the upper middle Rhine Valley (Oberes Mittelrheintal) is both beautiful and an outstanding example of how its role as one of the most important transport routes in Europe for thousands of years facilitated cultural exchange between the Mediterranean and the north. The steep slopes of the river have been terraced for agriculture for hundreds of years, and the warm, south-facing slopes make ideal areas for the cultivation of grapes for the region's famous wines and add to the beauty of the river valley. The captivating views of the narrow valley, dotted with pretty towns and ruined castles and surrounded by towering mountains, have made this one of Germany's most important areas for tourism. Its waters are plied by both commercial and pleasure craft, especially cruisers.

WHAT IS THERE TO DO?
Wander through cobbled alleys, sip delicious wines at one of the many vineyards or take a boat cruise down the river.
WORTH A SPLURGE:
Stay overnight in one of the restored castles.

MUSICAL AND LITERARY INSPIRATION
Since the Age of Enlightenment, the remarkable beauty of the middle Rhine has captured the imagination of musicians, artists and writers such as Lord Byron, Alexandre Dumas, Victor Hugo and Richard Wagner.

OKTOBERFEST
Germany

WHAT IS IT?
The largest beer festival in the world.
WHERE IS IT?
Munich, in Bavaria, southern Germany.
WHAT IS THERE TO DO?
Drink beer, listen to the traditional Bavarian music and watch the parades.

The Oktoberfest is the largest beer festival in the world, attracting up to six million visitors annually to the beer gardens of Munich, Germany every September–October. A truly riotous festival with crowds that rival those of Carnival in Rio, this event has inspired many celebrations around the world, but there is only one true Oktoberfest. The first Oktoberfest took place on 12 October 1810, in celebration of the marriage of Prince Ludwig of Bavaria to Princess Therese of Sachsen-Hildburghausen. All of the citizens of Munich were invited to a meadow in front of the city tower, to raise a glass or two in honour of the union, and this became an annual tradition. Nowadays, enormous tents are filled with teeming throngs of locals and visitors from all around the world, and traditional musicians lead the crowds in well-known drinking chants. As well as drinking roughly six million glasses of *wiesn*, the crowd gets through some 91 oxen, 383,000 sausages and 630,000 chickens as well as tonnes of local favourites such as cheese noodles and sauerkraut.

RIGA
Latvia

Riga has become the Baltic's most cosmopolitan city. Its cultural claim to fame is that it has more Art Nouveau buildings than any other city in the world. The city is full of architectural gems, both ancient and relatively modern. Possibly the best examples of medieval residential buildings are the Three Brothers, a picturesque row of houses, the oldest of which was built in the 15th century. The Doma Cathedral dominates the old town. It was founded in 1211 and has been partially destroyed and then restored several times since then. The old town is full of streets and squares of 16th- and 17th-century German buildings, decorated with carvings and statues, and it is a joy to wander here. The Art Nouveau buildings stand just outside the old city. Whole streets here are lined with flamboyant architectural beauties.

ART NOVEAU
The gorgeous group of buildings on Alberta Street (Alberta iela) was designed by Mikhail Eisenstein, father of the celebrated Russian filmmaker Sergei Eisenstein.

WHAT IS IT? The Baltic's most cosmopolitan city and a World Heritage Site.
WHAT IS IT KNOWN FOR? It has more Art Noveau buildings than any other city in the world.
DON'T MISS: Riga Castle, St Peter's Church, Three Brothers, Cat House, St John's Church.

AMSTERDAM

The Netherlands

Amsterdam, the largest city in the Netherlands, is known for its liberalism, stunning architecture, friendly locals, culture and history. It has winding canals, cobbled streets, some of the world's greatest art collections, fascinating old buildings and even cannabis and sex museums.

The Golden Age (1585–1672) was the high point of Amsterdam's commercial success and some of the most important buildings from this period are the classical Royal Palace on Damplein, the Westerkerk, Zuiderkerk, and many canal houses including De Dolfijn (Dolphin), De Gecroonde Raep (the Crowned Turnip), the Huis met de Hoofden (the House with the Heads) and the Poppenhuis (dollhouse). Most of the houses in the city date from the 18th century.

WHAT IS THERE TO DO?

The city offers an incredible and dynamic diversity of attractions – cultural, historical or just plain fun. The nightlife in Amsterdam is notorious.

'VENICE OF THE NORTH'

Nearly 1,300 bridges criss-cross the canals of this beautiful city, known as 'the Venice of the North'. The four main city centre canals are Prinsengracht, Herengracht, Keizersgracht and Singel, which are best enjoyed by taking a boat tour or exploring the surrounding streets by bicycle.

THE VAN GOGH MUSEUM

The Netherlands

WHERE IS IT?
On Museumplein in Amsterdam, between the Rijksmuseum and the Stedelijk Museum.

Van Gogh was a highly prolific artist, creating 864 paintings and nearly 1,200 drawings and prints during his ten-year career. Home to the largest collection of Van Gogh's work in the world, the Van Gogh Museum in Amsterdam exhibits more than 200 paintings, 437 drawings and 31 prints including the highly prized *Sunflowers*, *The White Orchard* and *The Yellow House*, as well as many of the artist's self-portraits.

Other works by various renowned 19th-century artists can also be found here, among them Paul Gauguin, Henri de Toulouse-Lautrec, Léon Lhermitte and Jean-François Millet. New acquisitions by the museum include Kees van Dongen's *Portrait of Guus Preitinger* and two paintings by Monet that date from his Dutch period.

THE RIJKSMUSEUM

The Netherlands

Home to nearly one million objects, Amsterdam's Rijksmuseum is the largest museum of art and history in the Netherlands. Designed by Pierre Cuypers and opened in 1885, the museum has become a city landmark with its combination of Gothic and Renaissance styles. Perhaps best known for its unrivalled collection of 17th-century Dutch Old Masters, the Rijksmuseum counts 20 Rembrandts and many other highlights of the period as part of its treasures, including works by Johannes Vermeer, Frans Hals and Jan Steen. The Rijksmuseum draws more than one million visitors a year, and ranks as one of the major museums of western European painting and decorative arts.

THE GOLDEN AGE
The landscapes, seascapes, individual portraits, domestic scenes and Dutch still lifes offer a good overview of the Dutch Golden Age.

WHERE IS IT? The Museumplein in Amsterdam.
WHAT IS THERE TO SEE? An impressive collection of 17th-century Dutch masters, 20 Rembrandts and works by Johannes Vermeer, Frans Hals and Jan Steen.
DON'T MISS: Rembrandt's *The Night Watch*.

KEUKENHOF GARDENS

The Netherlands

Every spring, more than seven million blooms open at the famous Keukenhof Gardens, including 1,000 varieties of tulips alone. A showcase for the Dutch flower industry, the gardens draw nearly a million visitors a year anxious to glimpse this phenomenal show of vivid colours bursting throughout the 28-hectare (70-acre) area. Daffodils, croci, narcissi, tulips and hyacinths in every combination of yellow, gold, purple, red, orange, and with heavenly scents, offer an unmatched spectacle. The Keukenhof Gardens were established in Lisse in 1949 in the grounds of a long-ruined castle, where a countess with an enthusiasm for Dutch flowers had lived during the 15th century. Interestingly the tulip, which everyone associates with the Netherlands, does not originate here. In fact, they were not brought to this country until 1593 at the request of the Flemish ambassador to Constantinople who was captivated by their beauty. Stories of the special flower spread rapidly and wealthy Dutchmen began to invest in importing bulbs, creating a prosperous trade that lasted until the market crashed in 1637 when the tulip was no longer a rarity. The over-supply problem brought the prices down and many fortunes were lost. Their production continued, however, and the tulip is once again one of the Netherlands most important export products.

> **WHEN SHOULD I GO?**
> Late March to mid-May.
> **WHAT IS THERE TO SEE?**
> Flowers, flowers and more flowers.

WEST NORWEGIAN FJORDS

Norway

Two of Norway's most spectacular fjords, Geirangerfjord and Naeroyfjord lie 120km (75 miles) apart in southwest Norway, north-east of Bergen. They are among the world's longest and deepest fjords, and are of exceptional natural beauty.

Geirangerfjord is a large fjord, about 16km (10 miles) long. The water is saline, so it does not freeze during the long winter months. There is virtually no tide, so the waters are still and beautiful, reflecting the sky, the 2,000-m (6,600-ft) mountain walls on either side, and the famous rock formation that stands at the head of the fjord. Naeroyfjord is said to be the narrowest in the world. At one point it is less than 250m (820ft) wide, with the steep-sided crystalline rock walls of the mountains towering some 1,500m (4,900ft) above the water.

> **WHAT ARE THEY?**
> Two of the worlds most beautiful fjords.
> **WHAT IS THERE TO SEE?**
> The Sogne fjord, Flam Railway, Stalheimskleiva.
> **DON'T MISS:**
> Taking a trip down the fjords and looking out for seals lying on the rocks.

Right: Geirangerfjord

MIDNIGHT SUN AND AURORA BOREALIS

Norway

The city of Tromsø is some 350km (220 miles) north of the Arctic Circle, and here you can experience both midnight sun and polar night. From 21 May to 21 July the sun never sets, but there is no real darkness between late April and mid-August, merely an extended twilight. Conversely, between 21 November and 21 January the sun never rises above the horizon, although there is always an hour or two of marvellous, blueish twilight. Svalbard is a group of islands lying just 1,000km (620 miles) south of the North Pole. At its largest settlement, Longyearbyen, the midnight sun can be seen from April to August.

The aurora borealis is easily seen during the winter from both Tromsø and Svalbard, though this can never be guaranteed. The phenomenon occurs when plasma particles from the sun are trapped in the ionosphere above the Earth's surface, resulting in surreal light shows that ripple in curtains overhead. These shifting, otherworldly lights dance and crackle their way across the night sky in one of nature's most stunning spectacles.

WHEN SHOULD I GO?
For aurora borealis go during autumn, winter or spring. Polar night occurs from November to February and the midnight sun occurs between 21 May and 21 July.

LOFOTEN

Norway

DID YOU KNOW?

The population of the five main islands is only about 25,000.

WHAT IS THERE TO SEE?

The villages of Flakstad and Moskenes, Kabelvag Cathedral, the Lofoten Museum.

DON'T MISS:

Take an adventure tour out to Maelstrom.

The Lofoten Islands are an archipelago situated off the north Norwegian coast, high above the Arctic Circle. They rise from the green water like a wall, to a height of about 1,000m (3,300ft), and are fringed with white sandy beaches. The scenery here is magnificent.

The main source of income for the islanders comes from fishing, in particular, cod. Known as *sprei*, mature Norwegian Arctic cod that are ready to spawn arrive at Lofoten towards the end of January, migrating here from the Barents Sea. Some of the large females can be as long as 2m (6ft) and their roes will contain about five million eggs. Some 4,000 fishermen are there to catch as many as they can, and so are pods of orca, looking for an easy meal.

Tourism is another source of income here, and visitors can take adventure tours to see the Maelstrom whirlpool and other sights such as the awe-inspiring Refsvikhula Cave with its Stone-Age wall paintings. There are seal colonies and sea eagles, puffins and otters to be seen here and the mountains are wonderful for hiking and climbing, with superb views over the jagged peaks.

URNES STAVE CHURCH

Norway

The Urnes Stave Church is in Sogn county, north of Bergen. It was built in about 1130 and is believed to be the oldest of its kind. Architecturally it provides a link between the Vikings, with their animal-motif decoration, and Christian religious design. Archaeological evidence suggests that this is the third church on the site and that the two previous ones were simple post churches, created by ramming posts into the ground, walling between them and roofing them. Beneath the remnants of the first church are the remains of Christian graves, evidence of the conversion of the Vikings to Christianity.

WHAT IS IT?
The oldest stave church of its kind.
YOU SHOULD KNOW:
There is an entrance fee and it is generally only open June–August.

The survival of this wooden church for nearly 900 years is unusual enough, but its highlights are even older and include a fantastically carved wooden doorway, some planking, two gables and a corner post, which are thought to be from one of the earlier churches dating to the 11th century. The wood is fantastically carved. The doorway portrays a four-legged animal (often known as a biting beast, and possibly meant to represent a lion) biting a snake that curls sinuously upwards among intertwining foliage. It is presumed to symbolize the fight between Christ and Satan, although no-one knows for sure.

ROCK CARVINGS IN TANUM

Sweden

WHAT IS THERE TO SEE?
Vitlycke Museum (May–September), Vitlycke Rock, Aspeberget, Torsbo and Greby Gravfalt.
WHAT IS THERE TO DO?
Explore the rocks and discover rock carvings dating back to the Bronze Age.

Northern Bohuslan is about two hours' drive north of Gothenburg, along Sweden's west coast, and here you will find the amazing Bronze-Age petroglyphs, or rock carvings, of Tanum. This is an area where rock carvings are being discovered all the time, but the 350 separate and very varied groups carved in the flat rock here make it unique. The site was not discovered until 1972, when Age Nilsen, a construction worker, found the first site exactly where he had been planning to place an explosive charge. The carvings are thought to have been made between 1800–600 B.C. They are in four distinct groups along a 25-km (15.5-mile) stretch of what was once a fjord, but which today is about 25m (80ft) above sea level. Archaeologists have found 13 types of motifs and figures, including ships, sleighs, people, weapons, animals and trees.

STOCKHOLM

Sweden

DID YOU KNOW?
Sweden still has a
royal family but one
without any political power.

WHAT IS IT?
The capital of Sweden.
DON'T MISS:
Kungliga Slottet and Gamla
Stan, Stadshuset
and Vasamuseet.
WHAT IS IT KNOWN FOR?
Colourful buildings painted
in their original colours.

Sweden's lovely capital is in an amazing location, on a series of islands on the edge of the Baltic Sea. In 1252, the Swedish statesman Birger Jarl erected a fortress on the small island of Gamla Stan, where the Royal Palace stands today. The settlement that grew up around the fortress eventually became the Stockholm that we see today. By 1436 it was the capital city and Sweden, Norway and Denmark, together with Finland, Iceland and Greenland, formed one huge Scandinavian kingdom. It was not until 1523 that the first independent King of Sweden, Gustav Vasa, was crowned.

The old town (Gamla Stan) retains its medieval street plan, while the city has buildings in almost every western European style. An interesting feature is that the city fathers have tried to ensure that houses are painted in their original colour, so many 17th-century buildings are red, and 18th-century buildings are yellow. Off-white and grey buildings tend to be much more recent. All of this makes the city really visually attractive. There are several royal palaces, including the Baroque Drottningholm and Kungliga Slottet. Museums include the National Museet, which has a wide range of fine art, the Modern Museet, which has works by, among others, Picasso and Dalí, the Vasamuseet, which has the famous reconstruction of an ancient ship, and the Nordiska Museet, dedicated to the culture and ethnography of Sweden.

BERN
Switzerland

Wandering through the UNESCO World Heritage Site of Bern's Old Town can be a magical and surreal experience, because its architecture and street plan are essentially unchanged since the late Middle Ages. Founded in the 12th century on a hillside by the River Aare, Bern has a variety of architectural styles and characteristics representative of its long history including 13th-century arcades and 16th-century fountains. Largely restored in the 18th century, Bern has managed to retain its original charm and character.

According to legend, in 1191 Duke Berchtold V of Zähringen commanded nobleman Cuno von Bubenberg to build a city on the narrow, oak-covered peninsula. Von Bubenberg felled the forest and used the wood to build his town. After a disastrous fire in 1405, new buildings were built in sandstone and by the 16th and 17th centuries most houses had been updated in the new material. The bear featured on the city coat of arms first appeared in 1224. Legend has it that the city was named after the first animal killed by the duke while he was out hunting. Along with the clock tower, the bear has continued to be the symbol of Bern to this day.

WHAT IS IT?
A city centre that dates back to the twelfth century, and is largely unchanged since then..
DON'T MISS:
The beautiful old city, the bear pits, the astronomical clock, shopping in the vast covered markets.

GENEVA
Switzerland

Geneva is known for many things: lakeside scenery, watches, knives and cutlery, chocolate, fondue and for being the site of several UN agencies. A stunning city in the shadows of the Alps, Geneva is a historical town filled with many interesting attractions.

In the lake, the monumental Jet d'Eau is one of the symbols of Geneva, its waters spurting an impressive 140m (459ft) into the air. Once an overflow valve for hydroelectricity generated on the Rhône River, it was turned into a fountain in 1891. The clear azure lake covers 582 sq km (225 sq miles). The easiest way to travel around the lake is to cross it by boat, and the popular steam ships have been here since 1823. Nearly all the cities, hamlets and towns along the lake have landing quays, with services usually running from Easter through to October.

WHAT IS IT?
A lovely city with many urban attractions in a largely rural setting.
WHERE IS IT?
Southern Switzerland, on the French border.
WHAT IS IT KNOWN FOR?
Its scenic lakeside beauty.
WHAT SHOULD I DO?
Play chess on a giant chessboard in the Parc des Bastions.
WHAT SHOULD I BUY?
Watches or chocolate.

THE JUNGFRAU

Switzerland

DID YOU KNOW?
Jungfraujoch railway station, at a height of 3,454m (11,333ft), is the highest in Europe.

WHAT IS IT?
The highest peak in the Jungfrau massif.
WHERE IS IT?
In the Bernese Alps of western Switzerland.
WHAT IS THERE TO DO?
Look at the views and visit the Ice Palace.

The Jungfrau is the highest peak of the Jungfrau massif in the Bernese Oberland region of the Swiss Alps overlooking Grindelwald. At an elevation of 4,158m (13,642ft), it is surrounded by two other notable peaks, the Eiger and the Mönch.

The summit was first reached by the Meyer brothers from Aarau in 1811, but now it is much easier as the Jungfraubahn cog railway runs inside the mountain up to the Jungfraujoch railway station. The first step in the journey up to the peak is the Wengernalp railway (WAB), a rack-and-pinion railway that opened in 1893 that takes you to Lauterbrunnen at 784m (2,612ft), where you change to a train heading for the Kleine Scheidegg station at an elevation of 2,029m (6,762ft). From here you can view the Mönch, the Eigerwand and the Jungfrau and change to the highest rack railway in Europe, the Jungfraubahn. Some 6.4km (4 miles) of its 9.6-km (6-mile) journey is through a tunnel carved into the mountain. There are two brief stops – at Eigerwand 2,830m (9,400ft) and Eismeer 3,110m (10,368ft) – where you can view the sea of ice from windows in the rock. As you emerge into the dazzling sunlight, you reach the Jungfraujoch terminus.

WENGEN

Switzerland

The Swiss holiday resort of Wengen, nestling at the foot of the imposing peaks of the Eiger, Mönch and Jungfrau is a stunning area of natural beauty. A completely car-free area, this pretty village in the Bernese Oberland is part of the Jungfrau region as well as the UNESCO World Heritage Site of Jungfrau.

The first guesthouse here appeared in the 1890s and proved to be so popular, following the development of the Wengernalp Mountain Railway, that a further 30 resorts were built over the next two decades. This era of prosperity, albeit interrupted by the war, continued, encouraging further growth of transport facilities including cable-cars, chairlifts and more railway construction. Once a sleepy farming village, Wengen has become a stunning, chalet-style resort town that has managed to retain its quaint charms.

WHAT IS IT?
A Swiss holiday resort at the foot of the Eiger-Mönch-Jungfrau range.
WHAT IS THERE TO DO?
Every outdoor activity imaginable.

WORLD-CLASS MARATHON
Wengen is home to the most difficult marathon in the world, the International Jungfrau Marathon. Every September thousands of runners from many countries scramble around the high elevations, attempting to make the best time over this difficult terrain.

THE OLD MAN OF HOY

Scotland

WHAT IS THERE TO DO?
Take a trip around the shore and be amazed at the sheer volume of sea birds and seal colonies.

Orkney is made up of about 70 islands off the north coast of Scotland, of which fewer than 20 are inhabited. Hoy is the second largest of the islands after Mainland. It is the only island that is not flat, and the views from its hills are of moorland, vivid green turf and vertical cliffs reaching down to white-sand beaches and turquoise bays. The Old Man of Hoy is a rock stack 137m (450ft) tall on a promontory in the sea, and it is a favourite of rock climbers from around the world. The first successful recorded climb was made in 1966 by Chris Bonington's team.

The remoteness of the Orkneys and their untamed landscape make them a haven for wildlife. The northern part of Hoy has been a Royal Society for the Preservation of Birds' reserve for more than 20 years.

THE SCOTTISH HIGHLANDS

Scotland

Soaring peaks, broken boulders tumbling down sheer rock faces, dark glens and forbidding castles, sparkling streams and purple heather, golden eagles and deer – all this and more makes up this majestic part of the world. Ben Nevis, which lies within the Lochaber region of Scotland, overlooks the beautiful valley of Glen Nevis. This is an area as popular with serious climbers and hikers as it is with amateurs, but hiking up Ben Nevis is certainly a serious undertaking, and the barren summit of the mountain is often shrouded with thick, cold mist. The lower slopes are covered in native pine, oak and beech and home to many different kinds of wildlife. Farther up, the trees give way to moorland hosting wild thyme and bilberries. Near the summit only the toughest lichens and mosses can survive the near arctic conditions that prevail in winter.

GREAT HEIGHTS
Ben Nevis is the highest mountain in the British Isles, reaching 1,344m (4,410ft).

WHAT IS IT? A region of mountains running across Scotland.
WHAT IS THERE TO SEE? Magnificent lochs, beautiful castles, Inverness, Fort William and Glencoe.
IF YOU DARE: Hike up Ben Nevis, but make sure you're wearing suitable clothing and footwear.

SCOTTISH LOCHS

Scotland

There are hundreds of stunning lochs splashed like raindrops all over Scotland and exploring them all could take a lifetime – this is some of the most beautiful landscape in the British Isles. The lochs were formed during the last Ice Age, which sculpted this dramatic landscape in combination with ancient volcanic activity. Loch Lomond is the largest and contains the greatest area of fresh water in the British Isles. Its shores are lined with native oakwoods and its waters are home to 17 native species of fish. Loch Lomond is the centrepiece of the Loch Lomond and Trossachs National Park. It is 39km (24 miles) long and incredibly beautiful. To the west of Loch Lomond, on the far side of the Cowal Peninsula, lies Loch Fyne, a sea loch that is renowned for its oysters and its sea fishing.

The most famous loch in the Scottish Highlands, is, of course, Loch Ness, thanks to the Loch Ness monster, which was first mentioned by Saint Adomnán of Iona (627/8–704). Although the deep waters have been explored many times during the last 70 or so years, the monster has not been found.

WHAT IS THERE TO DO?
Whether you like fishing, sailing or enjoying freshly caught, local food there is something for everyone in this beautiful setting.
HOW DO I GET THERE?
It is best to travel by car so you can see as many lochs as possible and enjoy the surrounding scenery.

EDINBURGH CASTLE

Scotland

Edinburgh Castle is situated on the crags of Castle Rock, perfectly positioned to defend itself against incursions from countless numbers of invaders from Roman times right up to the middle of the 18th century.

The castle has a dramatic and bloody history – before you even reach the Portcullis Gate, near the entrance to the Esplanade beneath, you pass the Witches' Well where over 300 women were burned some 250 years ago. Just before the gate itself is a memorial to Sir William Kirkaldy, who was implicated in the murders of Cardinal Beaton and David Rizzio, Mary Queen of Scots' secretary, and who was later hanged. Above the gate is Constable's or Argyll's Tower, where the Marquess of Argyll was imprisoned before his execution in 1661.

WHAT IS IT?
Edinburgh's most iconic image dating back to the 11th century.
WHAT ELSE IS THERE TO SEE?
The Royal Mile, Arthur's Seat, Camera Obscura, Kirk of the Greyfriars, the Scottish Parliament and the Palace of Holyroodhouse.

Right: Loch Lomond

DURHAM CASTLE & CATHEDRAL

England

Durham is a small and exquisite city set on a hilltop peninsula on a bend of the River Wear in northeast England. A lively university town since the early 19th century, its main attractions are its glorious Romanesque cathedral, founded in 1093, and its castle, originally built in 1072. Surrounding both these buildings is a maze of little cobbled streets and lovely walks down to the river.

WHAT ELSE IS THERE TO SEE?
Bishop Auckland, Raby Castle, Barnard Castle and Alnwick.

Durham Castle was the home of the prince bishops of Durham, (so called by William the Conqueror in order to pacify both the locals and the Scots), right up until 1837 when it became the original college of the just-founded university, and it remains a university hall to this day. Each prince bishop added and changed the castle in the centuries that followed its inception, but as it was built of soft stone onto soft ground, it needed constant restoration and renovation. The Norman chapel, which was built in 1080, is wonderfully preserved, and is only one of a number of highlights to be seen within this enormous castle. The cathedral is also vast, and the interior is spectacular – it was the first cathedral in Europe to be roofed with stone-ribbed vaulting, and the transverse arches were the first of their kind to be built in Britain.

THE LAKE DISTRICT

England

WHAT IS IT KNOWN FOR?
The biggest lake in England and a literary heritage.
WHAT IS THERE TO DO?
There are many hiking trails and the Cumbria Way for those looking for a challenging walk.
DON'T MISS:
Take a boat out onto Windermere for a better look at the area.

The Lake District of Cumbria lies between the Scottish borders and Northumberland, Durham, North Yorkshire and Lancashire. The beautiful landscapes of mountains, valleys, fells and lakes have appealed to visitors for centuries. In the Victorian era it became very popular as a holiday spot, and it remains so today. Its status as a national park ensures the careful management of its varied environment. The high ground of the central area is wonderful hiking territory, with valleys, lakes and ridges radiating from it in all directions. Windermere is the largest lake in England, and Bowness-on-Windermere caters for the huge number of visitors it receives. Keswick is situated in the north of the Lake District, beside Derwentwater, and is an important centre for walking and climbing. The Cumbria Way, a trail of almost 113km (70 miles), is accessible from here.

THE YORKSHIRE DALES

England

WHAT IS IT KNOWN FOR?
Exquisite, rugged beauty that has inspired many authors and painters.

The Yorkshire Dales National Park covers an area of 1,770 sq km (683 sq miles) of countryside between the Lake District and the North Yorkshire Moors. Made up of hills, moors and valleys, it is a marvellous place for cycling and walking trips. The Yorkshire Dales Cycle Way, a route of 209km (130 miles), shows the park's best scenery, or you could try one of the walks such as the Dales Way or the Pennine Way.

If you prefer, you can explore the dales by car, or take a trip on the Settle-to-Carlisle railway line. This is a fabulous journey and special passes are available so that you can see a bit at a time if you wish. Jump out at Dent station, one of the highest in the country, and walk down to the picturesque village in the valley below.

SALTAIRE

England

Salt's Mill was built by the wealthy textile magnate Sir Titus Salt, a philanthropist who decided to surround the mill with a complete village of 850 houses, almshouses, wash houses, public baths, schools, hospitals, parks and a railway station. Saltaire was designed in Italianate style, with the mill resembling an enormous palazzo, and it is all well preserved. The mill is still the heart of the place, and is now home to shops and a restaurant. One floor, called the 1853 Gallery, now has a permanent retrospective of the work of David Hockney. Hockney was born in Bradford and was a friend of Jonathan Silver, who had the idea for the gallery. The transformation of the mill has been sympathetically designed and it is easy to spend a day here. Saltaire is now a UNESCO World Heritage Site.

WORLD'S LARGEST FACTORY
When it opened in 1853, the mill was the largest and most modern factory in the world.

WHAT IS IT? A beautiful village in West Yorkshire built around a textile mill that dates back to the 19th century.
WHAT ELSE IS THERE TO SEE? The National Museum of Photography, Film and Television, Kirkstall Abbey, the Brontë Parsonage Museum and Harewood House.

ELY CATHEDRAL

England

Ely Cathedral is possibly England's most awe-inspiring cathedral. Visible from miles around across the flat fen country, it towers over the landscape and its nickname, the Ship of the Fens, is very apt. St Etheldreda founded a Benedictine monastery here in 673, on a clay island surrounded by boggy marshland, which was sacked by the Danes 200 years later. The new monastery became the centre of resistance by Hereward the Wake against the Normans. In 1081, after the conquest, Abbot Simeon began the masterpiece of Romanesque architecture that is the cathedral we see today.

As you enter the cathedral, you look down the very long nave, with its austere Romanesque arches and Victorian painted ceiling, towards the centrepiece of the building, the unique octagonal Lantern Tower built by Alan de Walsingham in 1322 to replace the collapsed central tower. The tallest oaks in England were used to support the 400 tonnes of glass and lead that form the starburst lantern, surrounded by stunning fan vaulting. The Lady Chapel, built at about the same time, also has an astonishing fan-vaulted and carved ceiling, although much of the carving and statuary within easier reach on the walls was defaced during the Reformation and Commonwealth.

WHAT IS IT KNOWN FOR?
Ely Cathedral is known as England's most awe-inspiring cathedral.
WHAT IS THERE TO SEE?
The Lantern Tower, the Stained Glass Museum and Wicken Fen.

LAVENHAM

England

Lavenham is possibly the prettiest village in Suffolk. Situated in the Stour valley, it is a marvellously preserved medieval wool town, with more than 300 listed buildings. Lavenham has existed since Roman times, and was mentioned in the Domesday Book.

Walking around this lovely village you can see marvellous buildings of all descriptions, some of the oldest of which are weavers' cottages in Water Street. There are ancient inns, crooked houses, thatched cottages painted the traditional Suffolk pink, thought to have been whitewash tinted with pig's blood, and higgledy-piggledy roofs. The early 16th-century Guildhall is one of the finest half-timbered buildings in the country. In the late 17th century the wool trade moved away from here, but it left behind a wonderful legacy.

WHAT IS IT?
A medieval wool town with more than 300 listed buildings.
WHAT IS THERE TO DO?
Visit the Guildhall and discover local history at its best.
YOU SHOULD KNOW:
Entrance fees are payable at most of the local museums.

THE SUFFOLK HERITAGE COAST

England

DID YOU KNOW?
Suffolk is famous for its churches. One of the most spectacular is 'the Cathedral in the Marshes' at Blythburgh.

WHAT IS THERE TO DO?
Enjoy the walks and trails along the coast that will reveal much wildlife.

WHEN SHOULD I VISIT?
Spring and autumn if you want to avoid the crowds.

Suffolk's Heritage Coast was designated as an Area of Outstanding Natural Beauty in 1970. Stretching from the Stour estuary in the south to Kessingland in the north, it encompasses a world of marshland, heaths, forests and shingle beaches as well as villages and historic buildings. The Royal Society for the Protection of Birds' flagship bird reserve at Minsmere is a microcosm of the landscape. Unlike much of Britain's coastline, the Heritage Coast is largely undeveloped and this contributes to its charm.

The coastal landscape, with its huge skies and beautiful light, has inspired artists and musicians down the years including the composer Benjamin Britten, whose vision has resulted in the world-famous annual music festival at Snape, and J.M.W. Turner who painted Dunwich beach. The area is full of painters, musicians, writers and actors and visitors flock to seaside villages such as Southwold and Walberswick in the summer to enjoy the unspoiled, old-fashioned atmosphere.

IRONBRIDGE GORGE

England

The UNESCO World Heritage Site of Ironbridge Gorge in Shropshire was designated in recognition of its importance as the birthplace of the Industrial Revolution, and there are ten museums in the area testifying to the transformation of industry that took place.

Three generations of the extraordinary Darby family helped shape history here. In 1709, Abraham Darby pioneered the smelting of iron ore with coke, thus enabling local factories to mass-produce locomotives, rails and iron wheels, and the beginnings of Britain's railway system. Abraham Darby II invented a new forging process that allowed single beams of iron to be produced, and enabled his son, Abraham Darby III, in 1779, to construct the first iron bridge in the world, here in Ironbridge Gorge.

The gorge itself is made up of a group of pretty little villages and there is even a completely reconstructed Victorian-village theme park, with a working foundry and craftsmen demonstrating various skills, all in authentic Victorian dress. There is even a Victorian pub if you need some time out. You can visit a splendid tile museum, a clay-pipe-making museum in the largely unchanged factory which only closed down in 1957, and many others charting the history of industrialization and engineering.

WHAT IS THERE TO DO?
Wander through the gorge and take in pretty villages and the Victorian-village theme park.

STRATFORD-UPON-AVON

England

WHAT IS IT KNOWN FOR?
Being the birthplace of William Shakespeare.

WHAT IS THERE TO SEE?
Anne Hathaway's Cottage, the Swan Theatre, Gerard Johnson's alabaster bust of Shakespeare in Holy Trinity Church and Charlecote Park.

WORTH A DIVERSION:
Venture away from Stratford and spend a day at the beautiful Warwick Castle.

Stratford-upon-Avon is renowned as the birthplace of William Shakespeare. The Shakespeare Birthplace Trust manages five properties relating to Shakespeare, all of which are worth a visit. Shakespeare's Birthplace Museum has a modern visitor centre situated next door to the half-timbered building in which the bard is thought to have been born. Nash's House was the home of Shakespeare's granddaughter and from there you enter New Place, a memorial garden that marks the site of Shakespeare's own house, which he inhabited from 1610 until his death. Hall's Croft is another pretty house in which Shakespeare's daughter Susanna and her husband lived. Two other properties, Mary Arden's House and Anne Hathaway's Cottage, can be found at Wilmcote and Shottery. The latter was the family home of Shakespeare's wife and is the prettiest of the Shakespeare buildings.

THE COTSWOLDS

England

The limestone hills of the Cotswolds are one of England's main tourist attractions. They encompass some of England's prettiest countryside and are peppered with picturesque villages all built in the local stone, which varies from honey coloured to silvery-grey. Cirencester was a busy town in Roman times, when it was second in importance only to London. Today it remains a bustling town and is the *de facto* capital of the south Cotswolds, dominated by a splendid 15th-century church. Bourton-on-the-Water is possibly the prettiest of the Cotswold villages with its many low, stone bridges crossing the little River Windrush. Farther north, Stow-on-the-Wold, the highest town in the Cotswolds, boasts a large square surrounded by imposing, honey-coloured houses. The 'tunes' or narrow alleyways leading into the square were originally used to run sheep into the market. Nearby Chastleton House is one of the most complete Jacobean manor houses in England. Chipping Campden is another lovely town, with its famous high street and gabled Jacobean market hall.

WHAT IS IT?
The Cotswolds are limestone hills in the southwest of England.
WHAT IS IT KNOWN FOR?
The Cotswolds contain some of the most picturesque villages in England.
WHAT SHOULD I BUY?
Locally made arts and crafts.
WHAT IS THERE TO SEE?
Prinknash Abbey, Chedworth Roman Villa and Sezincote.

OXFORD

England

Oxford stands at the confluence of two rivers: the Cherwell and the Isis, as the Thames is known at this point. Originally a Saxon town, it was not until the 12th century that its Augustinian abbey began to attract students. The first colleges were built in the 13th century, and others followed, right up to the 20th century, in order to keep pace with the growing student population. The divide between 'town and gown' has always been in existence and to this day students rarely mix with locals. Tourism is always evident in Oxford because its wealth of historic buildings and world-famous museums draw visitors from around the world. Colleges have visiting hours and entrance fees, but when they are off-limits there are plenty of other things to do and see: beautiful walks by the canal and rivers, and punting during the summer, museums such as the Ashmolean and Pitt Rivers, art galleries and of course hundreds of restaurants, pubs, bars and nightclubs. Stroll around this historic city and soak up the atmosphere by day, and in the evening listen to a classical music concert.

WHAT IS THERE TO SEE?
Magdelen College, Balliol College, Christ Church, New College, the Radcliffe Camera and the Sheldonian Theatre.
WHEN SHOULD I GO?
Arrive in the summer and enjoy an afternoon punting on the river.

THE HOUSES OF PARLIAMENT

England

DID YOU KNOW?

The best views are from the south side of the river. At night, the floodlit towers and spires look particularly romantic.

WHAT IS IT?

An instantly recognizable landmark of London and the seat of government.

WHAT IS THERE TO SEE?

The Lord Chancellor's Residence, Westminster Abbey and Downing Street.

WHAT IS THERE TO DO?

In the summer you can take a guided tour through both houses.

YOU SHOULD KNOW:

Entry is free.

In the 11th century the original Palace of Westminster was built by Edward the Confessor, on the banks of the River Thames. It remained one of the palaces of every monarch until Henry VIII moved out after a fire, and has been the seat of government more or less ever since. In 1834, the old palace was almost completely devastated by another fire, leaving only Westminster Hall and the Jewel Tower intact, and Sir Charles Barry and A.W.N Pugin were charged with the rebuilding. They designed the fabulous Gothic-Revival complex that we see today, which is better known as The Houses of Parliament.

Anyone can go to watch the business of the House of Commons and the House of Lords, which are open to the public throughout the week, at different times of day. Just join the queue outside St Stephen's Gate and, after passing through strict security measures, you will be able to find a seat in one of the Strangers' Galleries. In August and September, when parliament is not sitting, guided tours of the complex are available.

St Stephen's Tower was built in 1858. It is commonly known as Big Ben, although this is actually the name of the 13-tonne bell that chimes within it. The sound of Big Ben's chimes is known throughout the world, and the tower is an instantly recognizable London landmark.

TATE MODERN

England

Tate Modern is housed in a wonderful conversion of what was the looming and unprepossessing Bankside Power Station, on the south bank of the River Thames. Completely renovated and redesigned by Jacques Herzog and Pierre de Meuron, it is the largest modern-art gallery in the world. This section of the south bank has gone through an extraordinary regeneration during the past ten years, with the Thames Path allowing you to walk west or east via many other attractions.

The best way to reach it is by crossing the Millennium Bridge, the first pedestrian-only bridge in London and the first new bridge across the river for more than 100 years. Enter Tate Modern down the western ramp and into the vast Turbine Hall and the view will take your breath away. This superb space is used for specially designed shows that are changed every six months or so. It allows the display of monumental pieces of art, such as Louise Bourgeois' giant female spider, entitled *Maman* and her three towers, all of which made up the opening show.

WHAT IS IT?
The largest modern art gallery in the world.
YOU SHOULD KNOW:
The permanent exhibitions are free but the temporary exhibitions require an entrance fee.

THE BRITISH MUSEUM

England

WHAT IS IT?
One of the greatest museums in the world, with superb collections.
WHAT IS THERE TO SEE?
The Sainsbury African Galleries, Lindow Man, the Portland Vase and the Mildenhall Treasure.
WHAT IS THERE TO DO?
Visit the world-famous Reading Room.

The British Museum is one of the greatest museums in the world, not only because of the volume of treasures that it holds, but also because of the quality of the collections.

Situated in Bloomsbury, the present building dates from 1823, and is a most imposing example of 19th-century Neoclassical architecture. The collection began in 1753 when Hans Sloane offered his extensive collections of art and antiquities to Parliament for considerably less than their true value. Further collections were added, including the Royal Library, which was given by George II. The collection was soon too large to be housed in the existing house, and Robert Smirke began work on the building that we see today. Altogether, including prints and drawings, the collection numbers over seven million items.

THE TOWER OF LONDON

England

The Tower of London was begun in 1078 by William the Conqueror, with the building of the White Tower, the first stone keep in England. In the early 13th century Henry III founded a palace here, and although no monarch has lived in it since Henry VII, the Tower remains a Royal Palace.

DID YOU KNOW?
Legend has it that if the ravens leave the Tower, the kingdom will fall – so their wings are clipped!

WHAT IS IT?
A royal palace dating back almost one thousand years.
WHAT IS IT KNOWN FOR?
It is most famous for being a prison and place of torture.

At various times it has been home to the Astronomer Royal, the Public Records Office, the Royal Menagerie and the Royal Armoury. It also, famously, houses the Crown Jewels. The tower's main claim to fame, however, is its bloody history, gained through having been a prison and a place of torture and execution. Most executions took place in front of a screaming mob at Tower Hill, but Tower Green saw the deaths of seven major historical figures, including two of Henry VIII's wives.

Yeoman Warders in Tudor costume, known as Beefeaters, guard the tower, as they have done since 1485. One, the Ravenmaster, is responsible for the Tower raven.

2014 saw the First World War memorial *Blood Swept Lands and Seas of Red* – a stunning art installation in which the tower's moat was filled with 888, 246 ceramic poppies, each representing a soldier who died in the conflict.

BATH

England

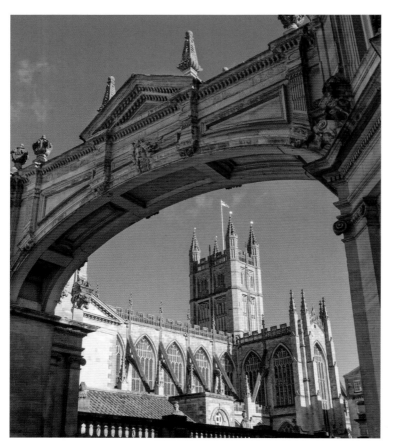

The city of Bath is a jewel of Georgian architecture but as long ago as 44AD it was known for its medicinal hot springs. The Romans built a temple and a complex of baths over one of the three hot springs and called the town that grew up around it *Aquae Sulis*. Medieval Bath was a prosperous wool-trading town as well as a religious centre, but it was not until the 18th century that, in part thanks to 'Beau' Nash, it became a fashionable resort.

The Royal Crescent is a magnificent terrace of Georgian houses built between 1767 and 1775. This is only a short walk from the Circus, a circle of 30 wonderfully preserved town houses. Plaques proclaim the many famous people who lived here – David Livingstone and Clive of India to name but two. The Roman Baths Museum gives a fascinating insight into the Roman complex that was here – you can even see the ruins of the 2,000-year-old temple or try to drink the waters in the Pump Room. Part of the complex has been refurbished to provide a modern spa.

WHAT IS IT?
A Roman site and the only hot springs in England.
WHAT IS THERE TO SEE?
Museum of Costume and the Assembly Rooms, the Jane Austen Centre, Castle Combe and Lacock Abbey.

STONEHENGE

England

WHAT IS IT?
The most famous prehistoric site in Europe, at 5,000 years old.
YOU SHOULD KNOW:
This is a World Heritage Site and there is an entrance fee.

The instantly recognizable 5,000-year-old stone circle at Stonehenge is the most famous prehistoric site in Europe. The outer, circular bank and ditch were constructed around 3,000 B C, and the inner circle of vast bluestones (granite that was originally blue) was added 1,000 years later. It is now believed that these granite stones, some of which weigh as much as four tonnes, were dragged all the way from the Preseli Hills of south Wales – some 400km (250 miles). Erected in pairs, each pair is topped by an equally huge stone lintel. Within the inner circle stand two horseshoe-shaped arrangements, one within the other, and at the centre lies what is known as the Altar Stone. Further stones are to be found here and there within the site, which is surrounded by barrow mounds. Archaeologically fascinating, the site remains a mystery, although many different theories have been advanced as to its original purpose.

SALISBURY CATHEDRAL

England

The city of Salisbury is dominated by the soaring spire of the cathedral, which stands in a beautiful walled close with verdant water meadows stretching away into the distance. It is a quintessentially English scene that looks much the same now as it did in John Constable's famous painting of 1823.

Salisbury Cathedral was designed and built in the almost miraculously short time of 38 years, between 1220 and 1258. It was made of Chilmark stone, quarried some 19km (12 miles) away and transported to the site. The octagonal Chapter House, started in the 1260s, took 40 years to complete. The spire was added in the 1320s and, at 123m (404ft), it is the highest in the country.

MEDIEVAL WORKMANSHIP
The building is an extraordinary feat of engineering – the spire leans less than 1m (3ft) out of true, and the foundations were only sunk a couple of metres deep in boggy ground.

WHAT IS THERE TO SEE? The Magna Carta, the cloisters, Mompesson House, Malmsbury House and St Thomas of Canterbury church.
WHAT ELSE IS THERE TO DO? Explore the water meadows in the surrounding area.

CHESIL BEACH

England

Chesil Beach is the most extraordinary part of the Dorset coastline and one of the strangest features of the whole of the English coast. Stretching for 29km (18 miles) it is a bank of pebbles about 170m (555ft) wide and 14m (45ft) high stretching from Portland to Burton Bradstock. The pebbles decrease in size from east to west – at Portland they are roughly the size of a fist, but at Burton Bradstock they have become pea shingle.

This pebble bank was formed by longshore drift: the powerful currents off the coast mean that the waves hit the shore obliquely, which has the effect of sorting the millions of pebbles deposited here over thousands of years. Chesil Beach is extremely popular with anglers, who enjoy the wild, unspoiled and atmospheric environment.

WHAT IS IT?
A bank of pebbles stretching for 29km (18 miles) from Portland to Bradstock.
WHAT IS THERE TO DO?
Enjoy a spot of angling or take a trip out into the Fleet in a glass-bottomed boat.

DANGEROUS CURRENTS
The powerful onshore currents make this one of the most dangerous beaches in Europe, and gravestones in many local churchyards testify to the many drownings and shipwrecks that have occurred here.

TRESCO

England

WHAT IS IT?
One of the prettiest of a group of 140 islands off the southwest coast of Cornwall.
DON'T MISS:
The Abbey Gardens, which contain 20,000 exotic plants from all over the world.

The Isles of Scilly lie 47km (29 miles) off the southwest coast of Cornwall and are made up of 140 islands, only five of which are inhabited. St Mary's is the largest and the most populated island, probably because it is the arrival point for ferries coming from the mainland, and it has an airport as well. Tresco is the second-largest island, and is much visited largely because it is the home of the Abbey Gardens, which are laid out on the site of a tenth-century Benedictine abbey. Myth and legend are part of the island's heritage — it is said that Tresco was part of Lyonnesse, the legendary 'land across the sea', and was King Arthur's final resting place.

Tresco draws loyal holidaymakers who return year after year to take a break from the real world and enjoy the wonderful scenery, sandy beaches, sparkling sea and unique atmosphere that exists here.

TINTERN ABBEY

Wales

Tintern Abbey is situated between the southern end of the village of Tintern and the River Wye. It was founded in 1131 by Cistercian monks. Rebuilt in the 13th century, it was home to about 400 monks, and despite the inroads made by the Black Death on the community, it survived until 1536, when Henry VIII brought about the dissolution of the monasteries and the abbey began to decay. Nowadays the ruins are well cared for by Cadw, Welsh Historic Monuments, and maintenance and restoration work is carried out to ensure their preservation. The imposing Gothic abbey church is the heart of the ruins and although it is roofless, it still looks fairly complete. The nave is 69m (226ft) long and most of the nave columns are still standing, as well as a complete southern arcade and part of the cloister.

HISTORY
Tintern Abbey was the first Cistercian monastery to be founded in Wales, and only the second in Britain.

WHERE IS IT? In south Wales, about 8km (5 miles) north of Chepstow, between southern Tintern and the River Wye.
YOU SHOULD KNOW: There is an entrance fee.

PORTMEIRION

Wales

Portmeirion is the brain-child of Sir Clough Williams-Ellis – a unique and bewitching fantasy village, set in a beautiful position by the sea. For 40 years, from 1926, this Welsh architect perfected his vision – a village of about 50 Italianate buildings, said to be modelled on Portofino, painted in pastel colours and built on sweet little streets around a piazza. The village has a hotel, a restaurant, a town hall, gift shops and several self-catering lets. The whole place overlooks a tidal estuary and a sweeping beach of pale sand.

The magic of Portmeirion has been the inspiration for many artists and writers, although it may still be best known for the cult television series, *The Prisoner*. Made in the late 1960s and starring Patrick McGoohan, *The Prisoner* was a bizarre and enigmatic story that kept audiences enthralled for weeks. Each spring, fans of the programme gather together in the village for a celebratory convention.

Portmeirion is only a couple of miles from Porthmadog, with its splendid views of Snowdon, and where visitors can experience the Ffestiniog Railway – a narrow gauge, vintage railway built in the 1830s.

WHAT ELSE IS THERE TO SEE?
The village of Tremadog, Harlech Castle.
WHAT IS THERE TO DO?
Spend a day at the seaside resort of Criccieth.
DON'T MISS:
Porthmadog and enjoy the views of Mount Snowdon.

DYLAN THOMAS'S BOATHOUSE

Wales

Half an hour's bus ride from Carmarthen, in south Wales, lies the pretty town of Laugharne, where Wales' favourite son, Dylan Thomas (1914–1953), spent the last few years of his life and produced some of his most famous works. Laugharne is set on the 'heron priested' Taff estuary which broadens out into Carmarthen Bay, and boasts the remains of a 12th-century castle. From the castle, which can be visited all year round, Thomas's home, The Boathouse, can be reached by a short walk down a path by the water's edge, or alternatively down a shady lane. The house, nestled in the cliffs over the estuary, is just as it was, perfectly preserved in honour of the poet and full of fascinating manuscripts, letters, photographs and even recordings of Thomas's voice reading his own works. The only additions are a bookshop, a tearoom and a viewing platform.

WHAT IS IT?
The home of the celebrated Welsh author, Dylan Thomas.
DON'T MISS:
A peek through the windows of 'the shack', as he called it – a wooden garage above the house where, amongst other things, he wrote *Under Milk Wood*, his best-known play.

SNOWDON AND SNOWDONIA

Wales

DID YOU KNOW?
Snowdon is the highest mountain in Wales, second in Britain only to Ben Nevis.

WHAT IS THERE TO DO?
As well as climbing and hiking in the area, you can also go mountain biking or pony trekking.
DON'T MISS:
Take the Snowdon Mountain Railway.

Snowdon is the highest mountain in Wales, standing at 1,085m (3,560ft) and is surrounded by a horseshoe of other peaks. Snowdonia National Park came into being in 1951 to ensure the area's protection. Hundreds of thousands of visitors every year come to scale Snowdon, either on foot or by taking the Snowdon Mountain Railway which runs from Llanberis to the summit. The views are magnificent, although the clouds may close in around the peaks here at all times of year, so check weather information before you start out. There are six main routes of varying difficulty to the top, most of which take about five hours.

This is a glorious part of the world with fantastic mountain scenery in all directions, and although Snowdon is the centrepiece, the park stretches 56km (35 miles) from east to west, and 80km (50 miles) from north to south, with mountain walks on the lower ranges, and beautiful forest and river walks lower still.

PEMBROKESHIRE COAST

Wales

The Pembrokeshire Coast National Park occupies almost all the coastline of south-west Wales. It includes the offshore islands of Skomer, Skokholm and Grassholm off the southern headland, and Ramsey Island off the northern headland of St. Bride's Bay as well as Caldey Island, which is further south, off Tenby.

> **IF YOU DARE:**
> Spend a day coasteering – a kind of rock climbing in the sea.

The Pembrokeshire coastal path stretches for 300 km (186 miles), which takes at least two weeks to walk and is a real test of endurance – most people opt for walking a section at a time. The rugged coastline and spectacular cliffs, probably the most spectacular in the country, are dotted with little fishing villages and vast sandy beaches. It is an austere and remote landscape filled with castles – more than 50 of them – and also St David's Cathedral, which is the most significant religious site in Wales. Generally speaking, tourists come for three reasons – to walk the coastal path, to look for wildlife (the islands are all marine nature reserves) and to practise outdoor pursuits.

THE DINGLE PENINSULA

Ireland

> **WHAT IS IT KNOWN FOR?**
> Spectacular scenery, early Christian monuments, Iron-Age fortifications and beehive huts.
> **WHAT IS THERE TO SEE?**
> Blennerville Windmill, Temple Monachan.
> **HOW DO I GET THERE?**
> It is best by car or walk the Dingle Way.

The Dingle Peninsula in southwest Ireland is the northernmost of five peninsulas that jut into the Atlantic like the fingers of a hand, and Dunmore Head has the distinction of being the far western point of mainland Ireland.

Each peninsula has a ridge of mountains, and the Dingle's are the Slieve Mish mountains. The highest peak, Brandon, at 953m (3,127ft), is Ireland's second-highest mountain. The peninsula is known for its spectacular scenery and its incomparable early Christian monuments, Iron-Age fortifications and beehive huts. Dingle itself is a beautifully situated village lying at the foot of Mount Ballysitteragh. It still has a fishing fleet in its almost land-locked harbour and is an excellent base from which to explore the antiquities on the peninsula.

THE GAP OF DUNLOE

Ireland

WHAT IS THERE TO DO?
Hike through the Gap of Dunloe for incredible views of the surrounding scenery.

The Gap of Dunloe lies to the east of Killarney, within the Killarney National Park. Killarney itself is the most-visited tourist attraction in Ireland and is the main town from where visitors can explore the sights around the lakes, and walk, cycle or ride through the Gap of Dunloe. This area has been praised by visitors since the middle of the 18th century; the climate is benign, the heather-clad mountains are dramatic and there are ruined castles and churches and glorious views of lakes and islands to be seen.

The gap itself was carved by glaciers and the route through it has extraordinary views of the three small lakes within it, and the boulder-strewn gorge that cuts between Purple Mountain and the MacGillycuddy Reeks – the highest mountain range in Ireland.

DUBLIN'S PUBS

Ireland

Dublin is the capital of the Emerald Isle, as Ireland is known, and it lies roughly halfway down the east coast, in the lovely Dublin bay. It is a compact little city, divided by the River Liffey into the north and south sides. Public transport is excellent, but the best way of seeing Dublin is on foot, which is particularly useful if you wish to sample either of the country's most famous exports – Guinness and Jameson whiskey. Dublin's pubs are famous the world over, and since Arthur Guinness founded his brewery at St James's Gate in 1759, they have been a focal point of the city's social life and the place to go to talk politics and literature, philosophy and sport. Music has also played a large part in Dublin's pub life, and you can still enjoy authentic traditional Irish music in many an old watering hole.

LITERARY CITY
Dublin is home to an astonishing array of literary giants, three of whom, Samuel Beckett, George Bernard Shaw and W.B. Yeats, received the Nobel Prize.

WHAT IS THERE TO DO? Have a drink in one of the best pubs, including the Dawson Lounge, Davey Byrne's, Toners, Doheny and Nesbitt's or Jonnie Fox's Pub.
YOU SHOULD KNOW: Dublin is really easy to get around on foot (just as well, really!).

KILLARY HARBOUR & CONNEMARA

Ireland

Connemara is a unique and beautiful part of western Ireland in County Galway, and Killary Harbour, which separates Galway from County Mayo, is Ireland's only fjord. Enclosed by mountains on either side, this 16-km (10-mile) long deep-water inlet boasts some of Ireland's most spectacular scenery and fabulous opportunities for boating. Nowadays there are mussel farms in the fjord and plenty of opportunities to taste them. You can even harvest your own mussels from the shoreline and cook them yourself if you want. North Connemara contains the National Park, which covers 2,050 hectares (5,000 acres) of wild countryside and includes bogland, moorland, lakes and mountains. Plants and wildlife abound. Peregrine falcons and merlins can be seen, as can otters, red deer, Connemara ponies and grey seals around the rocky coastline.

WHAT IS IT?
Ireland's only fjord.
DON'T MISS:
Harvesting and cooking your own mussels in Connemara.

POTATO FAMINE

This area of Connemara was seriously affected by the potato famine, which was sparked by the failure of the potato crop in 1845/6 and 1848. Today you can walk the famine relief road that was built in 1846 by local people in exchange for food.

THE GIANT'S CAUSEWAY

Northern Ireland

It is thought that the Giant's Causeway was formed some 60 million years ago. As a result of a series of underground volcanic eruptions, a vast amount of molten basalt was pushed through the surface. As it cooled, the basalt shrank and cracked into the 37,000 largely hexagonal columns that are found today, extending from the cliffs right into the sea. It is such a weird and wonderful place that it is the stuff of many legends, the most common of which tells of the giant warrior, Finn MacCool, who laid the causeway across the sea to the Isle of Staffa in Scotland, where his lover lived. Today it is the only UNESCO World Heritage site in Northern Ireland and attracts a great many visitors. The Causeway coast is a fascinating area in its own right, with spectacular caves to be visited, some on foot and some by boat, ruined castles, and lovely sandy bays.

WHAT IS IT?
The only World Heritage Site in Northern Ireland.
WHAT IS THERE TO DO?
Explore the caves on foot or by boat.

ALONG CAME A SPIDER

In Bruce's Cave, just off the coast on Rathlin Island, Robert the Bruce, King of Scotland, was said to have been inspired by a spider to win back his kingdom in 1306.

MIR CASTLE

Belarus

WHAT IS IT?
A 16th-century castle 85km (53 miles) southwest of Minsk.
WHAT ELSE IS THERE TO SEE?
Dudutki Open Air Museum, Njasvizh and Minsk.

Some 85km (53 miles) southwest of Minsk lies the small town of Mir, and its 16th-century castle. Founded by Duke Ilinich, it subsequently belonged to the powerful Radzivil family, who completed the originally Gothic construction in fine Renaissance style, adding a three-storey palace along the north and east walls. Its plastered façades are punctuated by limestone doorways and window embrasures.

Built predominantly of stone and red brick, the original castle forms a square, with a tower at each corner. The fifth tower, in the centre of the western wall, has a drawbridge that leads over the moat to the entrance arch. The five towers differ in design and decoration, including the number and design of the embrasures. Since 1994, when the castle was listed as a UNESCO World Heritage Site, further restoration work has taken place – and a museum, with an interesting display of weapons and costumes, has been opened in one of the towers. The history of the castle is rich and colourful and it is well worth taking a guided tour in order to appreciate it fully.

CHURCHES OF IVANOVO

Bulgaria

WHAT IS IT?
Churches carved into the limestone rock and natural caves of the area, dating back to the 13th century.
WHERE IS IT?
The monastery is on the banks of the Rusenski Lom River, 20km (12 miles) south of Ruse in northern Bulgaria.

A UNESCO World Heritage Site situated in the Rusenski Lom National Park, 20km (12 miles) south of Ruse, northern Bulgaria, high on the rocky banks of the Rusenski Lom river, this is an area full of natural caves. From the 13th century hermits and monks carved some 40 churches, chapels and monasteries and about 300 cells out of the limestone rock, on both sides of the river, using some of the natural caves as their starting point. In the 14th century wonderful murals were painted on the walls, and well-preserved examples can still be seen today in five sites. They testify to the exceptional talent and skill of the artists of the Tarnovo school. The caves remained inhabited until the 17th century. The Church of the Holy Virgin is the foremost of the churches, and contains a splendid portrait of Tsar Ivan Alexander.

SOZOPOL

Bulgaria

WORTH A DIVERSION:
Ivan Island and
Nesebar, Varna.
WHEN SHOULD I VISIT?
The Apollonia Festival
of Arts takes place each
September and is
worth visiting.

The Black Sea coast of Bulgaria has long been the most popular tourist destination in the country, both for northern Europeans in search of the sun and for Bulgarians themselves. Sozopol, which is about 30km (19 miles) south of Burgas, is the oldest of the Black Sea towns, and was first settled in 610 B C by the ancient Greeks.

Sozopol's old town lies on a small, rocky peninsula that is connected to the mainland by a narrow strip of land which is now a pretty park. There are some 45 architectural monuments in the town, including several interesting churches. The Renaissance St Zossima Chapel was built in the 13th century in honour of the patron saint of sailors. The 15th-century church of St Bogoroditsa contains gorgeous wooden screens embellished with ranks of icons, that separate the sanctuary from the nave.

PRAGUE

Czech Republic

Prague is set on seven hills surmounted by castles and churches, with Prague Castle on the west bank, dominating the city. The castle complex is home to the city's finest churches and museums. Founded in the ninth century, it has always been the seat of power. Outside the gate is the 18th-century Sternberg Palace, home to the National Gallery with its superb collection of Old Masters. The second courtyard contains the lovely Royal Gardens and in the third courtyard is St Vitus's Cathedral, a wonderful Gothic structure begun in 1344. The Old Town is a fascinating tangle of atmospheric alleyways and narrow, cobbled streets. Eight towers surround the enormous stone square at its heart, and there are superb churches and palaces to be visited.

DID YOU KNOW?
Prague is almost exactly halfway between Berlin and Vienna.

WHAT IS THERE TO SEE? The Old Town Hall, the synagogues of Josefov, Wallenstein Garden, Troja, John Lennon Wall, Vysehrad castle, Nové Mesto and the astronomical clock.
DON'T MISS: Crossing the Charles Bridge is a must for spectacular views over the river and city.

CESKY KRUMLOV

Czech Republic

Cesky Krumlov is set on a winding stretch of the Vltava River. It is a gorgeous, small medieval town in the southern Czech Republic, not far from the Sumava Hills and the border with Austria. Its magnificent Gothic castle was built in the 13th century, and revamped as a Renaissance chateau in the 16th century.

The chateau stands on the west bank of the river, opposite the old town centre, and is entered through the Red Gate. Crossing a bridge over a moated bearpit you reach the oldest part of the castle, which has round towers and Renaissance frescoes. The complex is so large, with more than 40 separate buildings, that there are three separate tours. The tours include the older, Renaissance rooms, as well as the Masquerade Hall with its superb eighteenth-century murals.

The pretty, old town centre lies within a horseshoe bend of the river and dates from between the 14th to the 17th centuries, and is in an excellent state of preservation.

DON'T MISS:
Take one of the tours around the chateau.
WHAT IS THERE TO SEE?
Egon Schiele Art Centre, the Eggenberg Brewery, St Vitus's Church, Zlatá Koruna monastery and the castle at Hluboká nad Vltavou.

TOKAJ WINE REGION

Hungary

Tokaj, with its population of less than 5,000, is a picturesque little place at the foot of the Kopasz Mountains with the Zemplén Hills to the north and the Tisza and Bodrog rivers to the south. The Zemplén Hills are volcanic and the autumns are mild, which may go some way towards explaining why this area produces such fine wines and has done so continuously since the 17th century.

Unlike Eger, the main city in northern Hungary which is famous for its red wines, including the well-known Bull's Blood, Tokaj, farther to the northeast, produces only white wines. It is known throughout the world, however, for its sweet dessert wines – Louis XIV said of Tokaj that it was 'the wine of kings and the king of wines'. In fact Tokaj produces various different types of white wine, all worth a try.

WHAT IS IT KNOWN FOR?
Tokaj is known throughout the world for white wine, and particularly for its sweet dessert wines.
WHAT IS THERE TO SEE?
Rákóczi Pince cellars, the Tokaj Museum and the Tokaj Himesudvar Winery.
HOW DO I GET THERE?
By train from Budapest.

BUDAPEST

Hungary

DID YOU KNOW?
Originally Budapest was three towns that merged in 1873.

WHAT IS THERE TO SEE?
The Great Synagogue and the Jewish Museum, Parliament, Gellert Hill, Heroes' Square, Esztergom and Szekesfehervar.
DON'T MISS:
The views of the city from the Panorama Tower of St Stephen's Basilica, spending a day at the thermal baths.

Budapest is really three distinct towns set on either side of the Danube, and linked by bridges. In 1873, the three towns merged. Óbuda and Buda (the historic medieval city on Castle Hill with the Buda Hills ranged beyond) are on the west bank, and Pest (the administrative and commercial city) is on the east. Large parts of the city are listed as a UNESCO World Heritage Site because of their architectural, archaeological and cultural importance.

Castle Hill, the heart of Budapest, is a beautiful area. It has suffered many times over the centuries from the ravages of war – but the Hungarians have painstakingly rebuilt their city and once again it stands proud. The neo-Gothic Mathias Church has a multicoloured, tiled roof and a wonderful interior, and the castle itself is now home to some excellent museums. Pest too has some marvellous museums – including the National Museum – and churches, of which St Stephen's Basilica is the city's largest. Its neo-Renaissance dome shelters a glorious interior, and the balcony of its Panorama Tower provides 360-degree views of the city and surrounding area. The National Opera House is a spectacular building in Andrassy Ut, the grandest boulevard in the city built during the glory days of the Austro-Hungarian Empire. The Parliament building dominates the river bank and its spectacular interior is worth seeing.

AUSCHWITZ CONCENTRATION CAMP

Poland

Auschwitz I, with its sister camp Auschwitz II-Birkenau, was the largest Nazi concentration camp. It is 60km (40 miles) west of Kraków, on the site of a Polish army barracks outside the town of Oswiecim. It was originally intended to house Polish political prisoners, but was instead developed into an enormous death factory, exterminating between 1.5 and 2 million 'undesirables', about 90 per cent of whom were Jews. Over the camp's gate is the chilling legend *Arbeit Macht Frei* ('work will make you free'). The camp authority's attempt to destroy the evidence of genocide before they fled the advancing Soviet army did not succeed and about 30 prison blocks remain, some of which house part of the Auschwitz-Birkenau State Museum. The visitor centre screens a bleak, 15-minute documentary about the camp's liberation in 1945. Auschwitz-Birkenau, just 3km (2 miles) away, was where most of the exterminations took place. At the height of its operation it could hold 200,000 people at once. It enclosed 300 prison barracks, five huge gas chambers, each built to hold 2,000 people, and crematoria. The ruins are haunting and utterly shocking. The site is well worth visiting, although it is not for the faint of heart. The unspeakable horror of the sight of thousands and thousands of toys, shoes, spectacles and bundles of human hair, heaped up in neat mounds, makes an impression that will never leave you.

YOU SHOULD KNOW:
It is not for the faint hearted. The horrific nature of some of the images and installations will remain with you.

BIALOWIEZA NATIONAL PARK

Poland

WHERE IS IT?
The national park is located on the border with Belarus, 200km (120 miles) east of Warsaw.
YOU SHOULD KNOW:
It is a UNESCO Biosphere Reserve and World Heritage Site. The park is off-limits without a licenced guide.

Bialowieza National Park is one of the last virgin forests left in Europe, a remnant of the primeval forest that once covered much of the European plain. It was once a favourite hunting spot for the kings of Poland, and the site of the former residence of Tsar Nicholas I, in the Palace Park. The ancient forest's huge trees and pockets of dense vegetation provide shelter for a wealth of biodiversity. It is home to some 11,000 species of flora and fauna rarely seen elsewhere in Europe.

The European Bison Reserve enables you to see some of these animals within the confines of a small park, or you can tour around the Strict Nature Reserve, really the main attraction here, with a licenced guide, either on foot or by horse-drawn cart.

GDANSK

Poland

DID YOU KNOW?

It was here that World War II started in September 1939.

WHAT IT IS IT?

A beautiful old port city on Poland's Baltic coast.

DON'T MISS:

The National Museum, the seaside town of Sopot, Oliwa Cathedral and Monastery.

Gdansk is a beautiful, old port city on the Baltic Sea, in the north of Poland. First settled in the ninth century, it became the thriving city of Danzig after being conquered by the Teutonic Knights in the early 14th century. By the middle of the 16th century it was the most important Baltic port, and Poland's largest city.

Gdansk used to be one of the richest port-cities in northern Europe and it shows — the buildings are bigger and the streets are broader than in other medieval cities. St Mary's Church is possibly the largest brick church in the world. Dlugi Targ is the splendid main square at the heart of Glone Miasto, Main Town. From here you can easily walk to the huge, 14th-century town hall and many other architectural gems, such as the unique, 17th-century houses lining St Mary's Street. You can stroll for hours along the picturesque old streets and river banks of this ancient port, which has been so significant in European history.

GRUNWALD

Poland

WHAT IS IT?
The site of the largest battle
in medieval Europe.

Southwest of Olsztyn, in northeast Poland, stands the Monument of the Grunwald Battlefield, in an area of gently rolling meadows. This monument, unveiled in 1960, celebrates the Polish victory over the Teutonic Knights in 1410, in what was the largest battle in medieval Europe.

The battle was won by the stratagems and cunning employed by the Polish king, who had been fighting the Tartars, Turks and Cossacks since his early childhood. To him the rows of noble knights in heavy armour marching into battle resembled cattle led to slaughter. They proved to be no match for the lightly armed and highly mobile Polish, Lithuanian and Tartar cavalrymen. After ten hours of carnage, half of the 27,000 Teutonic Knights were dead or captured and the rest routed. In World War I, on this same spot, the Germans took their revenge and beat the Russians at the Battle of Tannenberg.

The victory at Grunwald is widely regarded as a turning point in Polish history, and the battlefield and the small museum about the battle are frequently visited. Standing on the hill beneath the monument, where the king stood, one can imagine this clash of civilizations, and looking out over the grassland and forests below there is a certain sense of eeriness.

KETRZYN

Poland

WHAT IS IT?
The site of the
'Wolfsschanze',
Adolf Hitler's wartime
headquarters.
WHAT IS IT KNOWN FOR?
Site of the attempted
assassination of Adolf Hitler.
WHAT ELSE IS THERE
TO SEE?
The Great Masurian Lakes
and Olsztyn.

Ketrzyn is a charming village in northeastern Poland, dominated by a 14th-century castle, which houses an interesting regional museum. However, the main reason visitors make their way here is the 'Wolfsschanze', Adolf Hitler's wartime military headquarters. The so-called Wolf's Lair is located in the forest east of the town, and what remains of it, after it was blown up by the retreating Germans in 1945, is both historically important and a major tourist attraction well worth seeing. It was here, in July 1944, that a group of high-ranking German officers headed by Baron Claus von Stauffenberg tried to kill Hitler.

The ruins of 'Wolfsschanze', with 2–3-m (6–10-ft) thick concrete walls, endless fortified underground corridors, conference rooms and living quarters, all bear witness to Hitler's paranoia.

KRAKÓW

Poland

WHAT IS THERE TO SEE?
The Barbican, Czartoryski Museum, the church of St Peter and Paul, the Old Synagogue.
WHAT IS THERE TO DO?
Visit the Gallery of 19th-Century Polish Painting for an insight into the art of the area.

Kraków is the only large city in Poland that remained intact during World War II and today it is a well-preserved, charming, medieval city, with picturesque cobbled streets, numerous churches, museums, cafés, restaurants and bars.

It boasts an impressive central square with the 14th-century St Mary's church, and a 16th-century Renaissance cloth hall. The square is filled with countless stalls, selling numerous products from local artisans. The painstakingly restored Jewish quarter Kazimierz feels eerie and haunted – here is a Jewish neighbourhood without Jewish residents. At the start of World War II 65,000 Jews lived here, but they were exterminated in the nearby Plaszów Concentration Camp, made famous in Steven Speilberg's film *Schindler's List*. South of the Old Town is the splendid royal castle and cathedral.

MARIENBURG CASTLE

Poland

Marienburg Castle is the ancient seat of the Grand Master of the Teutonic Knights. It is situated in Malbork on the Nogat River, a branch of the Vistula River, about 50 km (30 miles) from Gdansk and 250 km (155 miles) from Warsaw. The Marienberg Castle is a classic example of a Gothic medieval fortress, one of the best of its kind in Europe, and the largest brick castle in the world. Together with a system of multiple defensive walls with gates and towers, it covers over 32 ha (80 acres). The interior houses several exhibitions, including a permanent exhibition detailing the castle's history, together with collections of medieval sculpture, stained-glass windows, coins and medals, weaponry, iron and foundry work, pottery, tapestries and a priceless collection of amber art.

HISTORY
During World War II the castle housed the prisoner-of-war camp Stalag XXB.

WHEN SHOULD I GO? In the summer for the *son et lumière* spectacles held in the castle courtyards.
WHERE IS IT? On the Nogat River, a branch of the Vistula River between Gdansk and Warsaw in northern Poland.
YOU SHOULD KNOW: There is an entrance fee.

WIELICZKA SALT MINE

Poland

One well-travelled Frenchman observed in the 18th century that Kraków's Wieliczka Salt Mine was no less magnificent than the Egyptian pyramids. Millions of visitors, crowned heads and celebrities such as Goethe and Sarah Bernhardt have appeared to share his enthusiasm when exploring the subterranean world of labyrinthine passages, giant caverns, underground lakes and sculptures of Polish heroes, all carved from the crystalline rock salt. They have also marvelled at the ingenuity of the ancient mining equipment. The mine is fully operational and produces about 20 tonnes of salt each day. Increasingly, since the mid-18th century, it has become a tourist attraction. Every last inch of it has been carved out and fashioned by hand and the chapel, measuring 54x17m (177x56ft) and rising to 12m (39ft) in height, took 32 years to make, entailing the removal of 20,000 tonnes of salt. The chapel is richly ornamented, and everything is made of salt. The altarpiece, the chandeliers and the sculptures and other religious artefacts are incredibly beautiful.

WHAT IS IT?
A fully operational salt mine, dating back 900 years.
YOU SHOULD KNOW:
The unique acoustics of the place make listening to music here an exceptional experience.

ZAKOPANE

Poland

WHAT IS THERE TO SEE?
The Tatra Mountains Museum, Mount Gubałówka, and Lake Morskie Oko.
WHEN SHOULD I GO?
In summer to enjoy hiking in the mountains and the abundant wildlife, or in winter for skiing.

Zakopane is a beautiful mountain resort nestled in the Tatras, the highest range in the 1,000-km (620-mile) long Carpathian Mountains, not far from the border with Slovakia, in southern Poland. Towering above the town is Giewont, a mountain in the shape of a sleeping giant, topped with an enormous cross.

Zakopane is popular both in the summer and in the winter. It is a great place for both outdoor activities and for a more relaxed contemplation of nature. The main summertime activity is hiking in the mountains of the magnificent Tatra National Park area, with its many fine peaks and alpine meadows. Here you can see a good variety of birds and animals – even the rare brown bear. In winter, the skiing is excellent, with four major ski areas and more than 50 ski lifts to transport you from peak to peak. Laid-back apres-ski spots are numerous and lively.

THE GREAT MASURIAN LAKES

Poland

Northeast Poland's Great Masurian Lakes are the most extensive system of lakes in the country. The region is a beautiful landscape of hills, forests, farms and lakes, many of which are connected by a network of canals and rivers. Altogether there are 45 lakes, 12 canals and eight rivers, making up the most extensive stretch of water in Europe, and the area is extremely popular for sailing and canoeing as well as hiking, mountain biking and fishing.

If you are not a sailor, it is easy to travel the lakes in comfort on a pleasure boat from any of the lake ports, or take a trip on the Elblag Canal.

NATURAL PARADISE
The whole area is home to an extraordinary range of plants and animals. Lake Luknajo Reserve is the largest central European breeding ground for mute swans.

WHAT IS IT? The largest lake system in Poland with 45 lakes, 12 canals and eight rivers.
YOU SHOULD KNOW: This is a UNESCO World Biosphere Reserve.
WHAT IS THERE TO SEE? Pisz Forest, Swieta Lipka Monastery and the towns of Gizycko, Mikolajki and Sztynort.

SIGHISOARA

Romania

Sighisoara is an exquisite, fortified medieval town set in the Tarnarva Mare River valley in Transylvania. Once a Roman fort, it was founded by craftsmen and merchants, known as the Saxons of Transylvania, in the 12th century, and was the birthplace of Vlad the Impaler, Count Dracula -- his house is now a restaurant.

WHERE IS IT?
Sighisoara is in Translyvania, central Romania.
DON'T MISS:
The Monastery Church, the Tailors' Tower, the Venetian House, the Medieval Art and Theatre Festival, Biertan.

The medieval citadel is entered through the Clock Tower, one of nine remaining towers out of the original 14. It was built in 1360 to defend the main gate, and in 1604 was topped with a wooden clock. This was remade by Johann Kirschel, who constructed two groups of limewood figures beside the two large dials. The clock mechanism moves the figures – for example, a soldier, representing Mars, and the angel of the night who carries two candles. At the southern end of the citadel is the Gothic Bergkirche, with a beautiful interior that includes remnants of 15th-century frescoes. It is reached by a covered, wooden stairway, which was built in 1642 to help people reach both the church and the school on the hill. The streets and houses within the citadel, which is still lived and worked in, are all wonderfully preserved. Narrow, cobbled streets wind past tiny craftsmen's cottages and wealthy merchants' houses, painted in pink, green and yellow ochre. Sighisoara richly deserves its title of 'the pearl of Transylvania'.

WHAT IS IT?
The biggest lake in the world, holding a rich variety of aquatic life.
WHAT IS THERE TO DO?
Take a boat trip on the lake or spend a few days on Olkhon Island.
DON'T MISS:
The Circum-Baikal railway from Slyudyanka to Port Baikal; the hot springs in Arshan; hiking in the Sayan Mountains.
ALSO KNOWN AS:
The Blue Eye of Siberia, Ozero Baykal and Dalai-Nor.

LAKE BAIKAL

Russia

Lake Baikal is special. Very special. It is the deepest, purest, oldest and, in volume, the biggest lake in the world. It holds 20 per cent of the world's unfrozen fresh water. It is so large that all the rivers in the world combined would take a year to fill it. It is in an active continental rift, which is spreading by about 2cm (¾in) a year and earthquakes occur regularly.

No fewer than 336 rivers and streams flow into the lake, while only one, the Angara, drains out of it. About 636 by 80km (395x50 miles), with a coastline of about 2,100km (1,305 miles) and containing 30 islands, Lake Baikal is in an immense area of breathtaking physical beauty, surrounded by mountains and forests in southern Siberia close to the Mongolian border.

ST PETERSBURG

Russia

DID YOU KNOW?
The astonishing St Isaac's Cathedral's enormous dome is covered with 100 kg (220lb) of gold.

WHAT IS IT?
The former capital and cultural centre of the Russian Empire.
DON'T MISS:
Nevsky Prospekt, the Russian Museum, the Steiglitz Museum and Yusupov's Palace.

Tsar Peter the Great of Russia founded St Petersburg in 1703. He had a vision of a great city dedicated to art and culture, providing a 'window on the west', and decided to build it on what was then a large, Finnish swamp, the delta of the Neva River, on the edge of the Baltic Sea's Gulf of Finland.

St Petersburg is unlike any other Russian city. Dominated by the Winter Palace, which stretches for 200m (660ft) along the river front, it is imbued with a sense of Russian imperial history. The Baroque palace was commissioned by the Tsarina Elizabeth for use by the imperial family during the winter, and its lavish interior gives an insight into the opulent lives of the tsars. Catherine the Great added the Hermitage in 1764 to house her private art collection, which has now grown so large that it is housed in five beautiful buildings and is second only in size to that of the Louvre's.

There are dozens of Baroque and Neoclassical palaces within the old centre of St Petersburg and an amazing array of churches. The area was declared a UNESCO World Heritage Site in 1990.

THE MOSCOW METRO

Russia

The Moscow Metro was designed as a hymn of praise to socialism. The beauty of the stations is renowned, and their sumptuous décor should be seen and enjoyed by everyone visiting the city.

DON'T MISS:
Komsomolskaya, the most beautiful of all the stations.

The outbreak of World War I, followed by the revolution, delayed its construction until 1931. This line originally had 13 stations, the most interesting of which is Kropotkinskaya. The walls and columns of the station were faced with marble taken from the demolished Cathedral of Christ the Saviour. In 1950 the ring line was opened and its Komsomolskaya station (1952) is the best of all. Designed by Shchusev, its underground pavilion is topped with a steeple crowned with a five-pointed star. The interior is sumptuous, full of astonishing mosaics depicting military victories and Russian heroes, marble, granite, multicoloured glass and chandeliers.

The Moscow Metro carries an average of 8.1 million passengers each day, making it one of the busiest in the world. Visitors should not miss this gorgeous underground art gallery-cum-museum — and you can travel on it too!

THE KREMLIN AND RED SQUARE

Russia

WHERE IS IT?
The Kremlin and Red Square are in the centre of Moscow.
WHAT IS IT KNOWN FOR?
The colourful domes of St Basil's Cathedral are an iconic image of Red Square.

Right: St Basil's Cathedral, Moscow

The Kremlin is a vast, fortified, roughly triangular complex of buildings at the heart of Moscow, and its name conjures up visions of Stalinism and KGB agents. In the 14th century it became the headquarters of the Russian Orthodox Church, and three great cathedrals were built here during the 15th and 16th centuries. There is a great deal to be seen.

The 700-m (2,300-ft) Red Square is dominated by the glory that is St Basil's Cathedral, its fabulously colourful onion domes topped by golden needles and its main tower topped with a smaller, golden dome of its own, the epitome of a Russian church. Red Square's sheer scale and the contrast between the beautiful churches and palaces and the stark Kremlin wall create a lasting, if unsettling, impression.

LEVOCA

Slovakia

The Spis region is generally regarded as the most beautiful part of Slovakia and Levoca, one of the finest walled towns in the whole country, is often known as the 'jewel in the Spis crown'.

The wealth of Renaissance structures that the town possesses today is mainly the result of extensive and elaborate construction work that followed a major fire in 1550, in which many of the town's buildings were destroyed. One that did survive, however, is the magnificent 14th-century St Jacob's Church, home to the world's tallest (over 18.5m/60ft) Gothic wooden altar which was hand-carved over a period of ten years by the great carver and sculptor Majster Pavol, after whom the town's splendid medieval main square is named. Other notable buildings include the town hall, the trade house, the theatre and more than 60 burghers' houses, mostly from the 14th and 15th centuries, in the main square.

With its medieval walls, its fine collection of well-preserved old buildings, its attractive setting and interesting history, Levoca – long a source of pride to the local Slovak population – has over recent decades begun to attract an increasing number of admirers from many other countries.

DON'T MISS:
Central Europe's largest castle at Spisské Podhradie; the cathedral and Gothic houses at Spisské Kapitula; the murals in the church at Zehra.
WORTH A DIVERSION:
Spend a day hiking in nearby Slovensky Raj national park.

YOU SHOULD KNOW:
On the island in Lake Bled there is a picturesque little white 17th-century church complete with a wishing bell. Legend has it that a husband who can carry his new bride up the 99 stone steps from the dock to the church will enjoy a happy marriage, and ringing the bell will make the couple's dreams come true.

BLED

Slovenia

Known in Slovenia as the 'alpine pearl', Bled is a particularly attractive small town in a fairy-tale location. Set against the backdrop of the forested slopes of the Julian Alps in northwest Slovenia and the peaks of the Karavanke Mountains, it sits beside a beautiful, emerald-green lake with an island in the middle. Looming over all, perched high up on the rocky cliff on the northern side of town, is the awe-inspiring red-and-white Castle of Bled, the origins of which date back to the 11th century. It was rebuilt in the 17th century, renovated and remodelled in the 1950s and now houses a museum. Once home to the Yugoslav royal family, famous as a health spa at the beginning of the 20th century and later the summer residence of President Tito, Bled has naturally always been something of a magnet for visitors – from the pilgrims of many centuries ago to the honeymooners of today.

Right: Beautiful Bled

ST SOPHIA CATHEDRAL

Ukraine

Kiev is the capital city of the Ukraine, and Saint Sophia's Cathedral is its best-known landmark. The monastery complex is large and elaborate. It was built between 1017 and 1031 in honour of Prince Yaroslav the Wise, to commemorate his victory over the nomadic Asian Pecheneg tribe, but has been added to and renewed over the centuries. The cathedral was named after the Aya Sophia cathedral in Constantinople, and was surrounded by other churches dedicated to patron saints. The exterior that we see today dates from the 17th and 18th centuries, when Baroque modifications were made to conceal the original structure.

DON'T MISS:
The tomb of Yaroslav the Wise, the cycle of frescoes in the lofts, the Golden Gate and St Michael's Monastery.

The cathedral has 13 golden onion domes, five naves and five apses, with two-tiered galleries on three sides. The interior walls are covered with frescoes and mosaics of the highest order, dating back to the 11th century, but including work from the 17th and 18th centuries as well. The mosaics in the cathedral are notable for their rich tones, made up of 177 different shades against a gold background. Possibly the most magnificent example is the 6-m (20-ft) high image of the Virgin Mary at prayer. The 21 shades of blue in her clothing convey the folds and flow of the fabric.

KIEV PECHERSK LAVRA

Ukraine

WHAT ELSE IS THERE TO SEE?
All Saints' Church, the Historical Treasures Museum and the Wax Figures.

WHAT IS THERE TO DO?
Climb the the Great Bell Tower for fabulous views across the city.

YOU SHOULD KNOW:
This is a UNESCO World Heritage Site.

The Kiev Pechersk Lavra (Kiev Cave Monastery) is built over wooded slopes above the Dnieper River. The name Pechersk refers to caves in the rocky banks of the river, where two monks founded the monastery in the 11th century. 'Lavra' comes from Greek and means a monastery of the Eastern church, living communally but inhabiting detached cells, or, as in this case, caves. This complex, believed to have been erected on a site chosen by God, is the spiritual home of the Ukranian people. Today some of the buildings are museums, but it is also a functioning monastery. The original few inhabited caves grew into two independent cave systems, each of which has three underground churches lit by candles and displaying wonderful icons. The monastery grew to cover several hectares and was surrounded by walls and towers, within which the monks built beautiful churches with spires and golden domes.

DUBROVNIK

Croatia

Dubrovnik stands on the coast of south Dalmatia, the most southerly region of Croatia. Its ancient city walls, reinforced with towers in the 15th century, surround and protect a wonderfully preserved historic city centre that was designated a UNESCO World Heritage Site in 1979.

WHAT IS THERE TO SEE?
The city walls, the Orthodox Church, the Synagogue and the Summer Festival.
DON'T MISS:
Do some island hopping on the Elafiti Islands for secluded sandy beaches and beautiful scenery.

Known as Ragusa from the 12th century until 1918, it became a rich and powerful republic thanks to its location. By the 16th century it had a huge fleet of merchant ships, carrying goods to western Europe, but its decline began after a terrible earthquake in 1667, which razed many Gothic buildings and killed some 5,000 people. New Baroque buildings were erected, and to this day those fortified medieval walls have largely protected the city from the wars that have raged around it. In the early 1990s the Yugoslav People's Army besieged Dubrovnik and ruined many of its famous terracotta-tiled rooftops. However careful restoration work since then has returned the city to its former glory. The old city is pedestrianized and a joy to stroll around. The main street, Placa, is paved with gleaming white limestone dating from the 1460s, although the buildings to either side were erected after the earthquake. The Sponza Palace dates from the 1520s and is one of the few buildings not to have been damaged by the earthquake.

KORCULA ISLAND

Croatia

WHAT IS THERE TO SEE?
The Icon Museum, Marco
Polo House.
WHAT IS IT KNOWN FOR?
A medieval sword dance
called the Moreska.
HOW DO I GET THERE?
By ferry from Dubrovnik
or Split.

Korcula is a long, narrow island, situated just south of the Peljesac Peninsula of south Dalmatia. The island is thought to have got its name from the Greek *korkyra melaina* after the dense pine forests that once covered it. It is a just a short ferry ride away from the mainland and was first settled in 6,500 B C.

The town of Korcula, on the northeast coast, is often described as being like a mini-Dubrovnik because of its roofs of terracotta tiles set above the sea on a small, fortified peninsula. The island has changed hands several times over the centuries, but the architectural legacy left by the Venetians between 1420 and 1779 is second to none.

The Land Gate is the main entrance to the old, fortified town, and the symbol of Venice, the winged lion of St Mark, can be seen above the arch. The Gothic-Renaissance Cathedral of St Mark stands on the main square. The doorway, built by Bonino of Milan in 1412, has Adam and Eve to either side and St Mark above. There is a lovely rose window in the centre of the façade. The Renaissance interior was carved by a local stonemason, and contains treasures such as an early Tintoretto.

SPLIT

Croatia

WHAT IS IT?
The second largest of
Croatia's cities.
WHAT IS THERE TO SEE?
The Bronze Gate, Jupiter's
Temple, Marjan Hill,
Diocletian's Mausoleum,
Mestrovic Gallery and the
Archaeological Museum.
WHEN SHOULD I GO?
Arrive in the summer and
soak up the atmosphere at
Split Summer Festival.

Set on a peninsula jutting out into the Adriatic, Split is the second largest of Croatia's cities, with a fascinating history. In 295 AD the Roman Emperor, Diocletian, ordered an enormous palace to be built here, and the heart of the city still lies within its ancient walls. For almost 400 years, from 1420, Split came under the authority of Venice, and became a wealthy trading port. Gorgeous Venetian-Gothic palaces were built and the resulting mixture of architecture is unique. The Bronze Gate, one of four, leads from the seafront into the Podrum, a series of underground halls said to have been Diocletian's prison. His mausoleum, guarded by an ancient Egyptian sphinx, is now the site of one of the oldest Catholic cathedrals in the world, dedicated to St Domnius, whose remains replaced those of Diocletian in the seventh century. If you can face climbing the steps of the bell tower, you will have an amazing view of the whole area.

HVAR ISLAND
Croatia

Hvar is a long and narrow island, which in 1997 was nominated as one of the ten most beautiful islands in the world by *Traveller* magazine. It is a perfect place to escape to from the mainland, an island of lavender fields and vineyards and hills giving fabulous views to the mainland mountains. The island has many pretty Venetian villages, and if you just want to relax, head for the southeast, which is still largely untouched.

St Stephen's Square is the largest in Dalmatia. It is lined with shops and cafés, with one end opening onto a small harbour and the other occupied by the magnificent 16th-century cathedral. On the southern corner of the square is the former arsenal, which now houses an art gallery that leads to the old theatre. The arched vault beneath the gallery used to allow Venetian ships to anchor safely while undergoing repair. In 1610 a democratic agreement was signed giving all citizens equal rights. For a short time the years were counted from that date, and the Latin inscription over the door reads 'the second year of peace'.

WHAT IS IT?
One of the ten most beautiful islands in the world.
WHAT IS IT KNOWN FOR?
Pretty Venetian villages and lavender fields.
WHAT IS THERE TO SEE?
Stari Grad, Church of St Lawrence at Vrboska and the vineyard of Zlatan Otok at Sveta Nedjelja.
HOW DO I GET THERE?
Take a ferry from Split.

THE BLUE CAVE

Croatia

YOU SHOULD KNOW:
The best time to see the Blue Cave is between 11am and 12 noon, on a sunny day when the sea is calm. This is when the sunlight sneaks through a submerged opening in the rock and, reflecting off the white sandy floor, floods the cave with a superb shade of blue – a sublime, once-in-a-lifetime experience.

The coast of Dalmatia is scattered with islands across its entire length. There are more than 1,100 of them, of which fewer than 100 are inhabited. Vis Island is the farthest inhabited island from the mainland, and until 1989 it was a base for the Yugoslav navy. This fact, combined with its relative isolation, has enabled Vis to remain fairly unspoiled despite the rugged, natural beauty of its interior and 16th-century Venetian fortress and monasteries.

Just 5km (3.1 miles) south-west of Komiza, Vis's second town, on the west coast lies the tiny island of Bisevo. Formed from limestone, the island is less than 6 sq km (2.5 sq miles) in area and has a permanent population of only about 20 people. To the east, Bisevo rises to 240m (790ft) and in the centre is an area of olive groves and vineyards, but what it is most famous for is its coastal caves. There are 26 caves around the coastline, all of which can be visited by boat, and the Blue Cave (Modra Spilja) in Balun Cove is by far the best known, and is often favourably compared to Capri's Blue Grotto.

ZAGREB

Croatia

WHAT IS IT?
The capital of Croatia, with beautiful old buildings and teeming with museums.
WHAT IS THERE TO SEE?
St Catherine's Church, Mirogoj Cemetery and Maksimir Park.
WHAT IS THERE TO DO?
Take a stroll round Medvednica Nature Park and get away from the bustle of the city.

Zagreb is a lovely Austro-Hungarian-style city, full of glorious churches, museums and art galleries. It is divided into an upper and lower town, each with its own distinctive character, which meet at the vast, paved main square, Trg Bana Jelacica.

The upper town, Gornji Grad, is the oldest part of the city, and is set on two hills. It is easy to spend time wandering through the winding cobbled streets that lead you from one splendid building to another.

A funicular railway goes down to the lower town (Donji Grad), which was built to a grid design in the late 19th century and is made up of handsome squares set around central gardens, wide boulevards and parks. Most of the museums are here.

THE ACROPOLIS

Greece

The word 'Acropolis', is synonymous with Athens in the minds of many people. In fact 'acropolis' means 'high city', and there are many other towns and cities in Greece built around a mount or peak. The Acropolis in Athens is a limestone outcrop surmounted by the distinctive shape of the Parthenon, a constant reminder of the glory of ancient Greece.

The Propylaea is the superb marble entrance gate to the Acropolis, built in about 430 B C, and considered by many to be architecturally the equal of the Parthenon. Built on a slope, it has five gates with enormous doors and wings to either side. The Parthenon, a Doric temple constructed between 447 and 432 B C, is made of about 13,500 blocks of marble, no two the same. It is a masterpiece of design, using sophisticated techniques to counteract optical effects that would have made the columns look too thin and the building squat. The outer colonnade consists of 46 columns supporting 96 metopes (carved panels) with battle scenes. The inner, Ionic, frieze was a majestic 160m (524ft) long but was removed and taken to Britain by Lord Elgin in the early 19th century. The aura of this extraordinary place is redolent with the weight of the history of civilization.

DID YOU KNOW?
The Parthenon is considered the most famous building in the world.

WHAT IS IT?
A limestone outcrop that stands above Athens, Greece's capital.

WHAT IS THERE TO SEE?
The Acropolis Museum, the Theatre of Dionysus Eleuthereus, the Panathenaic Way and the ancient Agora.

DELPHI

Greece

WHERE IS IT?
About 160 km (100 miles)
north-west of Athens.
WHAT IS THERE TO SEE?
The Museum, the Treasury
of the Athenians, the
Sanctuary of Gaia-Themes
and Mount Parnassos

The ruins of the great complex of Delphi are situated in a suitably awe-inspiring position on a ledge beneath the towering cliff face, with the clear waters of the Gulf of Corinth sparkling 600m (1,970ft) below. When consulted, Apollo's priestess was believed to deliver the gods' response in the form of esoteric riddles. The ancient Greeks considered Delphi to be the centre of the world, and it is mentioned in almost every Greek myth.

The site consists of two separate sacred areas, little more than 1km (0.5 miles) apart. The Sanctuary of Athena Pronaia has two ruined temples, ruined altars and treasuries and the Tholos. The Sanctuary of Apollo is more extensive and is covered with an astonishing collection of ruins, monuments, friezes and altars linked by the paved Sacred Way, which leads to the Temple of Apollo. To the west, Roman steps lead to the well-preserved theatre, which has 35 tiers of seats. Right at the top of Delphi is the stadium, which is also wonderfully preserved, and has stands cut into the rock face capable of seating 7,000 spectators, and a triumphal arch at the end. Here the Delphic games took place every four years.

WHAT IS IT?
A self-governing monastic
republic dedicated to the
worship of God.
HOW DO I GET THERE?
By boat from Ouranopoulis
to Daphne.
WHAT SHOULD I KNOW?
Only men can apply to
visit and must do so via the
Mount Athos Pilgrim's Office
in Thessaloniki at least six
months in advance. Only ten
non-Orthodox pilgrims are
allowed per day and only
one night is allowed at any
one monastery.

MOUNT ATHOS

Greece

Mount Athos (Agio Oros) is situated on the most northerly, and most beautiful, peninsula of the three that spread out like fingers from Halkidiki, in the Macedonian region of northeastern Greece, some 140km (90 miles) southeast of Thessaloniki. Known as the Holy Mount, it is the treasury of the Greek Orthodox faith, and the entire peninsula is dedicated to the worship of God.

It is the oldest monastic republic in existence and among its rules, which have been enforced for more than 1,000 years, are those stating that no women are premitted within 500m (1,650ft) and that no images of women are allowed. The Holy Mount covers an area of 350 sq km (135 sq miles) and is divided into 20 self-governing monasteries and some smaller monastic communities known as *sketae*.

WHAT IS IT?
The highest mountain in Greece.
HOW DO I GET THERE?
By road or rail from Athens or Thessaloniki to Litochoro.

MOUNT OLYMPUS
Greece

At 2,919m (9,570ft), Mt Olympus is the highest mountain in Greece, its rugged precipices rising to a broad summit covered in snow. It is on the east coast of mainland Greece, looking over the Aegean Sea. Mount Olympus is part of a mountain chain that runs north into Bulgaria and south into Turkey and it straddles the border between Thessaly and Macedonia.

According to Greek mythology, Mount Olympus was where Gaia gave birth to the Titans. They were so enormous that they used the Greek mountains as their thrones, and Cronos, the most powerful Titan, sat on Mount Olympus itself. It was later the home of the principal gods in the Greek pantheon who, according to Homer, lived in palaces of crystal on the summit, eating nectar and ambrosia, the food of the gods, which reinforced their immortality. Alexander the Great came to make sacrifices at ancient Dion, at the foot of Olympus, before he went to war, and today you can visit the museum and archaeological park there.

THE SAMARIA GORGE
Greece

The Samaria Gorge is in one of the national parks of Greece, and the only one situated on Crete. Set in the White Mountains of western Crete, the gorge is 16km (10 miles) long, starting from Omalos at an altitude of 1,250m (4,100ft) and dropping all the way down to sea level, at the village of Agia Roumeli. It is a hike that can take anything from four to seven hours. The first mile is a steep drop of 1,000m (3,300ft) that follows a tricky trail called the Wooden Stairs – this is the hardest part of the trek, after which the slope is more gentle. The path follows the river bed, so the park is only open from late spring when the river is dry. The vegetation is at its best in spring, when there is a mass of wildflowers and the scent of mountain thyme and oregano fills the air.

CONSERVATION
This is one of the last areas still inhabited by the rare, horned wild mountain goat known as *kri-kri*.

WHAT IS IT? A 16-km (10-mile) gorge in Crete's only national park.
HOW DO I GET THERE? By bus to Omalos from Chania. After the descent, most people get a boat back to Chania.
YOU SHOULD KNOW: There are guards to help walkers and make sure they are safe. There is an entrance fee.

PATMOS

Greece

Patmos is the most northerly island of the Dodecanese. The islands lie strung out, like jewels in a necklace, between Samos and Rhodes off the southwest coast of Turkey.

In 1088, the Emperor Alexius I Comnenus granted Patmos to St. Christodoulos, so he could found a monastery here in honour of St John. He chose a spectacular site that dominates the whole island, and the Greek Orthodox rituals still practised here are virtually unchanged from the 11th century.

The Cave of the Apocalypse is also a place of pilgrimage – in it St John wrote the Book of Revelation after God spoke directly to him from a crevice in the rock face. At the mouth of the cave is the late 11th-century chapel of St Anne.

WHAT IS THERE TO SEE?
The Monastery of St John, Patmian School, Ecclesiastical Museum and the Cave of the Apocalypse.

MYSTICAL ISLAND
Patmos is where St John the Divine wrote the Book of Revelation and is also known as the 'Jerusalem of the Aegean'. The island has a mystical, otherworldly atmosphere, and many visitors report having extraordinarily vivid dreams here.

TEMPLE OF POSEIDON

Greece

DON'T MISS:
Watching a spectacular
sunset from here.

Cape Sounion is the southernmost tip of the region of Attica, 65km (40 miles) southeast of Athens. The Temple of Poseidon is dramatically poised on a 60-m (200-ft) cliff, with stunning views over the Aegean Sea and islands beyond.

The temple was built about 440BC, to replace an earlier temple that had been destroyed by the Persians. Numerous archaeological finds on the promontory prove the area was in use as long ago as 700BC, and the existence of a sanctuary here was mentioned in *The Odyssey*. The classical temple seen today is thought to have been built by the architect of the Theseum in Athens, and is made of Agrileza marble. Fifteen columns still remain, standing on an imposing base, but much of the west side of the temple has been destroyed. The Propylon, or entrance gate, was added a little later.

SANTORINI

Greece

Santorini is the epitome of a Greek island, reached through a huge circular bay that was once covered by an enormous volcano. At some point around 1650BC the volcano erupted with such force that 30 cubic km (7 cubic miles) of magma was ejected causing the top of the mountain to collapse and an 8-km (5-mile) bay to be formed from the sunken crater. The cliffs are formed of bands of multicoloured rock and your first view of the island, with its sheer cliffs curving around the bay and rising almost 350m (1,150ft) from the sea, is breathtaking. Thanks to the volcanic nature of the island, the soil is extraordinarily fertile, and Santorini is famous for its grapes. Unusually, the vines are grown low to the ground and trained in circles to protect them from strong winds from the north. The white wine produced here is some of the best in Greece.

WHAT'S IN A NAME
The classical name of the island
was Thera, and Santorini comes
from the patron saint of the island,
Santa Irina.

WHAT IS THERE TO SEE? The Historical and Cultural Museum of Santorini in Phira, the traditional village of Oia, the Prehistoric Thera Museumand the excavations at Akrotiri.
HOW DO I GET THERE? Travel by ferry, catamaran, cruise ship or plane from Athens.

SYMI

Greece

The lovely, mountainous island of Symi lies 41km (25 miles) from Rhodes. Part of the Dodecanese group, the island is small, only 57 sq km (22 sq miles), with a rocky coastline with small coves and sandy beaches. The town is divided into upper and lower parts, dominated by the fortress of the Knights of St John and linked by 500 steps lined with Neoclassical, pastel houses with flower-filled courtyards. The harbour is utterly beautiful, surrounded by hills forming a natural amphitheatre. On a still day, in the upper town, it is possible to hear conversations taking place right down on the waterfront. Many visitors discover Symi on a day trip from Rhodes, but the island is so relaxing and has such natural charm and beauty that some of them return year after year to stay for as long as they can.

WHAT IS THERE TO DO?
Hire a boat to a secluded beach or hike to any of the isolated chapels.
HOW DO I GET THERE?
By boat or hydrofoil from Rhodes or Piraeus.

HISTORY
In 1309, Symi was conquered by the Knights of St John, who developed both a boat-building industry and the sponge-diving trade. In the 1830s it came under Turkish rule, followed in 1912 by Italian rule. Then the capital of the Dodecanese, it was home to the world's largest sponge-fishing fleet, and had a population of 30,000.

VATICAN CITY

Holy See

Although the Vatican City covers less than 1 sq km (0.4 sq miles) in Rome, it is in fact a sovereign state governed by the pope. It is the administrative headquarters of the Roman Catholic Church. Stroll across the gigantic, 17th-century St Peter's Square towards the basilica, passing Bernini's quadruple rows of Tuscan columns crowned with statues of the saints, and the Egyptian obelisk, brought to Rome from Heliopolis by Caligula.

St Peter's Basilica is enormous and can hold 60,000 people. Its spectacular interior is unbelievably opulent. The extraordinary dome, designed by Michelangelo, is 119m (390ft) high, its balconies decorated with reliefs. Inside the basilica Bernini's Baroque canopy towers over the altar, Michelangelo's *Pietà* is exquisite, and everywhere you look there are works of art by the Italian masters.

As if this were not enough, the Vatican Museums, housed in a collection of sumptuously adorned wings, boast one of the finest and most extensive collections of art in the world, including Michelangelo's Sistine Chapel frescoes, the suite of rooms Raphael painted for Pope Julius II and Fra Angelico's exquisite chapel for Nicholas V, as well as staggering amounts of Egyptian, Etruscan, Roman and Renaissance sculpture, paintings and porcelain.

DID YOU KNOW?
Climb to the top of St Peter's Basilica for the finest views of the Vatican City and Rome itself.

WHY IS IT IMPORTANT?
It has a wealth of beautiful architecture steeped in religious history.

WHAT IS THERE TO SEE?
The Cupola, the Treasury of St Peter, the tomb of St Peter and the Necropolis, where more than 90 popes are interred.

ROME

Italy

Rome is two cities — ancient and modern — and it is hard not to be awestruck by its blend of noise, excitement and bustle threaded with sudden calms of tranquil reflection. Some 2,500 years as a political and economic centre have defined its insouciant but passionate sophistication. Whether they have shopping on the Via Veneto, ancient ruins, historic churches, art or the *dolce vita* in mind, no visitors ever go away disappointed.

The rich Roman ruins range from the remains of the sumptuous imperial palaces on the Palatine Hill and the temples in the forum to the arresting simplicity of Augustus's *Ara Pacis* (altar of peace), the huge Baths of Diocletian, the exquisite beauty of the Pantheon, the eeriness of the catacombs and the chill of the Colosseum.

DON'T MISS:
The Palatine Hill, Trajan's Forum, the Castel Sant'Angelo, the Spanish Steps and the Borghese Gardens.

RELIGIOUS HERITAGE

As the centre of the Christian world for centuries, Rome has more than 900 churches and basilicas, among the most important of which are San Giovanni in Laterano (St John Lateran, the pope's church as Bishop of Rome), Santa Maria Maggiore and San Lorenzo Fuori le Mura.

VENICE

Italy

Venice shimmers in the middle of a huge lagoon on the northwestern edge of the Adriatic. Built on wooden piles dug into a series of mud flats and islets, it appears to float on water. Its realities — looming through a winter mist or sparkling in sunshine — are more beautiful even than its myths and legends.

The Grand Canal, at the heart of Venice, sweeps in a majestic S-shape through its centre. On either side, the shabby grandeur of more than 300 palaces bears witness to Venice's 1,000-year-old blend of Europe and Byzantium. Their collective elegance and richness of detail make a powerful reminder of the wealth and confidence of Venice in its imperial heyday, culminating in the Doge's Palace and St Mark's Square (Piazza San Marco). The palace dominates Venice in every direction — as befits the ducal home and seat of a government for 700 years. A *vaporetto* (water-bus) trip from San Marco to Piazzale Roma and back again is a good introduction to the city.

Save your gondola ride to explore some of the 177 canals spanned by 450 bridges linking Venice's six districts, or lose yourself in the narrow alleys away from the super-smart shops and hotels, where the only noise is of water slapping walls and washing flapping overhead.

DID YOU KNOW?
During Carnival the city is a swirl of outrageously glamorous masked decadence.

DON'T MISS:
Take a water taxi down the Grand Canal for the best view of the city.
WHEN SHOULD I GO?
Take in the atmosphere of the Carnival during the two weeks before Lent.

FLORENCE

Italy

Florence is the soul of Italy. Its centre, closed to traffic, still looks and feels like the late-medieval city state it once was. It resonates with the historical impact of its contribution to the cultural and political development of all Europe. It has an almost overwhelming range of galleries, fabulous buildings and treasures crammed into and between its churches. Its heart is the Duomo, dedicated to Santa Maria del Fiore, a perfect Gothic masterpiece, topped by Brunelleschi's dome and full of frescoes by some of Italy's greatest artists. Next door, the baptistery is a re-used Roman temple, with three sets of bronze doors that were among the earliest large bronze castings in the Renaissance. Renaissance Florence is dominated by the Medici and the works of the artists they patronized. Florence's two major art galleries – the Uffizi and the Palazzo Pitti – were built for their art collections. The third major gallery, the Accademia, houses Michelangelo's monumental statue of David.

Florence is the birthplace of Renaissance architecture, and such monuments as Brunelleschi's Ospedale degli Innocenti (foundling hospice) and the Pazzi chapel in the church of Santa Croce, and Michelangelo's work at San Lorenzo in the Medici Chapel and Laurentian Library, are perfect examples of their type.

DON'T MISS:
A stroll along the banks of the Arno to enjoy Florence's unspoiled skyline of russet domes and towers. It also offers you the Ponte Vecchio, the only surviving original bridge, with its houses and shops, still bustling.

POMPEII

Italy

Pompeii is a city frozen in time. It was destroyed by a volcanic eruption in 79AD, caught between Vesuvius and the sea. The eruption was two days old when a sudden change of wind brought a huge cloud of burning hot ash crashing down without warning – catching most of the population. Aristocrat and slave died together.

It is a city, not a village, and is known to have been where many wealthy Romans had holiday villas. You can walk through its streets and see its shops, houses, theatre, gladiator school, forums and markets. In the haunting Garden of the Fugitives you can even see its people: 17 casts made from the pockets of air found during excavation. Throughout the city, some of the best revelations are public and private frescoes, which give clues to daily life in Pompeii, its festivals and routines.

WHERE IS IT?
On the Bay of Naples in the region of Campania in southwest Italy.
WHAT IS IT?
One of Italy's most famous cities, frozen in time.
DON'T MISS:
The House of Vettii, the best example of human life in Pompeii.

Right: The Duomo dominates the skyline of Florence

SIENA

Italy

Siena is the classic image of Tuscany. Set amongst a landscape of soft, rounded hills bathed in warm, golden light, Siena's tranquil air of antiquity makes exploring it a delight.

Dominated by the Romanasque *duomo* (cathedral) at the top of the hill, the city's historic centre is a maze of little alleyways. Carved shadows mark every twist, opening suddenly onto sunny squares and ancient churches. But everything radiates from the enormous, scallop-shaped Piazza del Campo in the centre. One of the greatest squares in the world, it is overlooked by the Palazzo Pubblico and the soaring Torre del Mangia. Collectively, they are a UNESCO World Heritage Site and represent a millennium of Siena's cherished aspiration of independence and (not always successful) democracy.

DON'T MISS:
The Palazzo Pubblico and the Torre del Mangia, the duomo and the Museo dell'Opera del Duomo, the Pinacoteca Nazionale and the Piazza del Campo – one of the greatest squares in the world.

THE PALIO
Twice a year, the Piazza del Campo hosts the Palio, a frantic, bareback horse race round the cobbled streets Habitual calm is shattered by rival processions, each a kaleidoscope of colourful medieval dress, screeching bands driven by remorseless drums, and flags.

HERCULANEUM

Italy

WHERE IS IT?
On the Bay of Naples in the region of Campania in southwest Italy.
WHAT IS IT?
A Roman resort destroyed by Vesuvius in 79AD.

Herculaneum is the Roman resort town destroyed by Vesuvius in 79AD, at the same time as neighbouring Pompeii. All the evidence confirms that Herculaneum was an upmarket seaside resort. It feels different to Pompeii, because people were there to enjoy themselves, or to provide services for those on holiday. Appearances mattered to Roman visitors who were comfortable but not wealthy. For example, many of the columns were made of brick, then rendered to approximate fluted marble that resembled the real thing found in Pompeii. You can see metal bathtubs whose shape proves that there is no need to change a good design over 2,000 years; an early immersion heater in the men's communal baths; a price list painted on a wall; a poster advertising a shop's range of wines; and a fast-food restaurant where the counter is set with fixed earthenware pots that would have kept the food hot. All the shops and houses used brightly coloured, extensive mosaics and frescoes to foster a holiday atmosphere, and many have survived.

TORRE ANNUNZIATA

Italy

Torre Annunziata is a modern seaport in the shadow of Vesuvius, between Pompeii and Herculaneum. In 1842, the remains of three buildings were discovered and identified from a 13th-century map of Roman roads as the hamlet of Oplontis. This is the name sometimes given to the third and smallest of the amazing excavations of the ruins caused by the volcanic eruption of 79AD. The discovery included a bath house, a rustic villa crowded with victims of the eruption (and a hoard of gold coins and jewellery), and possibly the greatest of all the finds associated with the Pompeii area. This is a huge residential villa, now fully excavated and partly restored, that was part of the Imperial family's estates. It is believed to have belonged to Poppaea Sabina, the slave mistress of the Emperor Nero, who became his second wife, so the house is often called the Villa Poppaea.

RICHES OF THE PAST
Villa Poppaea offers an unparalleled insight into the lives of wealthy Romans.

DON'T MISS: Villa Poppaea – the long colonnaded walks, the *trompe l'oeil* and perspective in the frescoes (that survive in many of the rooms) and the internal courtyard decorated with landscapes – it all reeks of luxury and excess. What a place it must have been.

URBINO

Italy

Urbino is a pinnacle of Renaissance art and architecture. It is a hill town in the Marche region of central Italy that achieved cultural importance for a short period and then fell back into obscurity, which had the happy effect of preserving its harmonious 16th-century appearance. The centre of the city is a UNESCO World Heritage Site. The Palazzo Ducale dominates the city. It provided a standard for all Renaissance palaces that followed it and is still a worthy setting for one of the greatest collections of Renaissance paintings in the world, the Galleria Nazionale delle Marche. It is appropriate that the duke who built it was the legendary *condottiere* (aristocratic mercenary soldier) Federico II da Montefeltro, honoured throughout Europe as a diplomat and patron of art and literature. The city was also home to the painter Raphael, and his family home is now a museum. Raphael even influenced the majolica pottery for which Urbino is still known 500 years later.

Urbino remains a favourite with many visitors because of its fairy-tale skyline and the harmonious blend of the medieval cityscape and the Renaissance palace, which was designed to complement its surroundings, not to dominate them.

WHAT IS IT KNOWN FOR?
The Galleria Nazionale delle Marche, one of the greatest collections of Renaissance paintings in the world.
WHEN SHOULD I GO?
Visit Urbino's flower festival in May or the Jazz festival in June.

THE AMALFI COAST

Italy

The Amalfi Coast stretches for just 40km (25 miles) along the south side of the Sorrentine Peninsula, between Positano and Vietri sul Mare. It is stunningly beautiful. Backed by the spine of the harsh Lattari mountains, it consists of vertiginous slopes plunging 210m (700ft) into the deep, intensely blue Tyrrhenian Sea. Broken by rocky spurs and ravines into tiny bays and secret coves, it appears to be completely wild and even hostile. But every twist and turn of the switchback coast road reveals a dramatic new vista of ancient fishing villages clinging to the mountainside, tumbling down to quayside huddles of colourful boats and café awnings. Positano is becoming the resort of choice for the rich, powerful and famous. Its multicoloured houses crowd together, interwoven by a million steps, arcades, and arched passages full of shops, lively bars and excellent restaurants.

WHAT IS THERE TO DO?
Explore the 'Path of the Gods' and walk from Positano to Praiano.
WHAT IS THERE TO SEE?
The gardens of the Villa Cimbrone and Villa Rufolo in Ravello and the old paper mill in Amalfi, Capri.

Right: Positano on Italy's stunning Amalfi Coast

ASSISI

Italy

Assisi is an exceptional Umbrian hill town whose development since the 13th century has been guided by an idea. As the birthplace of St Francis (in 1182), and site of his most significant revelations and works, the town has ever since been the repository of masterpieces of art and architecture created to honour his legacy.

WHAT IS THERE TO SEE?
The monastery of St Francis and the Basilica of Santa Maria degli Angeli.
WHEN SHOULD I GO?
The annual Palio, an archery contest in August, and the Festival of St Franci in October.

The process began only two years after his death and swift canonization. Assisi had flourished under the Umbrians, Etruscans and Romans – but only now did it expand beyond its Roman walls. Nearly all of Assisi's art and architecture, through the Renaissance and later centuries, reflects St Francis's precepts of simplicity, humility and tolerance of differing beliefs. The church of Santa Chiara heads the list with its simple Gothic interior; the Renaissance finds some of its most harmonious expression in the Basilica of Santa Maria degli Angeli (1569), and (remarkably in an age of flamboyance) the peaceful ambience of the 17th-century palaces of the Bernabei and Giacobetti. This basilica houses the Porziuncola, Assisi's most moving treasure, the little chapel ('of the Angels') that Francis restored, and in which he died. Today Assisi attracts many groups and individuals looking to share the town's beauty, simplicity and tranquillity.

THE AEOLIAN ISLANDS

Italy

The now sparsely populated Aeolian Islands (Lipari, Panarea, Salina, Vulcano, Stromboli, Filicudi and Alicudi) are a volcanic archipelago. The earliest settlers, the Cnidians (580 BC) named the islands after Aeolus, the keeper of the winds, and Homer's Odysseus faced the mighty Cyclops here. More recently, Rossellini's 1950 film, *Stromboli*, was inspired by the active volcano of the same name, where regular eruptions still send special-effect, red, molten lava down the scarred rocks. The charming *Il Postino* was filmed on Salina in the 1994. The archipelago was designated a UNESCO World Heritage Site in 2000 because of its importance to the fields of geology and vulcanology, in particular because Stromboli and Vulcano are the archetypes of two different forms of eruption and have been studied for more than 200 years.

DON'T MISS:
The archeological museum in Lipari, the lighthouse with the horse's head on Strombolicchio, night trips up Stromboli and the Valley of the Monsters.
NOTABLE GEOGRAPHY:
The Bay of Fumarole offers incredible rock formations and black beaches.

SAN GIMIGNANO
Italy

The astonishing and beautiful old walled hilltop town of San Gimignano 'delle Belle Torri' in southern Tuscany displays one of the best-known skylines in Italy. Set amongst cornfields, olive groves and vineyards in the verdant Val d'Elsa with its 14 remaining towers (there were once 72), symbols of the wealth of the town's medieval families, the place took its name from the Bishop of Modena who is said to have repelled Atilla and his Huns. To walk into San Gimignano on a pulsatingly hot July afternoon, when the shutters are down as people take their siestas, is an extraordinary experience. The tallest tower, at 54m (177ft), and the only one that can be climbed, is the Torre Grossa, which has spectacular panoramic views. The Palazzo del Popolo has a charming courtyard with frescoes on the walls, and in the museum upstairs you can enjoy Memmo di Filipuccio's wedding scene frescoes. Wander through the town to the Rocca, the old ruined fortress, and walk up the valley to the Balze, a deep ravine where, since the middle ages, churches and other buildings have fallen into the depths.

WHAT IS THERE TO SEE?
The Collegiata (the former cathedral), Palazzo Vecchio del Podestà, the Museum of Wine and the Archaeological Museum.
DON'T MISS:
Climbing the Torre Grossa for stunning panoramic views.
HOW DO I GET THERE?
By bus from Florence or Siena.
YOU SHOULD KNOW:
The historic centre is a UNESCO World Heritage Site.

ORVIETO

Italy

YOU SHOULD KNOW:
Orvieto is a byword for good restaurants and fine wine, and you can enjoy both in sumptuous medieval surroundings. In fact, even 1,500 years ago, Orvieto earned the nickname *Oinarea*, 'where wine flows'.

Orvieto is a particularly charming Umbrian hill town. It perches on a huge outcrop of soft volcanic tufa (porous rock), with its steep cliff served by a funicular railway that isolates the spectacular Etruscan and medieval centre at the top from the modern area of Orvieto Scalo at the bottom. Its small historic area and easy accessibility make it a magnet for both day-visitors and for people seeking a special base from which to explore the region.

Orvieto's political importance throughout history is legendary. It was *primus inter pares* (first among equals) of the original Etruscan Federation. It resisted every attack – the Etruscans dug a honeycomb of deep wells (Pozzo della Cava is amazing), underground chambers, passages and openings looking out over the plain into the soft tufa. Later residents, ever threatened by siege, added underground mills and stables. In 1527, during the sack of Rome, Pope Clement VII took refuge here and had a spectacular well, with a double ramp to allow easy access, constructed. Above ground, the 12th-century black-and-white cathedral dominates the winding lanes. It is Orvieto's most dramatic attraction, and has some fantastic frescoes by Luca Signorelli and Fra Angelico, but scarcely less beautiful are the myriad pretty churches and *palazzos* crowding round it.

CASTEL DEL MONTE

Italy

WHAT IS IT?
A 13th-century castle 16km (10 miles) from Andria, built for the Emperor Frederick II Barbarossa.
INTERESTING FACT:
Castle del Monte appears on the reverse of the Italian one cent coin.
WHAT ELSE IS THERE TO SEE?
Bari, Barletta and the Castellana Grottoes.

Castel del Monte is a unique masterpiece of medieval military architecture and a strong statement of imperial might. Standing proud on the top of a hill and visible from kilometres around, it was built in about 1240 near Bari, in the southeastern Italian region of Puglia. Castel del Monte is a successful blend of elements from classical antiquity, the Islamic Orient and north European Cistercian Gothic. It is a UNESCO World Heritage Site.

The castle, which may not ever have been intended as a defensive structure, was the inspiration of the Holy Roman Emperor Frederick II Barbarossa on his return from the Crusades, where he had seen the octagonal base of the Dome of the Rock, although he could equally have been inspired by the imperial example of Charlemagne's chapel in the cathedral at Aachen.

GUBBIO

Italy

WHAT IS THERE TO SEE?
Palazzo dei Consoli and civic museum, Church of San Francesco; Monte Cucco, Valle di Spoleto, Perugia.
WHEN SHOULD I GO?
Arrive in May and see the Corsa dei Ceri.

Gubbio's historic centre is a crash course in medieval architecture. It is a town of Gothic austerity, dark-grey stone and narrow streets, developed to defend the wealth and power acquired as a city state. The Romans constructed the second-largest theatre in the empire just outside the walls. Within them, the number and richness of merchants' houses are just as inspirational as the 12th-century cathedral with its striking rose window and symbols of the Evangelists, or the Palazzo Ducale, built in 1470 with the most extravagant flourishes late-medieval craftsmen could make, to show the grandeur and status of Federico II di Montefeltro, Gubbio's new conqueror. Gubbio is home to the Eugubine Tables, a set of bronze tablets that constitute the largest surviving text in the ancient Umbrian language. They are housed in the massive, early 14th-century Palazzo dei Consoli, itself a statement of how Gubbio prospered in the Middle Ages. Among the city's other treasures are the basilica of Sant'Ubaldo, a Roman mausoleum, the late 13th-century church of San Francesco, Santa Maria Nuova and the Pallazzo and Torre Gabrielli.

HADRIAN'S VILLA & VILLA D'ESTE

Italy

Hadrian's Villa (the Villa Adriana) is in spectacular ruins, yet it is still the greatest example of a Roman garden. Built by Hadrian at Tivoli, near Rome, early in the second century, its 30 buildings cover some 100 hectares (250 acres) of pools, grottos and wonderfully contrived settings and vistas. It recreates a sacred landscape that can still inspire – and which is still traceable despite Cardinal Ippolito d'Este, Lucrezia Borgia's son, stripping most of its marble to build his own gardens at the Villa d'Este nearby in the 1550s. Both villas have UNESCO World Heritage Site status. Hadrian drew on his extensive travels for the design of his imperial palace. By combining Greek, Egyptian and Roman architectural orders he turned the beautiful buildings into a personal statement and many of the structures have symbolic meaning.

CREATIVE INSPIRATION
Villa d'Este has been celebrated in poetry, painting and music like Franz Liszt's evocative *Les Jeux d'Eaux à la Villa d'Este*.

WHAT IS ELSE IS THERE TO SEE? Medieval Tivoli, with several tower houses, the temples of Hercules and the Tiburtine Sybil, the papal fortress of Rocca Pia and the beautiful waterfalls.
DON'T MISS: The fountains and water features of the Villa d'Este.

MOUNT ETNA

Italy

YOU SHOULD KNOW:
Climbing to the top is strictly forbidden, and if it is going through an active phase, or is showing signs of activity, routes lower down will be restricted. Closures may change depending on the wind direction.

Mount Etna is Europe's highest active volcano, at 3,323m (10,900ft), and Sicily's greatest natural attraction. To the ancient Greeks, it was the realm of Hephaestus, the god of fire, and home to the one-eyed Cyclops. Now it is a paradise for skiers in winter, and for hikers all year round. Although there are towns clustered around its base, there has been little building on the mountain itself because it has numerous vents and it is impossible to predict where the next eruption will be, whether it will produce large amounts of lava or just steam and ash. Today, its wilderness is protected by law.

Etna has several smaller peaks on its flanks that are beautiful places to walk. The hike up the Monte Gallo, on the western side, leads to the Rifugio della Galverina, an outpost in the heart of the oak, pine, beech and birch forest that surrounds much of the volcano. From Case Pirao on the north slope, climb to the dazzling beechwood of Monte Spagnolo, pausing to explore some of the caves that pepper the Etna complex. Away from the popular routes, nature trails offer a chance to see lizards, weasels, hares, porcupines, snakes and even wild cats. The spectacular landscape is also home to raptors such as falcons and golden eagles, as well as owls and shyer birds such as partridges.

TAORMINA

Italy

WHAT IS IT?
Sicily's most famous resort.
WHAT IS THERE TO SEE?
Torre dell'Orologia, Church of San Giuseppe, Villa Comunale, Isola Bella nature reserve and the Alcantara Gorge.
YOU SHOULD KNOW:
There is an entrance fee for the Roman theatre.

Taormina has long been Sicily's most famous resort. Set high above the Ionian Sea, it was for centuries a major crossroads of the ancient world. It is a gem of interlocked Greek, Roman and medieval styles – influenced by Phoenician, Carthaginian, Arab and Bourbon tastes, as each ruled the city in turn. Taormina's consequent reputation for lavish adornment in art and architecture is matched by the wealth and luxury enjoyed by its inhabitants. The maze of streets, alleyways and staircases harbours hidden squares, terraces looking out to sea, and a profound sense of balmy enchantment.

The town is still a playground for the rich, famous and beautiful and the sophisticated buzz reaches its height during the film festival, one of several to take advantage of Taormina's special blend of beauty and history.

NOTO

Italy

ALSO KNOWN AS:
The Baroque city of Sicily.
WHAT IS THERE TO SEE?
Syracuse, Modica
and Ragusa.
DON'T MISS:
If you are short of time,
make sure you see
Piazza Municipo.

Noto is the Baroque city of Sicily. The ancient city was totally destroyed by an earthquake in 1693; so Noto was rebuilt 13km (20 miles) away in the then-popular Baroque style. Noto is the place to see Baroque art and architecture not just in its grand expressions of palaces or great churches, but in lesser, domestic and secular forms. Even the smallest details are harmonious: if you walk down Noto's grand main street, Corso Vittorio Emanuele, it feels like you are entering a period film set.

Of course, the grandest buildings are still the most interesting and most beautiful. The best are concentrated in the Piazza Municipio, Noto's main square, where the cathedral of San Nicolò de Mira is flanked to its left by the Palazzo Alfano and the Palazzo Villadorta, a fantastic froth of late Baroque at its most fanciful: it is covered in wrought-iron balconies and fabulous lions, nymphs, ogres and mythical creatures.

PANTALICA

Italy

Pantalica is one of Sicily's special hidden surprises. Just west of Syracuse, the rivers Anapo and Calcinara converge in a spectacular limestone gorge in the Monti Iblei hills. The spectacular, but hardest way to explore Pantalica is to take the straggling road from Ferla. Just before it ends in a precipice, a rough track tumbles downhill to the Anaktoron – the remnants of the ancient capital of King Hyblon, a king of the Sikels, Sicily's original inhabitants. And this is Pantalica's real secret, for you will pass over 5,000 tombs cut into the limestone, part of a vast necropolis developed between the 13th and 8th centuries B.C. The tombs were re-used in the Byzantine era by refugees, who carved deep into the rock to build the church of San Micidario nearby.

WILD BEAUTY
Coming from Sortino, pass a wonderful, clear pool in the Calcinara, shortly before it joins the Anapo at the wildest and most beautiful part of the gorge, where eagles soar above. The gorge widens out to lush fields and orchards of citrus, almonds, walnuts and even persimmon.

WHAT IS THERE TO DO?
Follow the trails through Anaktoron and see the incredible rock tombs.

AGRIGENTO

Italy

Agrigento lies on Sicily's south coast, the modern city spreading untidily from its medieval core. Its real treasures lie a few kilometres away, in the site known as the Valley of the Temples, where the ruins of Agrigento's Greek, Carthaginian and Roman past are testimony to its earlier importance and glory.

WHEN SHOULD I GO?
The best time of the year to visit is in spring when the almond trees in the nearby orchards are in bloom.
DON'T MISS:
The sight of the Temple of Concord lit up at night.

Founded in about 582 B C, the wealthy and important Greek colony of Akragas had some of the best public monuments outside Greece itself. The colony was destroyed and rebuilt on several occasions, particularly during the Punic Wars between Carthage and Rome. Surrounded by olive groves and almond orchards, the city's ruins include necropoli, houses, streets, auditoria and a small theatre. However, it is best known for its group of seven Doric temples on the acropolis (high ground) above the colony. The largest temple on the site was that of Olympian Zeus, built in celebration of a military victory some time after 480 B C, but sadly little of it survives because of earthquake damage and the quarrying of its stones to help create the harbour of Porto Empedocle nearby. Other temples here were dedicated to Hephaestus, Hercules and Asclepius.

WHAT IS THERE TO SEE?
The theatre museum and the cathedral.
WHAT IS THERE TO DO?
Make sure you visit the refectory of Santa Maria della Grazia, containing Leonardo da Vinci's *The Last Supper*.
DON'T MISS:
Make sure you see an opera while you are here.
VITAL STATISTICS:
Total capacity is 2,200 people: 678 orchestra seats, 409 seats, first and second galleries and 155 boxes on four levels.

LA SCALA

Italy

Even if you are not that fond of opera, if you miss the opportunity to visit La Scala, you will regret it. Here, Rossini made his name and Puccini's magnificent *Madame Butterfly* made her debut. It is the epitome of architectural, acoustic and musical passion and excellence.

In 1776, the Regio Teatro Ducale was destroyed by fire and the great Neoclassical architect Giuseppe Piermarini was commissioned by Empress Maria Theresa of Austria to build a theatre to replace it. He chose the site of a demolished church, Santa Maria alla Scala. Piermarini must have had phenomenal builders, because what is probably the most perfect theatre in the world was completed in under two years. It opened on 3 August 1778 with a performance of Antonio Salieri's *l'Europa Riconosciuta*.

LAKE MAGGIORE

Italy

DID YOU KNOW?
Lake Maggiore straddles the border between north-east Italy and southern Switzerland.

WHAT IS THERE TO SEE?
The Alpine Botanic Garden in Stresa, the Palazzo Borromeo on Isola Bella and Palazzo Madre on Isola Madre.
DON'T MISS:
Stresa's cable-car for stunning views.

Like many of the world's most fascinating places, Lake Maggiore, the most westerly and second largest of the pre-alpine lakes of Europe, is a place where history, cultures and regions meet. To the west its banks are in Piedmont, to the east in Lombardy and to the north in Switzerland. Before the unification of Italy, Piedmont and Lombardy were separate nation states, guarding their lands from the greedy designs of their neighbours. At Ornavasso you can still see the medieval watchtower with its spectacular views over the Ossolo valley and the peaks of the Corni di Nibbio alongside the octagonal Baroque church of the Madonna della Guardia, built between 1674 and 1772.

This stunning waterscape boasts the perfect semi-Mediterranean climate, mild in both summer and winter, encouraging glorious lush and exotic flora such as the orchids to be seen on the Borromeo islands, Isola Madre and Isola Bella, which also boasts an exquisite palace. The Borromeo islands are visible from almost every part of the shore and can be reached by the frequent ferries and water taxis that cross and recross the lake. Visit Swiss Locarno in spring for the magnificent camelias, mimosa and forsythia.

LAKE TRASIMENO

Italy

Lake Trasimeno is a place of contrast and contradiction. Surrounded on three sides by hills, its tranquil green waters are home to an abundance of fish and breathtaking birdlife, from wild swans to herons, cormorants, widgeon, stilts and wild geese. This, the largest lake in peninsular Italy, is a haven of peace. Conversely, the medieval fortifications of Passignano, Monte del Lago and Castiglione del Lago and the remains of castles on the Polvese and Maggiore islands proudly bear testimony to its turbulent military history. Legend has it that when one of the most decisive battles of the Punic War was fought here in 217BC and Hannibal of Carthage defeated Gaius Flaminius of the Roman Republic, the fighting was so fierce that neither side noticed an earthquake, which happened in the heat of battle.

Nowadays, the luxuriant waterside flora is rarely disturbed except by wild boar and coypu. Olives and pines grow on the Perugian islands of Polvese, Isola Maggiore and Isola Minore, the last of which has been uninhabited for centuries. Frequent boat trips take visitors to the islands.

WHAT IS IT?
The longest lake in peninsular Italy.
WHAT IS THERE TO SEE?
Castiglione del Lago's Rocca del Leone and the nearby palace of Ascanio della Cornia, Palazzo Casali 12km (7.5 miles) from Cortona.

THE ROYAL PALACE AT CASERTA

Italy

The 18th-century royal palace at Caserta with its park, aqueduct and the San Leucio complex, in the region of Campania, was declared a UNESCO World Heritage Site in 1996. It was conceived by King Charles IV, later Charles III of Spain, as a majestic statement of the power, wealth and prestige of the Bourbon dynasty. The palace most nearly rivals the palace at Versailles. It has been said that it is the last great building of the Italian Baroque. The main palace has 1,200 exquisite rooms, 25 magnificent royal apartments and a main staircase that boasts 116 steps carved from one piece of stone. Vanvitelli designed and built a magnificent aqueduct to provide the water for the many fountains and pools, most of which featured glorious statues. The little theatre is modelled on Naples' Teatro San Carlo and the whole is set in vast, enchanting parkland with graceful Italianate gardens.

WHAT IS IT?
An 18th-century royal palace considered by many to be the last great example of Italian Baroque architecture.
WHAT IS THERE TO SEE?
The gardens feature a series of fountains and an 80m (260ft) waterfall fed by the specially built aqueduct. They are said to rival the gardens of Versailles.

THE LEANING TOWER OF PISA

Italy

The Leaning Tower of Pisa is often considered to be one of the Seven Wonders of the World, but would probably be so anyway, even if it was vertical Construction began in 1173, and by the time the third level was added in 1178, the lean was already noticeable. Work stopped for almost a century because of Pisa's almost constant wars with the neighbouring city state of Florence and began again in 1272 under the direction of Giovanni di Simone. Four further floors were added, at a different angle to the lower ones, but construction had to stop again in 1284 when Pisa was defeated in battle by Genoa. The bell-chamber was finally started in 1372, fully 199 years after building work had begun. It is now known that the tilt is caused by the inadequate foundations sinking into the weak subsoil. Work started in 1999 to strengthen the foundations and remove some of the subsoil on the high side, and the tower was brought back to a lean of 13 degrees. It is now hoped that it will remain a monument to the vision of its designer and a testament to the 12th-century prestige and wealth of the city of Pisa.

WHAT IS THERE TO SEE?
The cathedral, baptistery and museum, the Church of Santa Catharina and the National Museum of San Matteo.
YOU SHOULD KNOW:
There is an entrance fee. Numbers are strictly limited, and queues for the timed tickets are very long.

BOLOGNA

Italy

WHAT IS IT KNOWN FOR?
Bologna is famous for its food
and wine.
WHAT IS THERE TO SEE?
Piazza Maggiore and
Piazza del Nettuno, Palazzo
Comunale, Basilica of San
Petronio and the Basilica of
Santo Stefano.
WHAT IS THERE TO DO?
Climb the Asinelli tower for a
spectacular view of the city.
YOU SHOULD KNOW:
The Museo Civico
Archaeologico has one of the
best Etruscan collections
in Italy.

Bologna is the capital city of Emilia-Romagna in northern Italy. Since ancient times, this has been Italy's most fertile wheat and dairy region, and it is famous for its fine food and wine. Europe's oldest university was founded here in 1088 when Bologna was a wealthy, independent commune. In an effort to outdo each other, every family of note erected a tower in their own honour. There were once more than 170 of them, but only a handful remain today.

The two towers that rise above the Piazza di Porta Ravegnana are well-known landmarks. Leaning precariously they have both managed to defy gravity for hundreds of years. The Garisenda tower is 49m (160ft) high, but originally it was considerably taller. Unfortunately, the Garisenda family did not bother much with foundations for their tower – they were trying to out-do the neighbouring Asinelli family's tower, which is an astonishing 97m (318ft) high. Garisenda leans 3.2m (10ft) from the vertical, and as long ago as 1360 the top half was taken down as it was considered to be dangerous. It is still closed to the public to this day.

The Asinelli tower also leans, although not as much. Completed in 1119, it has 498 steps that you can climb in order to see the most breathtaking view of the red-tiled roofs of the city and the verdant countryside beyond. On a clear day you can see as far as the Adriatic and the Alps.

The historic centre of Bologna is beautiful and among its highlights is the church of San Domenico, which has the saint's shrine, made by Nicola Pisano, and some early sculptures by Michelangelo.

PADUA

Italy

Padua lies 37km (23 miles) west of Venice, on the River Brenta. There has been a town here since before Roman times, but the Middle Ages were its glory days. The university, founded in 1222, is the second oldest in Italy, and boasts many venerable figures such as Galileo, Petrarch and Dante amongst its professors and alumni.

Modern Padua is a lively city but is something of an urban sprawl surrounding a lovely medieval centre, which holds a remarkable treasure – the Arena Chapel. Fearing for the soul of his father, a money lender, Enrico Scrovegni used his ill-gotten gains to build this chapel, dedicated to the Virgin Mary. In 1305, he commissioned Giotto to paint a series of frescoes upon the walls, and the results are magnificent, illustrating the life of Christ and his mother.

YOU SHOULD KNOW:
Visitors must book at least one day in advance to visit the Arena Chapel, and can only spend 15 minutes there. It is, however, an experience not to be missed.

CHAPEL FRESCOES
One of the best-known of Giotto's images in the incredible Arena Chapel is the *Kiss of Judas*, and the series ends with *The Last Supper*.

OSTIA ANTICA

Italy

DON'T MISS:
The panoramic view from the theatre at Tuscolo.
WHAT IS THERE TO SEE?
The Etruscan remains at Civitavecchia, swimming at Lido di Ostia and the hill town of Frascati.

Ostia Antica is a 20-minute train ride from Rome, and a world away. Its 10,000 acres of excavations reveal more details of ancient Roman life than any other single site. The ruins are beautifully preserved – often up to the second storey of whole streets – and because it is impossible to glimpse any modern contrivances and the site is almost always nearly empty, Ostia is the perfect place to imagine what being a citizen of ancient Rome was really like.

Visitors are free to wander. There are mosaics and columns everywhere, but the highlights are such domestic details as the fishmonger's marble slab and the communal toilets that seated 20 at a time. Behind the 3,500-seat theatre, where live performances are held in summer, is the forum with the Temple of Ceres at its centre. In addition to temples, public baths and grand public spaces, you can explore the houses of the poor and the typical street plan and shops, and be a Roman for a day.

PAESTUM

Italy

The three glorious temples at Paestum are the most important Greek monuments south of Naples. The town was founded in the sixth century BC, and, being near the coast, was named Poseidonia. By the first century BC it had become an important Roman trading port, but was abandoned because of the decline of the Empire, Saracen raids and outbreaks of malaria. Today the temples are a UNESCO World Heritage Site. The Temple of Ceres (now known to have been dedicated to Athena) is the smallest, and the first you come to before strolling through the ruined city, which has several other buildings to explore. The Temple of Neptune (in fact dedicated to Apollo) which dates from around 450 BC, is both the best preserved and the largest of the three temples, missing only its roof and some of its interior walls.

HISTORY
The town was abandoned because of the decline of the Empire, Saracen raids and outbreaks of malaria and the temples were not rediscovered until the 20th century.

WHAT IS IT? Paestum contains the three most important Greek monuments south of Naples.
DON'T MISS: Visit the temple of Neptune for a look at the best-preserved temple.
YOU SHOULD KNOW: A visit to Southern Italy would not be complete without a visit to Paestum.

PORTOFINO

Italy

WHAT IS IT?
One of Liguria's most
exclusive seaside resorts,
east of Genoa.
WHAT IS THERE TO SEE:
Rapallo, the church of San
Giorgio, Santa Margherita
and the five villages of
Cinque Terra.

If you are looking for the high life, come to Portofino, one of Liguria's most exclusive seaside resorts, and also one of its most beautiful. It is situated on an idyllic promontory, its harbour is full of the elegant yachts of the international jet-set and its calm waters reflect the lovely ochre and yellow houses ringed around the water's edge. The village has long been a favourite with celebrities – Truman Capote and Guy de Maupassant both wrote here; Hollywood stars such as Greta Garbo, Clark Gable, Elizabeth Taylor and Rex Harrison stayed here; the Duke and Duchess of Windsor honeymooned here; and Aristotle Onassis arrived on his yacht. Today the rich and famous tend to holiday in private villas up in the hills behind the town but you never know who you might spot hiding behind sunglasses and sipping a Campari and soda at a waterfront bar.

Take a boat trip or a walk across the promontory to the 11th-century Abbazia di San Fruttuoso, set amongst pine trees and olive groves. Nearby, but out to sea, is a bronze statue of Christ, placed on the sea-bed in 1954 to protect sailors. You can either take a boat to see this, on a calm day, or dive down for a close-up look, if you are not too busy shopping in one of the expensive little boutiques around town.

CAPRI

Italy

WHAT IS THERE TO DO?
Ensure you visit the gardens
of Augustus and take the
chairlift up to Monte Solaro.
DON'T MISS:
The Blue Grotto.
HOW DO I GET THERE?
Take a ferry or hydrofoil from
Naples, Sorrento, Salerno,
Positano or Amalfi.

The enchanting island of Capri, in the bay of Naples, is one of Italy's loveliest resorts. This small island rises sharply from the sea and is a beautiful jumble of tumbling purple, pink and white bougainvillea, lemon trees, narrow, winding lanes, and pastel houses.

Visit the gardens of Caesar Augustus and admire the astonishing views across the sea to Faraglioni Rocks. Walk along the Via Tiberio to the Villa Jovis, the best and largest of the Roman villas, where both Tiberius and Caligula were reported to indulge in orgies and torture, although this rumour may have been anti-imperial propaganda. At Anacapri you can explore the Villa San Michele, and its superb gardens, built by Axel Munthe, a Swedish doctor, on the ruins of another Roman villa. Whatever you do, do not forget to visit the world-famous Blue Grotto, one of several sea caves along the rocky coast.

Right: The harbour of Portofino

SKOPJE

Macedonia

In 1963 a dreadful earthquake almost annihilated the town of Skopje, killing over 1,000 inhabitants and pulverizing their homes. The Old Bazaar and the ancient churches and mosques of the old town, north of the Vardar River, were spared.

At first glance Macedonia's capital city looks entirely modern, but in fact it has been inhabited since at least 3,500 BC. In 148 BC it came under Roman rule and subsequently passed into the hands of the Byzantine Empire. In 1392 it was conquered by the Turks and remained part of the Ottoman Empire for 500 years. A 15th-century stone bridge with 11 arches leads over the Vardar to the old city where you will find the Daut Pasha hamam, an extensive public bath complex that now houses the National Art Gallery's special collection, and the fascinating Old Bazaar, one of the largest of its kind in Europe. Here too is the 15th-century Mustafa Pasha's mosque. At the top of the hill stand the ruins of the fifth-century Kale fortress.

Skopje is a welcoming city that has a great deal of interesting historical monuments to see, as well as a burgeoning arts scene and vibrant nightlife.

WHAT IS IT?
Macedonia's capital city, in the north of the country and inhabited since 3,500 BC.
WHAT IS THERE TO SEE?
The Kursumli Han caravanserai or any of the many museums.

OHRID

Macedonia

The town of Ohrid is probably the most beautiful town in Macedonia, situated on the shores of Lake Ohrid in the southwest of the country, with steep, cobbled streets that wind through the old town beneath the tenth-century citadel of Tsar Samuil, which may be on the site of one built by Alexander the Great's father, Philip II of Macedon. The town became Christian early on – its first known bishop was Zosimus, in about 344 AD. Many fine churches and monasteries were built and there is a wealth of exquisite religious artwork here – fabulous icons, frescoes, moscaics and iconostases created in different eras. The 13th-century church of St Clement has beautiful frescoes, while the monastery of St Panteleimon has more than 800 icons from the 11th to 14th centuries. It is said that by the 15th century there was a chapel for each day of the year.

WHAT IS IT?
One of the most beautiful towns in Macedonia, set on the shore of Lake Ohrid.
WHAT IS THERE TO SEE?
Church of St Sophia, Church of St Naum, Church of St Clement, Church of St John the Divine and the Roman theatre.

VALLETTA

Malta

YOU SHOULD KNOW:
Valetta is not a museum-piece – as well as a tourist destination, it is a busy, working city with a lively arts programme and offers something for everyone.

The Baroque, fortified city of Valletta is built on the high, rocky Sceberras Peninsula, on Malta's northeast coast, and is surrounded on three sides by two of the most beautiful natural harbours in Europe, the Grand Harbour and Marsamxett Harbour. A panoramic harbour view can be seen from the Upper Barracca Gardens.

Explore the ancient fortifications, then wander through the narrow city streets and you will see statues, fountains and parapets above you sporting coats of arms as well as splendid Baroque architecture. St John's Co-Cathedral is magnificent. Its severe façade shelters an interior of lavish Baroque extravagance, with painted ceiling vaults, intricately carved stone walls and superb marble tombstones set in the floor. Among its many works of art is Caravaggio's late masterpiece, *The Beheading of John the Baptist,* while there are other important works in the museum next door.

KOTOR

Montenegro

First settled during Roman times, when it was part of the province of Dalmatia, and later becoming the ancient maritime centre of Montenegro, Kotor lies some 22km (14 miles) up the Adriatic coast from the busy beach resort of Budva. The attractions of the town owe much to its beautiful setting at the end of the Gulf of Kotor, a submerged river valley, surrounded by cliffs and steep-sloped hills. Despite being hit by earthquakes, most recently in the 1970s, Kotor is a particularly well-preserved medieval town, with no fewer than six Romanesque churches dating from the 12th and 13th centuries and a wealth of fine old buildings, from palaces to small private houses, all in a labyrinth of narrow cobbled streets and squares.

CITY WALLS
Kotor's city walls are one of the finest examples of fortifications in Europe. Reaching up to 20m (66ft) high and over 10m (33ft) wide in places, they wind for 5km (3 miles) around the city.

HOW DO I GET THERE? Travel by road from Podgorica or Budva.
WHAT IS THERE TO SEE? The view from the Fortress of St John and the city walls.
DON'T MISS: The mountain road from Kotor to Cetinje and Durmitor National Park.

THE ALHAMBRA

Spain

The city of Granada is dominated by the incredible Alhambra palace. The Alcazaba is the oldest part of the site, dating from the mid-13th century, and was built on the foundations of the original ninth-century Moorish fortress. From the watchtower of the Alcazaba you can see the Alhambra proper, a spectacular series of courtyards and halls decorated with carved wood, ornate stucco, fantastic ceiling paintings, horseshoe arches and the fabulous complex patterns of multicoloured glazed tiles. There are many fountains and pools throughout the site and the delightful sounds of water can be heard where ever you go. The pool in the Court of Myrtles is a perfect example of Moorish architecture, surrounded as it is by graceful columns and arches that are reflected in the water.

WHAT IS IT?
A Moorish palace dating back to 1238.
WHAT IS THERE TO SEE?
The Tower of Comares, the ceiling of the Hall of Abencerrajes and the Hall of the Kings.

HISTORY
In 1238, when Muhammad I took control of Granada, the Christians were regaining ground across the Iberian peninsula, and Granada became a Moorish vassal state of Spain. Under these unpromising circumstances, the caliphs of the Nasrid dynasty produced the finest flowering of their art and architecture ever to be seen.

BARCELONA

Spain

WHAT IS THERE TO SEE?
Palau and Park Güell, Palau
de la Música Catalana,
Museu Picasso, Las
Ramblas and Illa de
la Discordia.
DON'T MISS:
Spend an evening on Las
Ramblas soaking up the
atmosphere and enjoying
the street performances.
WHAT IS THERE TO DO?
Visit the Museu Picasso
and see original works in
an extensive installation.

Sitting on Spain's northeastern Mediterranean coast, the Catalan capital, Barcelona, is a great European city that, despite having a splendid medieval centre including the well-known Las Ramblas, is best known for the extraordinary Modernist buildings created by Antoni Gaudí (1852–1926) and other architects. Most of these buildings are to be found in the Eixample area.

The Casa Milà, known by the locals as La Pedrera, is perhaps the most famous example of Gaudí's domestic architecture – an apartment block whose undulating façade, supposedly inspired by the rock face of Montserrat, Catalonia's sacred mountain, appears to flow around the corner, and whose rooftop chimneys and air vents form a sculpture garden.

It is Gaudí's still-unfinished church, however, that is his greatest achievement. From 1884 La Sagrada Família became Gaudí's obsession and he even lived on the site for 16 years. It has four spires, each over 100m (330ft) high and topped with coloured ceramics, and stone porches that look as though they are made of dripping wax or a weird stalactite formation. The Nativity façade is the most complete part of Gaudí's church, with doorways that represent faith, hope and charity.

SANTIAGO DE COMPOSTELA

Spain

In the ninth century, a tomb supposed to be that of St James the Apostle was discovered at Santiago de Compostela, and by the Middle Ages this had become the third-most important place of Christian pilgrimage after St Peter's in Rome and Jerusalem. Today, both pilgrims and tourists still follow the ancient route across northern Spain to the towering cathedral.

YOU SHOULD KNOW:
There is an entrance fee for the museum and cloisters.

Santiago Cathedral was built on the site of a ninth-century basilica between the 11th and 13th centuries. Although there have been additions such as the Baroque Obradoiro façade, the interior remains as it was almost 800 years ago. Behind the Obradoiro façade stands the superb 12th-century Portico de la Gloria, with its three decorated arches.

During the Middle Ages, as many as two million visitors made their way here on foot each year, and in the 12th century a monk named Aymery Picaud wrote the first guidebook in the world in order to help them, describing in detail the best routes and the best places to stay. Today, visitor numbers have not changed, but although many people choose to walk at least part of the way, it is not strictly necessary.

A CORUÑA

Spain

WHAT IS IT?
A town in northwest Spain with the world's oldest working lighthouse.
DON'T MISS:
Climbing to the top of the Tower of Hercules for an amazing panoramic view of the ocean.

A Coruña (La Coruña or Corunna) is built on a narrow peninsula in the northwest of Spain at the tip of which stands the Torre de Hercules – the oldest working lighthouse in the world. Originally built by Gaius Sevius Lupus, it has stood and served for 1,900 years. It appears in many medieval manuscripts, including the Hereford *Mappa Mundi*, which dates back to about 1285. The naval architect Don Eustaquio Giannini completely overhauled it in 1785, in a very sensitive reconstruction that echoed the Roman design he found within. The tower, which had fallen into disrepair, was raised again in 1847 and stands 49m (161ft) high. Today the lighthouse has been fully modernized and its beacon has a range of 37km (23 miles). Climb the 242 steps to the top for a panoramic ocean view.

PAMPLONA

Spain

DID YOU KNOW?
Pamplona has been the capital of Navarre in northern Spain since the ninth century.

WHAT IS THERE TO SEE?
The Museo de Navarra, the citadel and the cathedral.
WHEN SHOULD I VISIT?
The festival runs from 6–14 July.
YOU SHOULD KNOW:
Every year there are serious injuries sustained in the *encierro*.

Ernest Hemingway put Pamplona and its 'fiesta' firmly on the map when he published his book *The Sun Also Rises*. At midday on 6 July the fiesta gets going with a bang as a rocket explodes outside the town hall, and the crowd tie their red handkerchiefs around their necks, singing and shouting 'Viva San Fermín!' On the last night, 14 July, the party comes to an end with crowds of people holding candles and singing Basque songs in the main square.

The eight-day fiesta of San Fermín is a week of non-stop riotous parties, fireworks, parades, music, dancing and, at 8am each day, the *encierro* (running of the bulls). Six bulls are released to run through the old town's cobbled streets, on their way to the bullring for the evening's bullfight. Every day, too, men take the opportunity to run through the streets with the bulls, risking injury and even death.

If this sounds too dangerous for you, Pamplona also has Spain's best medieval military architecture in the form of the star-shaped citadel and city walls that Philip II had built in order to defend against the depredations of the French.

GUGGENHEIM MUSEUM

Spain

Bilbao is in the Basque Country of northern Spain and since the 19th century has been Spain's leading commercial port. An urban development scheme was introduced to regenerate the industrial sprawl, complete with futuristic buildings and a stylish metro system, and the port was moved to the coast. In 1991 the Basque authorities and the Guggenheim Foundation agreed to found a new Guggenheim Museum as part of the revitalization of Bilbao. In 1993 Frank O. Gehry's design was accepted, the foundation stone laid and in October 1997 the museum opened. By October 1998, the museum had received more than 1.3 million visitors.

The building is a piece of art in its own right. Built in limestone, glass and titanium it covers a 3.25-hectare (8-acre) site that runs down to the river, 16m (55ft) below the level of the rest of Bilbao. Outside it are several fantastic installations by contemporary artists. Inside, the spectacular atrium, with its flower-shaped skylight, is the centrepiece of Gehry's vision and is surrounded by 19 galleries on three levels, connected by curving walkways suspended from the roof.

WHAT IS IT?
A world renowned art gallery.
WHAT IS THERE TO SEE?
The wide range of art from the last 40 years of the twentieth century.

SANTA MARÍA DE GUADALUPE

Spain

WHAT IS IT?
An revered monastery founded in 1340 by Alfonso XI.
DON'T MISS:
The Baroque sacristy; the church; the Ermita del Humilladero.

Right: The spectacular Guggenheim Museum

The monastery of Guadalupe was founded in 1340 by Alfonso XI, in gratitude to the Virgin Mary, who had helped him to win an important battle. Legend has it that the religious significance of the site came about thanks to a peasant who, whilst out searching for a missing cow, had a vision and discovered a statue of the Virgin, carved by St Luke. Over time, three hospitals and a school of medicine were built and a pharmacy, where monks made remedies from herbs picked in the sierras, and one of the largest libraries in Spain, were added. However, it was when the Conquistadors chose Guadalupe as their shrine and brought treasure to it from the New World that it became the sumptuous building that it is today. The stone monastery, with its battlements and towers, is magnificent. From its hill-top vantage point it completely dominates the village that has grown up around it.

MONTSERRAT NATIONAL PARK

Spain

The small wooden statue of the Black Virgin of Montserrat, revered locally as *La Moreneta*, is at the heart of Catalonia's most holy site, the basilica, monastery and hermitage of Montserrat. The complex is near the top of the spectacular, saw-toothed mountain of the same name, which was designated as Spain's first national park about a century ago.

Whichever way you approach the monastery, on foot, by car, rack railway or cable-car, the mountain views are marvellous. Drivers approaching from the north get a particularly wonderful view of the *sierra* at Manresa. The monastery, which is surrounded by small chapels and hermit's caves, was founded in 880 and enlarged in the 11th century. In the 15th century it gained independence from Rome and its fame spread. In the early 19th century it was badly damaged when the French attacked Catalonia, but was rebuilt in 1844. Today it is a Benedictine monastery, which holds a marvellous collection of art in its museum. El Greco, Caravaggio and Zurbaran's religious paintings are featured, as well as modern works including some early Picassos, and some pieces from ancient Egypt and the near east.

WHAT IS IT?
Spain's first national park.
WHAT IS THERE TO SEE?
Spectacular natural scenery, the basilica, the statue of the Moreneta, the hermits' dwellings.

CÓRDOBA

Spain

In 711 the Moors entered Spain and by the middle of the century Córdoba was ruled by Abd Ar-Rahman, a charismatic leader who set in train a building programme that dramatically raised Córdoba's profile. By the tenth century it was the most important city west of Constantinople, home to Andalucia's first university and a library of more than 4,000 books.

The Great Mosque, known as the Mezquita, was originally built by Abd Ar-Rahman, who was a great believer in religious tolerance. This is particularly interesting in view of the fact that some 500 years later Alfonso X decided to add a royal chapel. A little over 100 years later, a second chapel was added, and about 150 years after that, the church decided to build a cathedral within the mosque as well.

DON'T MISS:
The medieval Jewish quarter, where the cobbled alleys are far too narrow to accommodate cars. You can see little whitewashed houses and workshops with beautiful wrought-ironwork, and tiny fountains with water splashing into beautiful basins of glazed, ceramic tiles set in lovely patios.

THE ESCORIAL

Spain

WHERE IS IT?
In the foothills of the Sierra Guadarrama, 45km (28 miles) north-west of Madrid.
WHAT IS THERE TO SEE?
The Museum of Art, the library, the royal pantheon and the chapter houses.

Phillip II built the Escorial to fulfil a vow he had made after a hermitage dedicated to St Lawrence was demolished during a Spanish victory over the French in 1557. Previously his father had made a wish on his deathbed for a church with a royal mausoleum to be built, and the Escorial (Real Monasterio de San Lorenzo de El Escorial) accomplished both desires.

The palace stands in the foothills of the Sierra Guadarrama, and its vast grey, granite walls and austere appearance began a vogue for an architectural style known as *desornamentado*, meaning 'unadorned'. The bleak basilica and simple royal apartments belie the wealth of the Habsburg art collection, which is largely housed in other buildings on the site such as the library and the royal pantheon.

THE PRADO

Spain

The Prado was originally built by Juan de Villanueva for Charles III, as a natural history museum. Later, Napoleon's brother Joseph decided it should be an art museum, and by the time it opened in 1819, under Fernando VII, it housed the royal art collection. There is no doubt that the Prado is one of the world's finest museums, holding more than 9,000 works of art by, among others, Velázquez, Goya, El Greco, Raphael, Titian, Botticelli, Caravaggio, Veronese, Fra Angelico, Bosch, Rubens, Dürer, Rembrandt and the Brueghels.

Queen Isabella began the royal collection in the 16th century, and this was added to by her successors until the 19th century. Try to see both the Goya and the Velázquez collections.

ART
The Prado displays about 1,500 works, some of which are on permanent display with others on a rotation system.

WHERE IS IT? In the centre of Madrid.
WHAT IS IT? One of the world's finest museums.
WHAT IS THERE TO SEE? Fra Angelico's *Annunciation*, Bosch's *Garden of Earthly Delights*, Rubens' *The Three Graces* and Velázquez's *Las Meninas*.

LOS JAMEOS DEL AGUA

Spain

Los Jameos del Agua (meaning 'the water hollows'), is a section of a long, volcanic tube that formed within the lava flow of the extensive eruption of the Corona volcano, which occurred about 3,000 years ago. It is part of the large Atlantida volcanic cave system in Lanzarote.

WHAT IS IT?
A spectacular series of underground volcanic caves that now house a restaurant, garden and auditorium.

In 1965, a local artist, César Manrique, was inspired to landscape this volcanic tube with its caverns and hollows that were formed where parts of the volcanic roof collapsed. Opened to the public by the island administration in 1968 as a series of unique entertainment venues, it was finally completed in 1987 with the construction of a superb natural auditorium with incredible acoustics and a capacity of about 600 seats.

Steps lead down to an extraordinary underground restaurant, complete with dance floor and bar. A 100-m (330-ft) long path leads the visitor to the Jameo Grande, an enormous cavern, 62m (200ft) long, 19m (62ft) wide and 21m (69ft) high. The path crosses a crystal-clear, saltwater, tidal lagoon in which a rare species of almost blind albino crab lives. This cave has been transformed into a lush, tropical garden planted around an emerald-green, man-made pool.

OPORTO

Portugal

Oporto, known in Portugal as simply 'Porto', is the second-largest city in the country and stands at the mouth of the Douro River. Since the 1850s port wine producers have matured and stored their wine in warehouses in Vila Nova de Gaia across the river, and about 60 establishments scramble up the hill from the waterfront. It is possible to tour about half of them, and sample their wares. In the 1980s five dams with locks in were constructed along the Douro, enabling small cruise ships to sail through to the heartland, where port-wine grapes are grown on hot, steeply terraced hillsides.

WHAT IS THERE TO SEE?
The Ribeira district, the Douro Valley and its vineyards, Amarante and the Cathedral of Se.
YOU SHOULD KNOW:
The people of Porto have always prided themselves on their work ethic, but the lively restaurant and bar scene in the evenings show that they also know when to play.

The centre of Porto is dominated by the 12th-century Cathedral of Se, with its Romanesque rose window and Gothic cloister. Old areas of the city, such as round the cathedral, are a maze of twisting streets and pretty, if crumbling, buildings.

LISBON

Portugal

WHAT IS THERE TO SEE?
The National Museum of Ancient Art, the Museum Calouste Gulbenkian, the monastery of São Vicente de Fora and the church of São Roque.
DON'T MISS:
The panoramic views of the city from Castello de São Jorge.

Lisbon lies snuggled between seven hills on the northern side of the mouth of the River Tagus (Tejo). The Praca do Comercio by the harbour is one of the most distinguished squares in Europe, with three sides of handsome buildings over arcaded galleries and the fourth formed by the riverfront.

For at least 3,000 years this harbour has been in use by different powers, but Lisbon's heyday was between the 15th and 17th centuries, when Portugal was a wealthy and powerful empire-building nation. In 1755 Lisbon was severely damaged by an earthquake, and never regained its former glory. Nowadays, however, it is a successful European capital city, and a great place to visit.

Lisbon is a lovely place, full of contrasts, from modern high rises to Art Nouveau buildings, wonderful mosaic pavements, brightly tiled buildings and the medieval Moorish area of the Alfama. There are fabulous buildings, museums, monasteries and parks to see. Look out over the city from the top of any of the hills – the Castello de São Jorge has panoramic views – and don't miss the façade of the church of Nossa Senhora da Conceição Velha or the unique Manveline (Portuguese late-Gothic) architecture of the Jerónimos Monastery, with its delightful clouster, and the Belem Tower.

COIMBRA

Portugal

WHERE IS IT?
195km (120 miles) north
of Lisbon.
WHY IS IT IMPORTANT?
Portugal's oldest university
is here and is still
considered to be the main
seat of learning in
the country.

Coimbra is the seat of Portugal's oldest university, which was founded in 1290 in Lisbon but moved here in 1537 on the top of a hill by the River Mondego. The old town is built around and beneath it, while the new town is around the base of the hill and along the riverfront. The university is built around a large square, beneath which is the entrance to a Baroque chapel. The Library of João V is the main draw – a fabulous, decorative space holding more than 300,000 books, with a frescoed ceiling and beautiful tables made of fine woods. The cathedral, Se Velha, is a stark, late 12th-century Romanesque building; its plain interior is lit up by a gilded sixteenth-century altar.

Other highlights within the city are the university's 18th-century botanic garden and the Machado de Castro Museum, which is housed in the former bishops' palace. Portugal dos Pequeninos Park is a collection of child-sized scale models of important Portuguese buildings. Southwest of Coimbra, just 16km (10 miles) away, are the Roman ruins of Conimbriga, settled in the first century AD. Some 300 years later Conimbriga's inhabitants fled to Coimbra to escape invasion, leaving behind what are now Portugal's most important Roman remains.

ÉVORA

Portugal

WHAT IS THERE TO SEE?
Palace of Vasco da Gama,
St Francisco church,
University of Évora and the
aqueduct of Agua de Prata.
WHAT IS THERE TO DO?
You will be spoilt for choice
with the incredible number
of historical buildings within
the city walls.

Évora stands upon a gentle hill at the heart of the Alentejo plain, some 150km (93 miles) southeast of Lisbon. Its historic centre is protected by a ring of fortified walls and dominated by an imposing, fortress cathedral. Évora is the best example of Portugal's 'Golden Age' because, unlike many other towns and cities, it was unaffected by the terrible earthquake of 1755.

There are some 4,000 buildings of historical interest within the city walls: churches, palaces, gates and squares, yet it is a lively university town, surrounded by vineyards and beautiful, rural scenery. The Alentejo plain is one of the country's poorer regions, but it is rich in history.

SINTRA
Portugal

WHAT IS IT KNOWN FOR?
The varying types of architecture from very different eras.
WHAT IS THERE TO SEE?
Castelo dos Mouros, Cappuchin Monastery and the Queluz Palace.

Sintra stands on the northern slopes of the wooded hills of Serra de Sintra, 30km (20 miles) northwest of Lisbon, and only 12km (7.5 miles) from the sea.

In the centre of the town is Pena National Palace, dominated by two huge towers. The palace, surrounded by a beautifully landscaped park, was rebuilt in 1839 and is among the most notable examples of royal architecture in the country. The old Hieronymite monastery, which had been added to and extended over the centuries and had elements of Moorish, Gothic, Manueline and Renaissance architecture, appealed to King Consort Ferdinand Saxe-Coburg-Gotha's taste for the Romantic. He had this extraordinary Bavarian-inspired building constructed around the ruins to serve as the royal family's summer palace.

THE GRAND BAZAAR
Turkey

The Kapalıçarsi, or Grand Bazaar, of Istanbul, is the largest covered market in the world. As with most ancient *medinas*, the Kapalıçarsi is divided into separate areas that trade in specific goods, such as antiques, leather, jewellery, spices and carpets, but when you are deep inside you seem to be in a fantastic maze from which there is no way out. In fact, although it can be both hot and full of people, you are never far from a small café or stall selling cold drinks, and there are tiled water fountains at regular intervals. The merchants are often very friendly and it can be highly enjoyable to drink glasses of tea with them while discussing world affairs and haggling over some desirable object.

BIGGEST MARKET
The Kapalıçarsi spreads over an impressive 20 hectares (50 acres) and includes 4,000 shops.

WHAT IS THERE TO SEE? Keçeciler Caddesi for carpet shops, Ic Bedesten for jewellery and leather goods, the *hamam* (Turkish baths) on Yerebatan Caddesi.
WHAT IS IT? The largest covered market in the world.

TOPKAPI PALACE

Turkey

DON'T MISS:
The Treasury – four rooms
full of jewels including the
emerald Topkapi dagger,
the Spoonmaker's diamond,
which is the fifth largest
in the world, and two
enormous, uncut emeralds.

The Topkapi Palace (Topkapi Sarayi) stands on a promontory called Seraglio Point, at the eastern end of the Old City of Istanbul, looking out over the Bosphorus and the Sea of Marmara. The extensive palace complex covers about 70 hectares (175 acres), and was once home to 40,000 people. Mehmet II began the building in 1462, and the Ottoman empire was ruled from here for nearly 400 years.

Today, visitors enter the palace through the Middle Gate, which leads into the Divan Court where the Council of State assembled, presided over by the Grand Vizir. The Sultan was able to eavesdrop on the proceedings from behind a latticed window. To one side of the Divan Court is the harem – a maze of almost 400 apartments, rooms, halls and terraces grouped around two large chambers. The eunuch's quarters are near the entrance, and consist of uncomfortable little rooms no better than those of the lesser concubines. The eunuchs decided which of the concubines were presented to the Sultan, and his favourites walked the 'golden way' to his private apartments. Each of his four wives had her own quarters, but only the Sultan's mother had a whole floor to herself. The Third Court contains the magnificently decorated throne room, the library of Ahmet III and the amazing collection of robes that were worn by the sultans.

WHAT IS THERE TO SEE?
The nightly *son et lumière*
performances in summer.
YOU SHOULD KNOW:
You will not be admitted
unless you are dressed
modestly and you must
remove your shoes.

THE BLUE MOSQUE

Turkey

This magnificent building, with its six graceful minarets, overlooks the Sea of Marmara, the Golden Horn and the Bosphorus, and its silhouette dominates the skyline of Istanbul's old city.

The Blue Mosque was commissioned by Sultan Ahmet I and designed by Mehmet Aga. The interior of the domes and the arches are covered with decorative calligraphy, but it is the 20,000 or more blue Iznik tiles that cover the interior walls that have given it its name. The huge central dome is 33m (100ft) wide and, together with the smaller domes and half domes, rests on four enormous 'elephant's foot' pillars, each one of which is 4.5m (15ft) thick. The vast, enclosed interior is surrounded by 260 stained-glass windows through which daylight floods, enhancing the blue tiles within.

HAGIA SOPHIA

Turkey

DID YOU KNOW?
It is one of the largest enclosed spaces in the world, and an astonishing architectural feat.

WHAT IS THERE TO SEE?
The 18th-century fountain, the tombs of the sultans and the alabaster urns from Pergamon.
YOU SHOULD KNOW:
The Hagia Sophia is open daily except Monday.

Hagia Sophia, the Church of Holy Wisdom, is a former Orthodox church across from the Blue Mosque. The first basilica was completed in 360, but burned to the ground in 532 and was subsequently rebuilt by Emperor Justinian as the finest Christian church in the Roman Empire. Justinian almost emptied the empire's coffers in the lavish construction. He brought marble and other building materials from Asia and Egypt, and looted columns from Ephesus. The vast central dome, which spans a good 30m (100ft), rests on two half domes and the huge buttress around it, forming an overwhelmingly large space inside. The Weeping Column, made of porous stone, leaches water from the cistern beneath and is said to have curative properties.

In 1453, after the fall of the city to the Turks, Aya Sofya became a mosque and the four minarets that surround it were added later. Most of the sultans added something to the church, in particular Mahmut II who, amongst other things, built a beautiful library. Many of its treasures have been looted over the centuries; the Crusaders even took the carved, gilt-bronze doors. Both the original mosaics and their early replacements have largely gone, but of those that remain, the finest are in the women's gallery and even in their current condition, those such as Christ Pantocrator are awe-inspiring.

TROY

Turkey

The city of Troy is known throughout the world, thanks to Homer's epic poem, *The Iliad*, in which the Greeks, led by Agamemnon, laid siege to the city of Troy for ten years in order to retrieve his brother Menelaus's wife, Helen, who had been been abducted by King Priam's younger son, Paris. According to *The Odyssey*, the Greeks achieved victory by hiding soldiers inside a wooden horse and sailing away, apparently defeated. The Trojans brought the horse inside the city, and while they were sleeping off their celebrations, the soldiers crept out, opened the gates for their comrades who had secretly returned, and laid waste to the city. This story was thought to be a myth until the 1870s, when German amateur archaeologist, Heinrich Schliemann, used his fortune to finance a massive dig at his chosen site, the hill known as Hisarlik. Eventually nine successive settlements were uncovered, each one on top of the last. The oldest dated back 5,000 years. Among the unsolved mysteries about Troy is Schliemann's discovery of 'King Priam's treasure', most of which is now in the Pushkin Museum in Russia. Not only did it come from the wrong layer of the city, but the discovery may have been faked.

WHERE IS IT?
In Çanakkale province in western Turkey.
WHAT IS IT KNOWN FOR?
The site is steeped in history and legend, made famous by Homer's epic, *The Iliad*.

MOUNT ARARAT

Turkey

Mount Ararat is the highest peak in Turkey, at 5,137m (16,854ft). It is a dormant volcano that stands on an arid plain, its permanently snow-covered summit visible for miles around.

Mount Ararat is of great interest to both archaeologists and religious groups because of its importance in the Book of Genesis. Noah and his family supposedly found themselves here after the Great Flood. In 70AD Josephus mentions that the ark is on Ararat for all to see, as did Marco Polo in 1300, although both reports were second-hand. A text on tablets found at Nineveh, known as the Epic of Gilgamesh, which dates from the seventh century BC, tells the same story. In the Epic of Gilgamesh, the hero is called Utnapishtim, and it was the god of wisdom, Ea, who commanded him to build the ark.

YOU SHOULD KNOW:
In 2004, the area was designated as the Kackar Mountains National Park, in an effort to attract tourists. This has made visiting the area easier for foreign visitors, but permits must still be applied for at least two months before a proposed visit, because this is a politically sensitive region.

KARAPINAR CRATER LAKES

Turkey

WHERE IS IT?
On the central Anatolian
plateau, 100 km (60 miles)
east of Konya.

The crater lake of Meke sits in a caldera formed millions of years ago when the top of the volcano was blown off. The cinder cone in the middle formed in a smaller eruption about 9,000 years ago.

The lake is said to be the Nazar Boncugu (a blue glass bead that you will see all over Turkey, which is said to avert the evil eye) of the world. It lies at 981m (3,219ft) above sea level, is 4km (2.5 miles) in circumference and up to 12m (40ft) deep in places. The cinder cone is about 300m (1,000ft) high. The blue-green, saltwater lake sits in an eerie volcanic landscape, and is a haven for many migratory birds and home to a variety of waders, ducks and flamingos. The Karapinar volcanic field was formed by intense volcanic activity, and there are several other craters as well as five cinder cones and two lava fields.

EPHESUS

Turkey

The ancient city of Ephesus is the jewel in the crown of Turkey's archaeological sites. Founded in the 13th century BC, by the end of the first century BC it had become a major Aegean port with a population of more than 300,000. By the time of Augustus Caesar it was the capital of Roman Asia, but as the port silted up the city waned, and finally it was abandoned altogether. This is no doubt why it remains in such good condition, because despite all the wars that went on around it, there was no need to sack an already deserted city. The Temple of Artemis, one of the Seven Wonders of the Ancient World, was destroyed centuries ago. The last version is represented by a single column.

GLADIATORS
The first-century stadium is entered through a huge, vaulted arch. The track was where the races were held, and where gladiators battled to the death.

WHERE IS IT? Next to Selçuk, on the west coast of Turkey 70km (45 miles) south of Izmir.
WHAT IS THERE TO SEE? The Virgin Mary's House, the Basilica of St John, the Archaeological Museum and the Isa Bey Mosque.
WHEN SHOULD I GO? Enjoy the Ephesus Festival in early May.

CAPPADOCIA

Turkey

WHAT IS IT?
An area of outstanding geology, with caves, 'fairy chimneys' and
spectacular landscapes.
DON'T MISS:
The underground cities of Derinkuyu and Kaymakli, Ihlara
Canyon and the Byzantine cave churches.

Cappadocia is a huge, isolated plateau in central Turkey, dominated by the extinct volcano of Erciyesdagi. Frequent eruptions that occurred over millions of years covered large parts of the plateau with tufa, a soft rock formed by volcanic ash, which in turn has been eroded over the centuries into bizarre conical hills in an amazing range of colours – off-white, yellow, violet, red and pink. These hills have been sculpted by the wind, rain and snow into an extraordinary variety of forms, some as high as 50m (165ft). For centuries people have carved dwellings into the rock. The Hittites are believed to have begun the underground city of Derinkuyu some time after 2000 B C. It is many storeys deep and has stones that could be rolled into place to block doorways, plus a sophisticated ventilation system. It is thought that as many as 20,000 people could take refuge here. The Göreme and Ilhara valleys in particular had a large number of churches, chapels and monasteries dug out of the rock, sometimes below ground and sometimes above, and many of these retain their Byzantine decoration.

DIVRIGI
Turkey

WHY IS IT IMPORTANT?
The Great Mosque is an important early work of Islamic architecture.
WHAT IS THERE TO SEE?
The Castle Mosque and the tomb of Sitte Melik.

Situated in central Anatolia, the Great Mosque and Hospital of Divrigi were commissioned in 1228 by Ahmet Shah Mengusoglu and his wife, Turan Malik, and are one of the most important early works of Islamic architecture in the whole region.

The mosque consists of a single prayer room crowned by two cupolas. The one over the centre of the mosque has a lantern, and the other, over the *mihrab* (the niche that indicates the direction of Mecca) is larger, with an eight-sided, ribbed cupola topped with a pointed roof. The mosque has three massive, beautifully decorated doorways: the one to the east is no longer operational, while the northern one was obviously the original main entrance. The inside is divided into five aisles, each of which has five bays, by 16 pillars carrying the stellate vaulting. The stone and ebony *minbars* (staircase-pulpits) are beautifully carved. The style of carving in both buildings has been influenced by Armenian manuscript decoration.

KEKOVA

Turkey

Kekova is a lovely island on the Mediterranean coast, and it gives its name to the whole group of picturesque islands in this area. Earthquakes have shaken the ground so often that the larger part of ancient Apollonia on the north shore of Kekova island itself has slid into the sea, creating an amazing sunken city that can be seen through the clear blue water. You can swim here amongst the marble halls, columns and stone steps of buildings that date back to the fifth century B.C. On the shore of the Bay of Tersane, the remains of a frescoed Byzantine church can be seen. The survivors of the earthquake moved across the water to the mainland and established the ancient cities of Simena (which today is the site of the small fishing village of Kale), Theimussa and Aperlai.

HISTORY
Simena was founded in 3000 BC and was once a thriving city, minting its first coin in the fourth century BC.

WHAT IS THERE TO DO? Take a tour of the islands of Kekova, visit Kas and ancient Xanthos or walk on part of the ancient Lycian Way.
WHAT IS IT KNOWN FOR? The beautiful underwater city of Apollonia.
HOW DO I GET THERE? By boat from Kas.

SUMELA MONASTERY

Turkey

The Monastery of the Black Virgin of Sumela is carved into a hollow in the sheer rock face of a mountain, some 350m (1,150ft) above the valley floor. Often shrouded in mist, it appears to cling to the mountain above a steep gorge in an impossibly inaccessible situation, surrounded by tall, dark pine trees.

The monastery was founded in the fourth century by the Blessed Barnabas, a Greek monk who brought with him a miraculous icon of the Virgin Mary, thought to have been painted by St Luke. In 1340 the shrine was rebuilt and added to by Emperor Alexios III, and there are frescoes in the main church that tell the story of his coronation here. Over the centuries more treasures were brought to this sacred shrine, and more frescoes were painted. It continued to be one of the most important centres of the Byzantine Church.

A 40-minute hike up the mountain brings you to the steps of the monastery, which is a complex of dormitories, courtyards, corridors and chapels around the main church.

WHERE IS IT?
Near Trabzon on the Black Sea coast of northeast Turkey.
YOU SHOULD KNOW:
The monastery is open daily and there is an entrance fee.
WHAT ELSE IS THERE TO SEE?
Trabzon, the Black Sea coast and Amasya's rock tombs.

BITLIS

Turkey

WHEN SHOULD I VISIT?
Arrive in spring and late
summer for sightseeing or
winter for skiing.
DON'T MISS:
Lake Van, the largest lake in
Turkey, is almost the size of
Luxemborg.

The town of Bitlis stands in the middle of the region of the same name, in the midst of a green oasis, on a tributary of the Tigris River and nestled amongst the mountains in eastern Anatolia. Situated at about 1,500m (4,900ft) above sea level, the town is surrounded by walnut trees, and is also an important centre for tobacco and honey production.

The most visible monument in the town itself is the Byzantine castle, the polygonal towers of which rise above the 12th-century Ulu Mosque, the Serefhan Medrese, Serefi Mosque and the Bayindir Kumbet mausoleum, all built in the local dark stone. There are many old buildings in the town with Armenian inscriptions above the doors, and the Seljuk cemetery has tombstones with inscriptions from the 12th century.

NEMRUT DAG

Turkey

The cone-shaped pinnacle of Nemrut Dag rises to 2,150m (7,054ft) in a remote area of southeastern Turkey, not far from the town of Adiyaman. This monument was the brainchild of King Antiochus I and was erected during the first century B.C. Antiochus conceived the idea of a majestic burial chamber for himself, hidden within the mountain and topped with colossal statues of Greek and Persian gods and goddesses. His inscription reads 'I, Antiochus, caused this monument to be erected in commemoration of my own glory and of that of the gods'. The burial mound on the summit is 50m (165ft) high and 150m (500ft) in diameter and is formed from fist-sized stones. The whole area is littered with stone panels, carved in relief, and the heads of gigantic statues that have been decapitated by earthquakes and the passage of time.

EXCAVATION
This monument was not
discovered until 1881.
Excavations and restoration work
have been continuing since 1984,
and in 1989 Nemrut Dag was
declared a national park.

DON'T MISS: Seeing the sunrise from the peak.
WHAT IS THERE TO SEE? The rock carving of Mithradites and Hercules shaking hands at Eski Kale.
WHEN SHOULD I VISIT? Late spring or early autumn.
HOW DO I GET THERE? By air to Adiyaman.

PAMUKKALE

Turkey

The pools and terraces of Pamukkale are one of the wonders of the natural world. The name means 'cotton fortress' and legend has it that this was where the Titans spread out their cotton crop to dry.

This is a huge, dazzling white cliff that drops some 100m (330ft) from a volcanic plateau from which water gushes in every direction. Hot streams of milky water, full of calcium carbonate and other minerals, flow from the plateau and down the cliff, creating terraces and overflowing basins as they go, covering everything in their path with white mineral deposits. Over the centuries the cliff has come to look like solid, gleaming waterfalls and great curtains of water apparently frozen in mid-air. The sound of water bubbling and splashing can be heard everywhere.

WHY IS IT IMPORTANT?
The pools and terraces are one of the wonders of the natural world.
WHAT IS THERE TO DO?
Swim in the warm, milky pools at nearby hotels.

HEALING WATERS
Ancient Greeks and Romans believed the water had curative properties – and built the city of Hierapolis here from 190BC. It is a vast complex of arches, columns, hot baths, temples, churches and a fascinating necropolis.

PETRA

Jordan

DID YOU KNOW?

Petra is world famous as the 'rose-red city half as old as time'.

WHEN WAS IT FOUND?

Petra's existence was known only to a few local Bedouins and Arab tradesmen until 1812, when a young Swiss explorer rediscovered it to finally reveal its glories to the west.

Petra is one of the most spectacular sites in the Middle East and many regard it as the most impressive ancient city remaining in the modern world. Archaeologists believe that Petra has been inhabited since prehistoric times – the remains of a 9,000-year-old city have been discovered, making it one of the earliest known settlements in the Middle East.

Surrounded by mountains riddled with passages and gorges, Petra was constructed by the Nabateans, who half-built, half-carved into the solid rock to create this wonderland of temples, tombs and elaborate buildings. From its origins as a fortress city, Petra became a wealthy commercial crossroads between Arabia, Assyria, Egypt, Greece and Rome. Later it was incorporated into the Roman empire and is thought to have been home to some 30,000 people in its heyday.

Most visitors approach Petra – either by foot or on horseback – through the Siq, a cleft in the rock that sometimes narrows to less than 5m (16ft) wide. After winding around for 1.5km (1 mile), the Siq suddenly opens upon the most impressive of all Petra's monuments, the Treasury. Carved out of solid rock in the side of the mountain and standing over 40m (130ft) high, it is one of the most elegant remains of antiquity.

BAALBEK

Lebanon

One of the world's great historical sites, Baalbek (Heliopolis), some 85km (52 miles) north-east of Beirut, is a place of superlatives: it is the largest complex of Roman temples ever built, some of its columns are the tallest ever erected and its stones – some weighing nearly 1,000 tonnes – are the largest ever used in any construction. The site is on a high plateau in the fertile Bekaa valley and lies against the impressive backdrop of the parallel ranges of the Lebanon and Anti-Lebanon mountains.

The origins of Baalbek are in fact thought to predate the Roman conquest by at least 3,000 years. The Phoenicians chose the site of Baalbek for a temple to their god Baal-Hadad, and the massive stones here are evidence of an earlier civilization.

ALSO KNOWN AS:
Heliopolis (city of the Sun).
TRAVELLERS' TIP:
Check with the Foreign Office about the advisability of visiting the area.

STATUS
At the time of its inclusion on the UNESCO World Heritage list, Baalbek was acclaimed as 'one of the finest examples of Imperial Roman architecture at its apogee'.

KRAK DES CHEVALIERS

Syria

DID YOU KNOW?

Krak des Chevaliers
was acclaimed by T.E.
Lawrence 'the most wholly
admirable castle in
the world'.

WHERE IS IT?
East of Tripoli on the road
from Antioch to Beirut.
WHAT IS IT?
One of the best-preserved
fortresses in the world.
HOW DO I GET THERE?
By road from Damascus
via Homs, which takes
about four hours.

Looking like a child's fantasy castle brought to life, Krak des Chevaliers sits on a 650-m (2,130-ft) cliff along what was the only route from Antioch to Beirut and the Mediterranean Sea. In 1144 the Krak was given to the Knights Hospitaller as their headquarters in Syria to enable them to control and guard this important strategic corridor. The Hospitallers rebuilt and expanded it into the largest Crusader fortress in the Holy Land, adding an outer wall 30m (100ft) thick with guard towers 8–10m (26–33ft) thick to create this concentric castle, that today, is one of the best-preserved fortresses in the world. The castle encompasses an area of 3,000 sq m (32,300 sq ft) and has 13 huge towers, as well as many stores, cisterns, corridors, bridges and stables. It is thought that it could accommodate 5,000 soldiers with their horses, equipment and enough provisions to withstand a siege of five years. The fortress is one of the few sites where Crusader art, in the form of frescoes, has been preserved. The English king Edward I, while on the Ninth Crusade, saw the fortress and used it as a basis for his own castles in England and Wales.

The Krak des Chevaliers (which means 'Fortress of the Knights' in a mixture of French and Arabic) is without doubt one of the world's greatest masterpieces of military architecture. The view from its towers is stunning.

SANA'A

Yemen

Surrounded by mountains of basalt, and situated in a relatively flat plain, Sana'a was, according to legend, built by the son of Noah, and throughout history has always been one of the major cities in Yemen.

The old walled city is one of the biggest and best-preserved *medinas* in the Arab world and has some 50,000 inhabitants, many of whom live in homes that are more than 400 years old. The world's first high-rise houses were built here – six- and seven-storey houses built of dark basalt stone and sun-dried mud-bricks. Their window surrounds are intricately decorated with elaborate friezes and are a complex infrastructure of round and angular shapes. Together with their panes, which were until recently made of thin slices of alabaster, they represent a unique architectural heritage. The old, walled city contains a wealth of architectural gems, including the Great Mosque, which was built at the time of the Prophet Muhammed. The *souq*, a vast maze of narrow alleyways and winding streets, is one of the oldest in Arabia.

WORTH A DIVERSION:
Do not miss the rock palace of Dar al-Hajar 14km (21 miles) to the north-west, the mosque at Shibam 27km (17 miles) farther on and Husn Thula fortress and the town of Amran, about 55km (34 miles) north of Sanaa.

SOCOTRA

Yemen

YOU SHOULD KNOW:
Socotra is among the top-ten endangered islands in the world. The island's tourist infrastructure is a pioneering example of ecotourism and, in order to protect the island's unique heritage, visitor numbers are limited.

Situated 170km (100 miles) east of the Horn of Africa, the isolated and wonderful island of Socotra is actually part of Yemen, which lies some 500km (300 miles) to the north. It boasts an astonishing variety of plant and animal species that are unique to the island. There are no fewer than 300 plant species, 113 insect species, 24 reptile species and six bird species that you will find nowhere else in the world.

Most people in the mountainous areas still live in caves and light fires by rubbing sticks together. The 40,000 inhabitants of Socotra are thought mostly to be descended from the settlers who arrived some 3,000 years ago from the Queen of Sheba's ancient city state of Saba on the south Arabian peninsula. Yet the pale skin and green and hazel eyes of others would seem to be evidence of the Greeks, Romans, Portuguese and ancient Egyptians who have arrived over the centuries.

JERUSALEM

Israel

Jerusalem is a city rich in history – from its foundation 5,000 years ago and King David's rule 3,000 years ago, to the presence of Jesus 2,000 years ago, the capital of modern Israel has experienced a tumultuous past. Over the centuries the Egyptians, Assyrians, Babylonians, Persians, Greeks, Romans, Byzantines, Arabs, Crusaders, Mamaluks, Ottomans and the British have all fought for, ruled over and lost Jerusalem. An archaeologist's paradise, Jerusalem is home to relics dating back as far as 3000 B C. Relics discovered before 1948 are housed in the Rockefeller Museum, and those excavated after this time are housed in the Israel Museum's Samuel Bronfman Archaeology Wing, which has sections on prehistory, the Canaanites, Israelites and Second Temple, Roman and Byzantine periods.

CITY OF SUPERLATIVES
This is one of the oldest, most significant cities in existence. Its history dates back past the Bronze Age and it is one of the holiest, and most disputed, cities on Earth.

YOU SHOULD KNOW: The walled Old City is the centre of Jerusalem, with Jewish West Jerusalem on one side and Arab East Jerusalem on the other. The old city is made up of several different areas: the Muslim, Christian, Armenian and Jewish quarters as well as the highly contested Temple Mount, where Abraham is said to have prepared his son for sacrifice.

THE DEAD SEA

Israel

The Dead Sea, on the border between the West Bank, Israel and Jordan in the Jordan Valley, is the deepest hypersaline lake in the world, located at the lowest exposed point on the Earth's surface. The Dead Sea has attracted visitors from around the world for thousands of years. The saline waters and mud on the shores of the Dead Sea contain many minerals believed to have medicinal and theraputic benefits. Many visitors cover their bodies with the dark mud to try to benefit from the restorative effects.

The other common activity for visitors is to try to sink, but it is futile. The unusually high salt concentration means that the water is denser than the human body so it is impossible not to float. The sea is called 'dead' because its high salinity means no fish or other aquatic organisms of any size can live in it, although minuscule quantities of bacteria and microbial fungi are present. The surrounding mountains, however, are host to a variety of species including camels, ibexes, hares, hyraxes, jackals, foxes and even leopards. Hundreds of bird species inhabit the zone as well.

WHAT IS IT?
The lowest exposed point on the Earth's surface.
WHAT IS THERE TO DO?
Float weightlessly in this natural phenomenon and indulge in a mineral mud treatment.

PERSEPOLIS

Iran

Persepolis, the magnificent palace complex founded by Darius the Great in about 518 BC, was built over a century as the seat of government for the kings of the Achaemenid Empire as well as a centre for ceremonial events and festivities.

The ancient hub of the Persian empire, now a UNESCO World Heritage Site, was built of dark-grey marble from the adjacent mountain, on an immense half-artificial-half-natural terrace. The wealth of the city was reflected in the extravagant construction of the buildings, inspired by Mesopotamian models. The largest and most complex building was the audience hall, marked by a large terrace and dotted with more than 36 enormous columns, some of which are still standing. It was accessed via two monumental stairways. Even after 2,500 years, the ruins of Persepolis are still awe-inspiring.

WHAT IS IT?
The ancient ruins of the former Persian capital, which was founded by Darius the Great in 518BC.
WHERE IS IT?
644km (400 miles) south of Tehran.

ISFAHAN

Iran

Designated a UNESCO World Heritage City, Isfahan contains various Islamic architectural sites dating from the 11th century to the 19th.

Shah Abbas the Great brought the Golden Age to Isfahan when he made it the new capital of the Safavid dynasty during his reign in the 16th century. Under his rule, Isfahan became known by Persians as Nesf-e-Jahan, or 'half of the world', because it held so many riches – in wealth, geography, architecture, religion and culture – that to see it was to see half the world. In its heyday, Isfahan had some of the most impressive parks, libraries, religious schools, shops, public baths and mosques of any city in the world.

The city's monumental architecture, one of the most impressive aspects of Isfahan, is made up of seven traditional elements: gardens, platforms, porches, gateways, domes, arched chambers and minarets. Many of the great buildings still in existence are located in the Imam Square, a vast rectangular area spanning 512m (1,700ft) long by 159m (522 ft) across. Highlights include the fabulous Imam Mosque, a masterpiece of Chahar-iwan style and the Sheikh Lotf Allah Mosque. Both are well regarded for their coloured arabesque tiles, their domes and their Safavid-style decoration.

DID YOU KNOW?
Duke Ellington once wrote a song, *Isfahan*, in honour of the city.

WHAT IS IT?
A UNESCO World Heritage Site containing a variety of Islamic architectural treasures.
WORTH A SPLURGE:
While you're there, pick up an Isfahan carpet.

INDEX